Routledge Revivals

The Entrepreneurial Middle Class

This book, first published in 1982, is a study of the processes that
shape the reproduction of the entrepreneurial middle class. It identifies
the major dynamics surrounding stages of business growth. More particularly, it focuses upon obstacles and cleavages inherent within the
process of small-scale capital accumulation. This book is ideal for students of business and economics.

T0362376

The Entrepreneurial Middle Class

Richard Scase and Robert Goffee

First published in 1981
by Croom Helm Ltd

This edition first published in 2015 by Routledge
2 Park Square, Milton Park, Abingdon, Oxon, OX14 4RN
and by Routledge
711 Third Avenue, New York, NY 10017

Routledge is an imprint of the Taylor & Francis Group, an informa business

Publisher's Note
The publisher has gone to great lengths to ensure the quality of this reprint but points out that some imperfections in the original copies may be apparent.

Disclaimer
The publisher has made every effort to trace copyright holders and welcomes correspondence from those they have been unable to contact.

A Library of Congress record exists under LC control number: 81208110

ISBN 13: 978-1-138-84269-4 (hbk)
ISBN 13: 978-1-315-72723-3 (ebk)
ISBN 13: 978-1-138-84685-2 (pbk)

The Entrepreneurial Middle Class

RICHARD SCASE AND ROBERT GOFFEE

CROOM HELM
London & Canberra

© 1982 Richard Scase and Robert Goffee
Croom Helm Ltd, 2–10 St John's Road, London SW11

British Library Cataloguing in Publication Data

Scase, Richard
    The entrepreneurial middle class.
    1. Middle classes
    2. Entrepreneur
    I. Title   II. Goffee, Robert
    338'.04   HB601
ISBN 0-7099-0450-9

Typeset in Great Britain by
Pat and Anne Murphy Typesetters, Highcliffe, Dorset

Printed and bound in Great Britain by
Biddles Ltd, Guildford and King's Lynn

CONTENTS

Preface

1. Class Analysis and the Entrepreneurial Middle Class 9

2. Technological Change, the Occupational Structure and the Entrepreneurial Middle Class 32

3. The Formation and Growth of Small Businesses: the Case of the Building Industry 53

4. The Self-employed 70

5. Small Employers 98

6. Owner-controllers 126

7. Owner-directors and Family-owned Firms 153

8. Conclusions: Entrepreneurship and the Middle Class 185

Methodological Appendix 198

Bibliography 203

Index 211

PREFACE

This book is a study of the processes shaping the reproduction of the entrepreneurial middle class. It identifies the major dynamics surrounding stages of business growth. More particularly, it focuses upon obstacles and cleavages inherent within the process of small-scale capital accumulation. In a sense, this book extends upon many of the ideas posed in our earlier, *The Real World of the Small Business Owner.*

We are grateful to Gerda Loosemore-Reppon, the Social Science Research Council for funding the research and to the many business owners that we interviewed. We also appreciate the patience and secretarial skills of John Hales, Barbara Holland and Vicky Marriott. But we are primarily indebted to each other. At the end of a three-year research project we are still friends. This is how it should be; academic research must be serious but also enjoyable. This book, then, is for three years in NC 32.

Richard Scase and Robert Goffee

THE ENTREPRENEURIAL MIDDLE CLASS

1 CLASS ANALYSIS AND THE ENTREPRENEURIAL MIDDLE CLASS

In studies of the class structure, the major focus of attention has been the working class. If, in the 1960s research was directed to the effects of 'affluence' upon the attitudes and behaviour of industrial manual workers, in the late 1970s and 1980s studies have become more concerned with the consequences of economic recession.[1] In more theoretical analyses, particularly those concerned with the specification of class boundaries, the working class has again attracted the most attention.[2] Consequently, our understanding of the middle class is meagre, both conceptually and empirically. Indeed, it is treated as though it were a residual category which 'expands' and 'contracts' according to differing definitions of the working class. Further, the middle class has rarely been studied as a whole; in most empirical enquiries it tends to evaporate into the analysis of specific occupations.[3] Newby and his associates have neatly assessed the current state of research as follows:

> If we divide the middle class according to an admittedly somewhat dubious division of labour into entrepreneurial, professional, managerial and 'white-collar' groupings, then the bulk of research attention has been devoted to the latter group, for reasons of both theoretical importance (especially in relation to orthodox Marxist class analysis) and accessibility.[4]

A major concern, then, has been the implications of the growth of lower-grade, non-manual occupations for the class structure.[5] This, in turn, has often been related to studies of bureaucratisation and the effects of the alleged proletarianisation of many white-collar occupations.[6] When other occupational groupings within the middle class have been studied, managers and professional employees have attracted the most interest.[7] Such discussions have tended to concentrate upon three issues. First, the extent to which the bureaucratisation of the workplace has affected managerial authority and professional autonomy.[8] Secondly, the degree to which managerial ideologies have emerged which are different in character from those of business owners and entrepreneurs.[9] It has, for example, often been argued that a new 'class'

9

of managers, separated from the ownership function, are more committed to 'welfare' and 'collectivist' ideologies than their owner-manager predecessors.[10] Finally, the class location of managerial and professional workers has been the subject of considerable debate. Thus, they have been variously described as *bourgeois, 'new' petty-bourgeois* as well as a distinct *managerial-professional class*.[11] These discussions, however, have usually been pitched at an extremely high level of abstraction.

The emphasis upon the salaried middle class has meant that other groupings have been neglected. More specifically, little attention has been devoted to those who derive income from property and other personally-owned assets which are used for *productive* purposes; in other words, the entrepreneurial middle class. As Newby and his associates have suggested:

> That section of the middle class which is widely recognised as being of considerable theoretical interest remains largely unexamined and our overall perception of the middle-class has become distorted as a result. As it currently stands, the literature concentrates on the problems of middle-class *employees*, especially on the social accoutrements of managerialism and mobility, rather than on business owners and entrepreneurs.[12]

Thus, it is as though the growth of large-scale, joint-stock companies has created a dominant managerial class and virtually eliminated owner-managers who are dependent for their income not upon salaries but on personally-owned assets. It is assumed, in other words, that the split between ownership and control is such that there is little scope for incorporating within sociological analysis the study of an entrepreneurial middle-class which both owns *and* controls productive resources. This is a major omission in the analysis of class structure in view of the continuing importance of this class in modern society; it serves, for example, not only to legitimate private property ownership in general, but it also continues to fulfil a significant economic role.[13] How, then, is this class to be defined?

At the most general level, the entrepreneurial middle class consists of several diverse groupings which, nevertheless, share a common feature: their ownership of capital assets. These are typically exploited for productive purposes by use of the proprietors' and others' labour. However, the relative *mix* of labour and capital is highly variable. Thus, there can be instances when income is mainly derived from property ownership (as with small *rentiers*), when income is primarily acquired through the exercise of labour (as with craftworkers and freelance professionals), and other cases where there is a *mixture* of both elements (as with shopkeepers, garage proprietors and restaurant owners). In general, discussions of the entrepreneurial middle class have focused upon specific groups where property ownership is the more important component. In Britain, for example, Bechhofer and Elliott have investigated Edinburgh shopkeepers[14] and small landlords[15] while more recently, Newby and his associates have studied East Anglian farmers.[16] In addition to differences in the proportionate use of capital and labour, a further source of variation derives from the *size* of businesses which proprietors own. A small shopkeeper not employing labour, a farmer with a thousand acres and five or six employees, and a manufacturer with fifty workers, all actively use their own capital assets for the purposes of personal profit and are, therefore, all members of the entrepreneurial middle class. This, in turn, leads to another source of internal differentiation; namely, the *type* of capital assets employed. Whereas for farmers it may be land, it is machinery for industrial employers and simple hand tools for independent tradesmen. Thus, empirically, the entrepreneurial middle class is a 'mixed bag' consisting as it does of proprietors who actively use their capital for a variety of purposes within different sectors of the economy. It is not surprising, then, that their location within modern society is conceptually problematic. Indeed, the entrepreneurial middle class has been regarded in at least three distinct ways. First, as 'separate' and 'removed' from the two major classes of capitalist society. Secondly, as part-and-parcel of an emerging 'post-industrial' or 'service' society. Finally, as a legacy of an earlier or pre-capitalist stage of production.

The first perspective regards certain groupings within the entrepreneurial middle class such as small-scale manufacturers, traders and shopkeepers, as an independent 'stratum' — the petty bourgeoisie — which is separate from both the bourgeoisie and the proletariat. Bechhofer and his colleagues, for example, have argued that they represent a stratum which is 'in some sense marginal or detached from the major classes and interests of contemporary industrial societies'.[17] At one point, this leads them to suggest they are '*outside*' the class structure, whilst at another, they sit 'uneasily *between* the major classes' (our emphasis).[18] On the basis of their own empirical enquiry the authors conclude:

> In a very real sense the petite bourgeoisie is detached from the concerns of the working and middle classes. To a large extent the

small businessman finds himself a mere spectator at the arena in which the forces of labour and big business confront each other.[19]

Notwithstanding this, Bechhofer and his colleagues regard the petty bourgeoisie as fulfilling important ideological functions within contemporary society if only because they are the custodians of certain 'core' capitalist values. They claim that an overriding value of many small business owners is *independence*; the appeal is to be 'your own boss' and, thereby, avoid the constraints of employment associated with large-scale corporations. The strength of this appeal is sufficient to compensate for frequently long and arduous working hours; indeed, their 'autonomy' often turns into 'serfdom' such that 'theirs, it seems, is a freedom to establish an extraordinary form of self-exploitation'.[20] Despite this, most remain firmly committed to notions of 'individualism' and 'independence' and this is reflected in their attitudes, life styles and patterns of consumption.[21] In sum, society is seen to be 'open' and it rewards those prepared to work hard and make the necessary self-sacrifice. To quote the authors they are:

> the repository of many of the traditional values upon which a capitalist social order was built. The shopkeepers' passionate individualism and the moral evaluation of work emerge clearly enough. So too does the vision of a *laissez-faire* economy in which men like themselves will prosper. Moreover, their belief that by hard work and wit you can succeed is crucial to the conception of ours as an open society. Thus, the symbolic significance of the stratum resides in the fact that, to many, their lives appear to demonstrate the possibility of individual mobility. Despite the modesty of their origins many have succeeded, that is, in terms quite fundamental to a capitalist society. They have won, albeit in small measure, property and autonomy.
>
> Finally, we would argue that the significance of these central concerns in the political and social philosophy of the petty bourgeois is this: espousing an ideology of independence and hard work he is inclined to the belief that inequality is the result of the differential distribution of talent and effort. In doing so he buttresses the present system of inequality and offers it legitimation.[22]

Even though the development of large-scale corporations and the growth of the state has fundamentally altered the structure of the economy, such beliefs reinforce the desirability of capitalism as a socio-economic system. The persistence of small-scale enterprises — whether in farming, commerce or industry — preserves an *image* of competition, the market and opportunity behind which the growing domination of large-scale monopoly enterprises is concealed. In fact, research suggests that small business owners have only a limited awareness of the growing market control of national-based and multi-national corporations and of the extent to which their own trading prospects are increasingly dependent upon them.[23] This is so, even for those small enterprises which operate as the suppliers of commodities and services to one or a few large customers which determine their economic survival. Bechhofer and his colleagues summarise the economic position of small business owners as follows:

> Running their own enterprises, be they small workshops, or retail stores or service operations, they are forced into some awareness of their vulnerability to change, to the booms and recessions in the economy, to the fiscal and other measures of the state . . . The sense of precariousness, of contingency, leads to the awareness of life as 'struggle' and to ambiguity in their relationship to others in the major classes. Small capital is menaced from above and below . . . in all circumstances it is a dependent stratum, dependent first and foremost on the dominant economic groups and institutions. It is their decisions, their interests that do most to affect the size and circumstances of the stratum.[24]

If this view suggests that petty bourgeois elements persist in a 'marginal' sense, a second — but related — approach argues that the entrepreneurial middle class will fulfil an increasingly important function in an emerging post-industrial society.[25] Several factors are said to underlie this trend. Some writers have claimed that as a result of a growing concern with the 'quality of life' the number of independent small-scale enterprises is likely to expand.[26] Within this argument a heavy emphasis is placed upon the growing 'diseconomies' and 'dysfunctions' of large-scale bureaucratic organisations which are said to produce inferior quality goods under conditions that lead to work dissatisfaction amongst employees. Thus, 'small is beautiful' since it encourages the production of goods and services in the context of more 'meaningful', and, therefore, less alienating, work environments.[27] Boissevain has recently listed the various manifestations of this trend in the following terms:

First, increasing awareness of environmental pollution has furnished a niche for entrepreneurs able to provide natural products, whether for the stomach, the body or the mind . . . Secondly, both the increase of the size and the power of firms . . . has reduced the relative autonomy of managers . . . Many dissatisfied managers in large corporations strike out on their own . . . Thirdly, there is growing realisation that the quality of life in urbanizing Europe is adversely affected by the disappearance of neighbourhood shops offering varied products, repair services, flexible opening hours and credit facilities. Finally, . . . is the belief that a reduction in scale provides satisfaction. Many have stepped out and down.[28]

Employees who choose to set up their own businesses are helped, it has been argued, by recent technological developments which are encouraging the growth of the domestic economy. The microchip computer, for instance, allows relatively sophisticated software to be purchased cheaply and used in the home. This has led Martin and Norman to speculate that 'we may see a return to cottage industry, with the spinning wheel replaced by the computer terminal'.[29] More recently, Kumar has lent support to this view by suggesting:

The computer is the most powerful instrument of dispersal and devolution since the invention of cheap printing. Potentially every aspect of education, work, politics, domestic tasks and leisure can be affected by it.[30]

Clearly, if these predictions prove to be correct, there could be a substantial potential for the expansion of independent, small-scale production. Some commentators have argued that such opportunities will be increasingly exploited if only because of the marked decline in 'formal' employment over recent years which has forced many to consider alternative forms of making a living.[31] Consequently, the growth of 'informal' economic activity has attracted much attention and Pahl, for example, has claimed that '*the substitution of informal, household production of services for the purchase of services from the formal economy*' could serve as the basis for an alternative means of income.[32] He continues:

Unemployment in the 1980's may, therefore, be a different kind of experience from that described for the period half a century ago. A man with his own tools, his own time and a long-stop income in the form of unemployment pay may not be in such a vulnerable position: his *work* identity can still be maintained even if his employment identity is in abeyance.[33]

If 'informal' work in the 'cash economy' is increasing while 'formal' employment declines this, too, could provide new avenues for small business formation and growth. It has been suggested that this trend is further encouraged by the increasing 'burden' of state regulations, controls and taxes.[34] Thus, Boissevain concludes that, 'the desire to avoid progressively heavier levels of taxation and contributions for social services has stimulated . . . people to start up on their own'.[35] Taken together, these changes are leading, so it is claimed, to a fundamental alteration in both the pattern and nature of economic activity within modern societies. As such, they constitute the basis for a *regeneration* of the entrepreneurial middle class in the developing 'post-industrial' society. Such a view stands in distinct contrast to the classical Marxist position which is the basis of the final interpretation that is now considered.

There are, then, thirdly, those who regard some sectors of the entrepreneurial middle class as the legacy of an earlier type of production which persists within present-day society. Because this view is the best known and theoretically most developed of the three, rather more attention is devoted to its summary and critical appraisal. The Marxist approach suggests that, in the long run, the development of capitalism will lead to the *dissolution* of the entrepreneurial middle class within the bourgeoisie and the proletariat. As Marx claimed in the *Communist Manifesto*:

> The lower strata of the middle-class – the small tradespeople, shopkeepers and retired tradesmen generally, the handicraftsmen and peasants . . . sink gradually into the proletariat, partly because their diminutive capital does not suffice for the scale on which Modern Industry is carried on, and is swamped in the competition with the large capitalist, partly because their specialised skill is rendered worthless by new methods of production.[36]

This prediction is based upon an analysis of the capitalist mode of production which distinguishes the stages of *co-operation* and *manufacture* from *modern industry*.[37] Under conditions of *co-operation* the worker is an autonomous craftsman, but with the development of capitalist *manufacture* a division of labour emerges and he becomes a specialist in one rather than in a number of activities. To quote Marx, 'each workman (becomes) exclusively assigned to a partial function, and that for the rest of his life, his labour power is turned into the organ of this detail function'.[38] With the development of *modern industry*, characterised by mechanised factory production, the worker 'becomes a mere appendage to an already existing material condition of production'.[39] As a 'machine minder' his conceptual capacity is further reduced whilst at the same time, the amount of capital required for production becomes greater. Under these circumstances few workers will become capitalists and, furthermore, few small-scale producers will be able to compete with the production methods of *modern industry* which *inevitably* become 'the general, socially predominant form of production'.[40] Thus, 'the larger capitals beat the smaller' causing 'the ruin of many small capitalists, whose capitals partly pass into the hands of their conquerers, partly vanish'.[41] The growth of *modern industry*, then, restricts the opportunity for workers to function as independent tradesmen or to become business owners while, at the same time, it destroys the capital of existing small-scale producers and manufacturers.

Given these developments in the capitalist mode of production, the entrepreneurial middle class is typically viewed by Marxists as the legacy of either an earlier stage of *capitalist* production, as with small-scale capitalists, or of *pre-capitalist* simple commodity production, as with the self-employed and the 'traditional' petty bourgeoisie. Thus, although the capitalist *mode* of production may be dominant in a social formation, prior *forms* of non-capitalist production may persist within it.[42] Similarly, the existence of large-scale capitalist enterprises in the present stage of 'monopoly' capitalism does not preclude the persistence of small-scale capital units characteristic of 'competitive' or 'private' capitalism. However, to claim that sectors of the entrepreneurial middle class represent a legacy of declining importance does not explain *how* or *why* they are currently reproduced.

Poulantzas, for example, who defines the 'traditional' petty bourgeoisie as the *self-employed* and those '*not chiefly involved in exploiting wage labour*',[43] (our emphasis) merely states that 'the contemporary existence of the petty bourgeoisie in the developed capitalist formations . . . depends on the perpetration of this form in the extended reproduction of capitalism'.[44] This is cumbersome description rather than explanation and is indicative of the fact that Poulantzas sees this class as a declining vestige of the simple commodity form 'which was historically the form of transition from the feudal to the capitalist mode'.[45] Similarly, Wright tends to ignore the actual mechanisms which account for the persistence of small-scale commodity production in contemporary society.[46] He defines the petty bourgeoisie as *those who either work for themselves or, despite the employment of some labour, generate the bulk of surplus value.*[47] In a similar fashion to Poulantzas, he sees this form of production as subordinated to capitalism and yet fails fully to explore the implications. In his terms, the petty bourgeoisie have *full* economic ownership of the means of production and *full* control over the allocation of their resources and yet they control little or no labour power. As such, he regards their class position as unambiguous.[48] But obviously, if members of the petty bourgeoisie produce commodities they *are* affected by the conditions of the market as they exist under monopoly capitalism. Thus, the constraints exercised by, for example, financial institutions and large-scale capitalist enterprises may severely curtail the *real* control that 'independent' small-scale producers are able to exercise over the use of their investments and resources. If 'economic control' is diminished, on Wright's criteria, the class location of the petty bourgeoisie in contemporary capitalist society cannot be regarded as 'unambiguous'. Indeed, any analysis which views petty commodity producers as representative of a surviving 'simple' or 'feudal' form which somehow persists within contemporary capitalism is of questionable value.

The Marxist interpretation of small-scale capitalists is rather different. They, unlike the petty bourgeoisie, own and control larger capital assets and employ more sizeable workforces. They are, for example, the owners of family firms and of medium-sized, non-monopoly enterprises in general. According to Poulantzas:

> Non-monopoly capital is not a simple form that is preserved or conserved, as in the case of feudal forms surviving within capitalism, but a form reproduced under the domination of monopoly capital.[49]

If this type of small-scale capital is representative of an earlier *competitive* stage of capitalism it is, nevertheless, seen to be shaped by the contemporary forces of *monopoly* capitalism. Consequently, Poulantzas suggests a number of functions which small enterprises fulfil in the modern economy. They often operate, for example, in sectors characterised by low profits and high risks, and those which 'service' large corporations. They may also function as a 'staging post in the process of subjecting labour-power to monopoly capital', and as a means whereby prices may be set at a level which allows monopoly capital larger profit margins because of its cheaper production costs.[50] Poulantzas further argues that the apparent independence of small-scale capital is constrained by monopoly standardisation of products, the patenting of technological innovations and the 'leonine controls' imposed by finance capital as a condition for extending credit.[51] Consequently, the *real* economic boundaries of small-scale, non-monopoly enterprises – so clearly defined in *legal* terms – become increasingly indeterminate. In contrast to the petty bourgeoisie, Poulantzas emphasises that 'the criteria by which non-monopoly capital is defined are always located in relation to monopoly capital . . . There is in no sense a simple "co-existence" of two separate water-tight sectors'.[52] Thus, the relationship between the two forms of capital is variable and dependent upon 'the phase of monopoly capitalism and its concrete forms (branches, sectors, etc.) within a social formation'.[53] Despite the extent to which monopoly capital reduces the economic viability of small-scale enterprises, then, Poulantzas recognises their continuing *functional* importance and, hence, their persistence within contemporary capitalism.

Wright and Carchedi adopt a similar approach. Wright sees 'small employers' as caught between simple commodity production and the capitalist mode of production in a 'contradictory class location'.[54] This implies that 'small employers' are partially integrated within the capitalist mode in a manner in which the traditional petty bourgeoisie are not. Unfortunately, Wright does not elaborate upon this. Similarly, Carchedi considers the 'capitalist of private capitalism' as distinct from the petty bourgeoisie, and also outside the capitalist class under the conditions of monopoly capitalism.[55] As such, they constitute an 'old' middle class while the top managers in large-scale enterprises are seen as 'capital personified . . . the most representative part (of the capitalist class) from the point of view of the production relations typical of monopoly capitalism'.[56] The owner-managers of non-monopoly enterprises, then, are regarded as the embodiment of an earlier stage of capitalist production which has been superceded by, and subordinated to, monopoly capitalism. The precise nature of this subordination, however, is not considered in any detail.

To sum up, there is among these writers a neglect of the *actual* dynamics whereby the petty bourgeoisie and small-scale capitalists are reproduced under the conditions of monopoly capitalism. This is the result of excessively abstract analyses which assume their progressive decline and fail, therefore, to study specific empirical processes.

Westergaard, in assessing recent contributions, has professed to be:

> both puzzled and disturbed by contemporary western Marxist work
> in which the concrete differential impact of capitalist economic
> processes on people's lives and prospects . . . seems to recede into
> remote distance . . . or to be brought into the picture only in a
> context of abstraction which, untranslated, leave the reality of
> human experience difficult to recognise.[57]

Indeed, Wright, Poulantzas and Carchedi explicitly deny they are
concerned with the human actors who occupy the class 'places' or
'positions' which constitute the essential focus of their discussions.
According to Poulantzas:

> The principal aspect of an analysis of social classes is that of their
> places in the class struggle; it is not true of the agents that compose
> them. Social classes are not empirical groups of individuals . . . The
> class memberships of the various agents depends on the class places
> that they occupy; it is moreover distinct from the class origin, the
> social origin, of the agents.[58]

Carchedi confines himself to the *economic* identification of the new
middle class and so does not even 'descend' to lower levels of
abstraction in order to discuss the behaviour of actors occupying
particular class locations. Thus, he argues:

> The 'old' middle class, (i.e. the small entrepreneurs) and strata of the
> petty bourgeoisie which are only indirectly tied to the economic
> structure of the capitalist system and whose analysis can be more
> properly undertaken at lower levels of abstraction, will not be
> analysed here for lack of space.[59]

Even Wright, who is committed to the idea that 'Marxist theory should
generate propositions about the real world which can be empirically
studied',[60] and who attacks abstract class definitions which relegate the
complexities of 'concrete social structures' to a secondary role, does not
consider it necessary to 'discuss contradictory locations that occur
because an *individual* simultaneously occupies two class positions
within social relations of production' (our emphasis).[61] He argues that
dual class membership, although of significance 'in certain historical
circumstances', does not present 'the same kind of analytical problem

as positions which are themselves located in a contradictory way within class relations'.[62] Once again, then, the discussion of class *actors* – despite the professed importance of class *struggle* rather than class *structure* – is deemed to be of less significance than that of abstractly-defined class locations. This is because, as Parkin has stated:

> Notions such as the mode of production make their claims to explanatory power precisely on the grounds of their indifference to the nature of the human material whose activities they determine. To introduce (such) questions . . . is to clutter up the analysis by laying stress upon the quality of *social actors*, a conception diametrically opposed to the notion of human agents as *träger* or 'embodiments' of systemic forces.[63]

Clearly, the reproduction of the petty bourgeoisie and small-scale capital within economies characterised by the dominance of large monopoly enterprises requires detailed *empirical* study. Abstract analyses that attribute priority to *modes* and *stages* of production, and to class *positions* rather than to class *actors* fail to sufficiently account for the mechanisms whereby the entrepreneurial middle class is reproduced in present-day society. If, as in most Marxist analyses, the distinction between *actor* and *position* is too sharply drawn, then areas of the class structure within which there is a significant degree of social mobility may be inadequately understood.[64] Poulantzas acknowledges that some manual workers and artisans become petty bourgeois producers and small capitalists but he overlooks the actual material processes which allow this mobility.[65] Although, therefore, at the theoretical level the simple commodity form *can* be distinguished from the pure capitalist mode of production, this type of analysis detracts from the study of empirical relationships. Thus, while the petty bourgeoisie is seen to be fairly 'insulated' from the capitalist mode of production, small-scale capitalists are described in a functional manner by reference to the 'needs' of monopoly capital. This means that the concrete relationships between petty bourgeois producers and small-scale capitalists on the one hand, and the interconnections between these and large-scale corporations on the other, have been relatively unexplored. Further, there have been hardly any sociological studies of the processes whereby *actors* can experience upward mobility through the small-scale accumulation of capital.

In some ways it is surprising that contemporary Marxists have neglected the analysis of these processes, given the importance which both Marx and Lenin attributed to them. In their respective accounts of the development of capitalism in Britain and Russia, they recognised the continuing formation of small-scale enterprises, *despite* long-term trends. Thus, Marx pointed out that:

> individual capitals, and with them the concentration of the means of production, increase in such proportion as they form aliquot parts of the total social capital. At the same time, portions of the original capitals disengage themselves and function as new independent capitals . . . Accumulation and the concentration accompanying it are, therefore, not only scattered over many points, but the increase of each functioning capital is thwarted by the formation of new and the sub-division of old capitals. Accumulation, therefore, presents itself on the one hand as increasing concentration of the means of production, and of the command over labour; on the other, as repulsion of many individual capitals one from another.[66]

Similarly, although Lenin asserted that 'the fundamental and principal trend of capitalism is the displacement of small-scale by large-scale production',[67] he nevertheless emphasised the persistence of petty production which ensured the continuous formation of various intermediary strata:

> In every capitalist country, side by side with the proletariat, there are always broad strata of the petty bourgoisie, small proprietors. Capitalism arose and is constantly arising out of small production. A number of new 'middle strata' are inevitably brought into existence again and again by capitalism (appendages to the factory, work at home, small workshops scattered all over the country to meet the requirements of the big industries, such as the bicycle and automobile industries etc.).[68]

Both Marx and Lenin, then, acknowledged the continuing reproduction of the petty bourgeoisie and small-scale capitalists within capitalist society. Although the development of capitalism would ultimately lead to their dissolution, the conditions which enabled the reproduction of the entrepreneurial middle class persisted. But what is lacking in contemporary Marxist accounts, however, is any empirical analysis of the ways in which this reproduction now takes place.[69] As Miller has pointed out:

> The small business sector as a whole . . . is large and strong in most
> capitalist nations . . . *(It) should not be regarded as an anchronism
> that will surely and swiftly fade away as big enterprises grow.*[70]

The implications of this for class structure have been stressed by Mayer:

> The lower middle class was expected to shrink drastically in
> importance, perhaps even to sink altogether into the proletariat; but
> this expectation, which was so widely shared, has not been fulfilled.
> Even the old lower middle class of petty independence has displayed
> an extraordinary longevity. To be sure, since the mid-nineteenth
> century the economic and numerical weight of small craftsmen,
> tradesmen, and peasants has declined strikingly. But this decline has
> been less rapid than commonly assumed. In fact, now and then the
> number of small shopkeepers and service operators actually
> increased, especially under conditions of acute economic distress.[71]

A satisfactory analytical framework must take account of the fact
that small-scale enterprises *are embedded within a general process of
capital accumulation.* Although this assumption is explicit in, for
example, Lenin's discussion of the development of capitalism in Russia,
it is largely absent in present-day work.[72] Even though the possibilities
for actors to become proprietors of small businesses are generally less
now than during earlier stages of capitalism, they are certainly greater
than is widely assumed. As such, they constitute avenues for individual
mobility of a 'non-career' or 'non-meritocratic' kind. Whereas studies
of upward mobility have stressed the acquisition of educational and
technical qualifications and then promotion within and between
hierarchically-organised corporations, little attention has been devoted
to small-scale capital accumulation as an alternative channel for
personal success.[73] Thus, managerial, professional and manual employees
can, in various ways and for different reasons, become small-scale
proprietors. As Crossick has suggested:

> The lower middle class plays a very specific role in the process of
> social mobility, whether of a career or inter-generational type. It is
> available for those seeking to rise out of the working class, whether
> into white collar occupations by means of a fairly rudimentary
> education, or by small capital accumulation into the petty
> bourgeoisie.[74]

Similarly, Mayer has argued that the entrepreneurial middle class functions as:

> A buffer between capital and labour . . . (and) as a bridge and mediator between them. Moreover, the petite bourgeoisie is the predominant channel for social mobility; skilled manual workers can and do move into it from below, while from within its bulging ranks it raises its own spiralists to higher rungs on the income and status ladder. This lower middle class also serves as a net that cushions the fall of the skidders and the superannuated of both the higher middle class and the grande bourgeoisie.[75]

In this manner, the reproduction of the entrepreneurial middle class must be regarded as *integral* to contemporary class dynamics; it cannot be explained solely by reference to earlier *stages* or *forms* of production.

This, then, completes our review of the three major analytical approaches to the entrepreneurial middle class. In Marxist accounts, the class does not, as such, exist; instead, as we have already shown, there is only the petty bourgeoisie and non-monopoly capitalists. In the other two more empirically-based orientations, reference is usually to a *melange* of petty proprietors such as, for example, farmers, small manufacturers, hoteliers and self-employed artisans. But none of these approaches are entirely satisfactory. The composition of the entrepreneurial middle class needs to be more precisely defined and the inter-relationships of its constituent groupings more clearly delineated if its reproduction, and the processes of individual mobility through small-scale capital accumulation, are to be better understood.

As we have already stated, the entrepreneurial middle class consists of those who own property which, together with their own and others' labour, they use for productive purposes. More specifically, it can be defined as consisting of *four* sub-categories, each of which is distinguished by differences in the relative mix of capital utilised and labour employed. This, in turn, tends to be associated with the nature of the proprietors' functional contribution to their enterprises. In these terms it is possible to regard the entrepreneurial middle class as consisting of the *self-employed, small employers, owner-controllers* and *owner-directors.*

The *self-employed* constitute the largest proportion of small business owners.[76] By definition, they *formally* employ no labour. They are, however, generally dependent upon the unpaid services of their families and the utilisation of domestic assets for business

purposes.[77] In most discussions they are normally seen as having a
strong commitment to 'good workmanship'.[78] They regard their work
as a way of 'earning a living' without experiencing the constraints
usually associated with employment. As such, they are said to
emphasise the intrinsic satisfactions which they derive from self-
employment, the pride in the quality of goods and services they
produce, and the working autonomy which they are alleged to enjoy.[79]
Many regard themselves as 'tradesmen' rather than 'businessmen' since
they are often more interested in personal work satisfaction than
business growth; consequently, most of the self-employed choose to
remain as such. They overwhelmingly trade on their skills instead of
capital assets and any finance required for trading is normally obtained
by personal savings within the family. Thus, the self-employed are
'marginal' within the entrepreneurial middle class. If self-employment
offers opportunities whereby manual workers can 'escape' from the
employment relationship, and thereby enjoy social prestige and
economic gain, there are, nevertheless, forces conducive to their
reversions to employee status. The self-employed are, for example,
vulnerable to the vagaries of the market while, at the same time, their
personal skills are likely to deteriorate through ageing. As a result,
earnings tend to decline over time and there are normally few capital
assets which can be inter-generationally transmitted. Although some of
the self-employed may, then, accumulate capital, many others become
proletarianised.

Small employers work alongside their employees and, in addition,
perform administrative and managerial tasks.[80] They both labour and
own their means of production and yet, at the same time, employ
wage labour. They are *directly* involved in the production of goods and
services and, in this way, personally contribute to the creation of
profit. Small employers are often skilled manual or technical workers
who began their business careers as self-employed. However, the
employment of labour – even of one person – introduces a range of
novel problems with which, from occupational experience alone, they
are often unable to cope. Employees have, after all, to be recruited and
trained, organised and controlled, insured and paid. In other words, in
order to operate efficiently, small employers must be able to *manage*
both finance and labour and, at the same time, do 'a day's work'. Many
adapt by either working excessively long hours or by making use of
family assistance. As with the self-employed, then, the family and the
domestic sphere represent an integral, indeed, inseparable part of the
business enterprise. Similarly, small employers are subject to

considerable market uncertainties which, together with their heavy dependence upon personal skills rather than capital assets, can make their proprietorship vulnerable. Their position within the entrepreneurial middle class, therefore, is tenuous although less marginal than that of the self-employed. In fact, there is a significant degree of mobility – in both directions – between these two categories. It is only when small employers accumulate considerable capital assets that their membership becomes more firmly structured.[81] Only a minority, however, are able to accumulate sufficient assets to become owner-controllers, while many others revert to self-employment or become employees.

Owner-controllers do not work alongside their employees but, instead, they are singularly and solely responsible for the administration and management of their businesses. They are, perhaps, the closest present-day approximation to the classical entrepreneur and, as such, they are more likely to adopt a rational, cost-effective approach.[82] They, too, are subject to market fluctuations, but whereas the self-employed and small employers attempt to protect themselves by cultivating networks of regular customers, the generally larger size of the owner-controllers' businesses prevent them adopting this strategy. At the same time, their market position is more vulnerable than that of larger enterprises since the latter often have access to greater cash and credit resources which enable them to 'ride' periods of trading difficulty. Unlike the self-employed and small employers, owner-controllers depend primarily upon personal managerial and financial expertise rather than purely trade-based skills. This category, therefore, includes individuals with prior managerial experience as well as those who have been upwardly mobile through small-scale capital accumulation. Because owner-controllers do not work alongside their employees they must consciously develop systems of supervisory control. Further, obtaining worker commitment is more problematic than for small employers who are able to dictate work performance by personal example. The owner-controllers' more calculative approach is reflected in the greater separation of business and domestic spheres. Unpaid family labour, characteristically important in smaller businesses, is no longer significant. However, enterprises of this sort are usually family-owned and, because they have greater tangible capital assets, can be transmitted between generations. This acts as a buffer against downward mobility of the kind which is often experienced by the self-employed and small employers; as such, owner-controllers are more firmly rooted within the entrepreneurial middle class.

Owner-directors control enterprises within which there are managerial structures.[83] Administrative tasks are sub-divided and delegated to executive directors and other senior staff. In other words, the scale of business activities is such that the owners are no longer able to *personally* perform all the functions of supervison and control. Within this category, there is a diversity of trajectories to proprietorship; some may have inherited businesses from their fathers, while others will have founded their own enterprises or purchased them from other owners.[84] Consequently, managerial practices vary. In confronting the common problem of delegation, some owner-directors implement formalised, quasi-bureaucratic decision-making practices while others rely upon more personal systems; for example, the cultivation of an ethos of paternalism within which employee commitment is obtained. As with owner-controllers, the ownership of substantial capital assets firmly entrenches owner-directors within the entrepreneurial middle class. As a hedge against business failure a substantial degree of product diversification often occurs. However, despite differences in managerial strategies, all owner-directors are confronted with a common problem; the need to *delegate* control and yet *retain* personal ownership. Those who, through business growth, fail to do this, have often to 'go public'. They thereby threaten their position as active proprietors.

These, briefly, are the four types of business proprietor which constitute the entrepreneurial middle class. This typology is used in this book to investigate a number of issues which, as yet, have been barely touched upon in sociological debate.[85] The problems confronting individuals who experience mobility on the basis of small-scale capital accumulation rather than through organisational careers are unknown. There is also a general ignorance of the attitudes and beliefs found among different sectors of the entrepreneurial middle class and the extent to which these are shaped by varying material circumstances.[86] Further, little is known about the ways whereby petty capital accumulation is related to different family and employment relationships.[87] In addition, the linkages that develop between small- and large-scale business enterprises are largely unexplored.[88] These sociological issues have received scant attention since most analyses have typically regarded them from an almost entirely financial or economic perspective.[89] Until further research is directed to these areas, the reproduction of the entrepreneurial middle class will remain uncharted. In Chapter 2 then, the conditions conducive to the formation of small-scale businesses are discussed and it is suggested that they are more likely to develop within labour- rather than capital-intensive sectors of the economy. In Chapter 3 this discussion is continued by reference to the building industry where both the work process and market conditions encourage the formation of business enterprises. This industry is used as a *critical case* in order to *illustrate* the technological, economic and social processes that operate, to varying degrees, in many other parts of the economy and which, in turn, explain the structural conditions underlying the reproduction of the entrepreneurial middle class. In Chapters 4 to 7 a detailed analysis of the four types of business owner is presented on the basis of empirical evidence collected in the research. Finally, in the concluding chapter, the implications of our findings for the analysis of class structure are explored.

Notes

1. See, for example, R. E. Pahl, 'Employment, Work and the Domestic Division of Labour', *International Journal of Urban and Regional Research*, vol. 4, 1980; J. Gershuny and R. E. Pahl, 'Work Outside Employment: Some Preliminary Speculations', *New Universities Quarterly*, vol. 34, 1979/80; J. H. Goldthorpe, 'The Current Inflation: Towards a Sociological Account' in F. Hirsch and J. H. Goldthorpe (eds), *The Political Economy of Inflation*, London, 1978a.

2. See N. Poulantzas, *Classes in Contemporary Capitalism*, London, 1975; E. O. Wright, *Class, Crisis and the State*, London, 1978; F. Parkin, *Marxism and Class Theory*, London, 1979.

3. Useful reviews of such enquiries are available in C. Sofer, *Men in Mid-Career*, Cambridge, 1970; J. M. and R. E. Pahl, *Managers and Their Wives*, Harmondsworth, 1972; J. Raynor, *The Middle Class*, London, 1969.

4. H. Newby, C. Bell, D. Rose and P. Saunders, *Property, Paternalism and Power*, London, 1978, p. 18.

5. See Poulantzas, *Classes in Contemporary Capitalism* and Wright, *Class Crisis and the State.*

6. See H. Braverman, *Labor and Monopoly Capital*, New York, 1974.

7. See Pahl, *Managers and Their Wives*, 1972; J. A. Jackson (ed.), *Professions and Professionalisation*, Cambridge, 1970; T. Johnson, 'The Professions in the Class Structure' in R. Scase (ed.), *Industrial Society: Class, Cleavage and Control*, London, 1977.

8. These issues are discussed by Braverman, *Labor and Monopoly Capital*; Johnson, 'The Professions in the Class Structure'; P. D. Anthony, *The Ideology of Work*, London, 1977.

9. See, for example, T. Nichols, *Ownership, Control and Ideology*, London, 1969.

10. For broad-ranging discussions of this theme see D. Bell, *The Coming of Post-Industrial Society*, London, 1974; J. K. Galbraith, *The New Industrial State*, Harmondsworth, 1972.

11. See A. Giddens, *The Class Structure of the Advanced Societies*, London,

1973; Poulantzas, *Classes in Contemporary Capitalism*; Parkin, *Marxism and Class Theory*; P. Walker (ed.), *Between Labour and Capital*, Hassocks, 1979.
12. Newby *et al.*, *Property, Paternalism and Power*, p. 20.
13. For a detailed analysis of the contributions made by small business owners in different sectors of the economy see *Report of the Committee of Inquiry on Small Firms* (The Bolton Report), Cmnd 4811, London, 1971 and, more recently, *The Financing of Small Firms* (The Wilson Report), Cmnd 7503, London, 1979.
14. See F. Bechhofer and B. Elliott, 'An Approach to a Study of Small Shopkeepers and the Class Structure', *European Journal of Sociology*, vol. 9, 1968; F. Bechhofer, B. Elliott, M. Rushforth and R. Bland, 'The Petits Bourgeois in the Class Structure: The Case of the Small Shopkeepers' in F. Parkin (ed.), *The Social Analysis of Class Structure*, London, 1974a; F. Bechhofer and B. Elliott, 'Persistence and Change: the Petite Bourgeoisie in Industrial Society', *European Journal of Sociology*, vol. 17, 1976; R. Bland, B. Elliott and F. Bechhofer, 'Social Mobility in the Petite Bourgeoisie', *Acta Sociologica*, vol. 21, 1978.
15. B. Elliott and D. McCrone, 'Landlords in Edinburgh: Some Preliminary Findings', *Sociological Review*, vol. 23, 1975; B. Elliott and D. McCrone, *Property and Power in a City*, London, 1980.
16. Newby *et al.*, *Property, Paternalism and Power*; H. Newby, *Green and Pleasant Land*, London, 1979.
17. Bechhofer and Elliott, 'Persistence and Change', p. 77.
18. Bechhofer *et al.*, 'The Petits Bourgeois', p. 123; F. Bechhofer and B. Elliott, 'Petty Property: The Survival of a Moral Economy' in F. Bechhofer and B. Elliott (eds.), *The Petite Bourgeoisie*, London, 1981, p. 183.
19. Bechhofer *et al.*, 'The Petits Bourgeois', p. 123.
20. F. Bechhofer, B. Elliott, M. Rushford and R. Bland, 'Small Shopkeepers: Matters of Money and Meaning', *Sociological Review*, vol. 22, 1974b, pp. 473–4, 479.
21. Ibid.; Bechhofer, 'The Petits Bourgeois'.
22. Bechhofer, 'The Petits Bourgeois', p. 124.
23. It is control by the state rather than big business which attracts most opposition from small business owners. See the contributions in, for example, R. King and N. Nugent (eds.), *Respectable Rebels*, London, 1979 and F. Bechhofer, B. Elliott and D. McCrone, 'Structure, Consciousness and Action', *British Journal of Sociology*, vol. 29, 1978.
24. Bechhofer and Elliott, 'Petty Property', pp. 183–4, 187.
25. For a discussion of the economic changes underlying this trend see J. Gershuny, *After Industrial Society*, London, 1978.
26. This argument is summarised in J. Boissevain, 'Small Entrepreneurs in Changing Europe: Towards a Research Agenda', unpublished paper presented at the European Centre for Work and Society, Utrecht, 1980.
27. See, for example, E. F. Schumacher, *Small is Beautiful*, London, 1973; K. Kumar, *Prophecy and Progress*, Harmondsworth, 1978.
28. Boissevain, 'Small Entrepreneurs in Changing Europe', pp. 21–2.
29. J. Martin and A. R. D. Norman, *The Computerized Society*, Englewood Cliffs, New Jersey, 1970, p. 32.
30. Kumar, *Prophecy and Progress*, p. 320.
31. For empirical evidence see F. Blackaby (ed.), *De-Industrialisation*, London, 1979; Pahl, 'Employment, Work and the Domestic Division of Labour'.
32. Pahl, 'Employment, Work and the Domestic Division of Labour', p. 4.
33. Ibid., p. 5.
34. See R. Scase and R. Goffee, *The Real World of the Small Business Owner*, London, 1980.

35. Boissevain, 'Small Entrepreneurs in Changing Europe', p. 11.

36. K. Marx and F. Engels, *The Communist Manifesto*, (1848) in K. Marx and F. Engels, *Selected Works*, London, 1968, p. 42.

37. See K. Marx, *Capital*, (vol. 1), London, 1954.

38. Ibid., p. 320.

39. Ibid., p. 364.

40. Ibid., p. 478.

41. Ibid., pp. 586–7.

42. The Marxist concept of 'mode of production' refers to an abstract combination of relations and forces of production. A 'social formation' is comprised of several modes and forms of production although one mode will be dominant. When Marx analysed nineteenth-century England the capitalist mode was predominant and all other types of productive activity were subordinate to it. At any particular stage the dissolution of prior modes of production may reach the point where only forms or elements of that mode persist. For further discussion of these points see Poulantzas, *Classes in Contemporary Capitalism*, and A. Friedman, *Industry and Labour*, London, 1977.

43. Poulantzas, *Classes in Contemporary Capitalism*, p. 151.

44. Ibid., p. 286.

45. Ibid., pp. 285–6.

46. Wright, *Class Crisis and the State*, Chapter Two.

47. Ibid., pp. 79–80.

48. Wright's schema is summarised diagrammatically as follows:

Capitalist mode of production   Simple commodity production

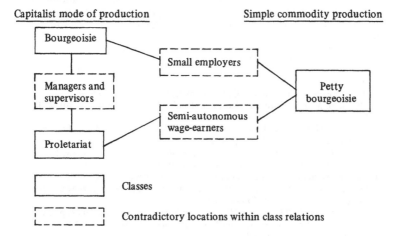

The criteria employed by Wright to define class position are derived from an historical analysis of three major changes in capitalist relations of production. The first concerns the loss of control by direct producers over the labour process as a result of the division of labour and technological changes associated with the stage of 'modern industry'. The second involves the separation of 'legal' and 'real' economic ownership, as stocks are dispersed and propertyless managers hired, in large corporations during the stage of monopoly capitalism. Consequently, economic 'possession' (control over the immediate labour process) is separated from economic 'ownership' (control over investments and resource allocation). Third, the functions of economic 'possession' are further differentiated in terms of 'control over the physical means of production' and 'control over labour power'; there is, then, the emergence of specialist managers and supervisory hierarchies. Class relations and class locations, may therefore be defined according to control over (1) the physical means of production; (2) labour power and (3) investments and resources. See Wright, *Class, Crisis and the State*, pp. 61–83.

49. Poulantzas, *Classes in Contemporary Capitalism*, p. 143.

50. Ibid.

51. Ibid., p. 147.

52. Ibid., p. 140.

53. Ibid.

54. Wright, *Class, Crisis and the State*, pp. 79–80.

55. G. Carchedi, 'On the Economic Identification of the New Middle Class', *Economy and Society*, vol. 4, 1975, p. 50.

56. Ibid., p. 48.

57. J. Westergaard, 'Class, Inequality and "Corporatism" ' in A. Hunt (ed.), *Class and Class Structure*, London, 1977, p. 168.

58. Poulantzas, *Classes in Contemporary Capitalism*, p. 17.

59. Carchedi, 'On the Economic Identification of the New Middle Class', p. 2.

60. Wright, *Class, Crisis and the State*, p. 10.

61. Ibid., pp. 74–5, note 67.

62. Ibid.

63. F. Parkin, 'Social Stratification' in T. Bottomore and R. Nisbet (eds.), *A History of Sociological Analysis*, London, 1978, p. 625.

64. For recent discussions of this distinction and the implications for research into social mobility and class structure see R. Blackburn, 'Social Stratification', unpublished paper presented to BSA Conference, Lancaster, 1980 and A. Stewart, K. Prandy and R. Blackburn, *Social Stratification and Occupations*, London, 1980.

65. Poulantzas, *Classes in Contemporary Capitalism*, p. 329.

66. Marx, *Capital*, (vol. 1), p. 586.

67. V. I. Lenin, *Collected Works*, (vol. 22), London, 1949, p. 70.

68. Ibid., (vol. 15), p. 39.

69. An exception is the work of Friedman, *Industry and Labour*.

70. S. M. Miller, 'Notes on Neo-Capitalism', *Theory and Society*, vol. 2, 1975, p. 15.

71. A. J. Mayer, 'The Lower Middle Class as Historical Problem', *Journal of Modern History*, vol. 47, 1975, p. 417.

72. V. I. Lenin, *The Development of Capitalism in Russia*, Moscow, 1956.

73. Most social mobility studies assume that the pre-eminent channel for upward movement is through occupational positions within large-scale bureaucracies on the basis of meritocratic criteria. For a recent review of such work see A. Heath, *Social Mobility*, Glasgow, 1981.

74. G. Crossick, *The Lower Middle Class in Britain*, London 1977, p. 35.

75. Mayer, 'The Lower Middle Class as Historical Problem', p. 432.

76. It is extremely difficult to present accurate statistical data in support of this assertion. Definitions of 'small businesses' and 'self-employed' vary (the latter often including those who formally employ others). Further, as recent discussions of the 'informal' economy suggest, many self-employed proprietors are not 'officially' recognised or, therefore, counted. Nevertheless, most aggregate data on the small firm sector strongly suggest that 'the vast majority of small firms are very small indeed'. *Report of the Committee of Inquiry on Small Firms*, (The Bolton Report), p. 3. More recent estimates suggest that of 1.9 million employers and self-employed, 1.1 million are sole traders without employees. See J. McHugh, 'The Self-employed and the Small Independent Entrepreneur' in King and Nugent (eds.), *Respectable Rebels*, pp. 47–8. For evidence that the

self-employed represent the largest proportion of small businesses owners in the USA see K. Mayer, 'Business Enterprise: The Traditional Symbol of Opportunity', *British Journal of Sociology*, vol. 4, 1953.

77. See the evidence reported in F. Bechhofer *et al.*, 'Small Shopkeepers'; H. Newby *et al.*, *Property, Paternalism and Power*; R. Gasson, 'Roles of Farm Women in England', unpublished paper, 1980; C. Delphy and D. Leonard, 'The Family as an Economic System', unpublished paper presented to Institutionalisation of Sex Differences Conference, University of Kent, April 1980.

78. This is particularly the case in discussions of independent craftworkers. See, for example, W. M. Williams, *The Country Craftsman*, London, 1958.

79. See, for example, the discussion in C. W. Mills, *White Collar*, London, 1951.

80. A substantial proportion of the Edinburgh shopkeepers and East Anglian 'family' and 'active managerial' farmers studied, respectively, by Bechhofer *et al.* and Newby *et al.* would fall into this category.

81. For a recent discussion of the 'marginal' and 'established' components of the 'old' middle class see J. H. Goldthorpe, 'Comment', *British Journal of Sociology*, vol. 29, 1978a.

82. For discussions of the historical role of the entrepreneur see, for example, M. W. Flinn, *Origins of the Industrial Revolution*, London, 1966; J. Boswell, *The Rise and Decline of Small Firms*, London, 1973. Entrepreneurial ideology is discussed in Nichols, *Ownership, Control and Ideology*.

83. The historical emergence of such structures is examined in A. Francis, 'Families, Firms and Finance Capital', *Sociology*, vol. 14, 1980 and S. Nyman and A. Silbertson, 'The Ownership and Control of Industry', *Oxford Economic Papers*, vol. 30, 1978. For contemporary analyses see M. Stanworth and J. Curran, *Management Motivation in the Smaller Business*, Epping, 1973 and Boswell, *The Rise and Decline of Small Firms*.

84. See Boswell, *The Rise and Decline of Small Firms*. One particular trajectory (inheritance) and one particular managerial style (paternalism) is discussed in G. M. Norris, 'Industrial Paternalist Capitalism and Local Labour Markets', *Sociology*, vol. 12, 1978.

85. Marx made a similar distinction in his discussion of independent artisans and handicraftsmen, small masters and 'full blown' capitalists. See Marx, *Capital*, (vol. 1).

86. Notwithstanding the various contributions of F. Bechhofer *et al.* and H. Newby *et al.*, *Property, Paternalism and Power*, as well as King and Nugent, *Respectable Rebels*.

87. These issues are discussed in Boswell, *The Rise and Decline of Small Firms* and Boissevain, 'Small Entrepreneurs in Changing Europe'.

88. See, however, Friedman, *Industry and Labour*.

89. This emphasis is reflected in much of the recent debate concerning the role of small businesses in the economy. For a critique of many contemporary assumptions of this sort see R. Scase and R. Goffee, *The Real World of the Small Business Owner*.

2 TECHNOLOGICAL CHANGE, THE OCCUPATIONAL STRUCTURE AND THE ENTREPRENEURIAL MIDDLE CLASS

In this chapter we discuss those features of the economy which are conducive to the formation and growth of small-scale enterprises. Although the general direction of economic and technological change has reduced the opportunities, a modern economy consists of different sectors and some are more conducive to small business growth than others. In their description of present-day capitalism, observers have stressed the growth of large-scale bureaucratic structures and the increasing concentration of industrial production.[1] These developments have had implications for the nature of the occupational structure and the demand for various work skills; while the proportion of manual workers has declined, there has been an increasing need for administrative, professional, technical and white-collar employees.[2] More importantly for our purposes, the growing domination of large-scale bureaucratic enterprises has led to a reduction in the proportion of business proprietors.[3] Indeed, no other group has experienced such a decline; between 1911 and 1971 it fell by 50 per cent. In other words, the growth of the corporate economy during the twentieth century has apparently witnessed the almost complete demise of the entrepreneurial middle class. In its place, the expanding ranks of administrative, professional and technical *employees* now constitute the core of a large, corporate-based middle class. These trends are clearly illustrated in Table 2.1 which documents the overall pattern of occupational change during the present century.

The degree to which these changes have been related to the growth of large-scale organisations and the increasing concentration of production is confirmed by Hannah and Kay's analysis which shows that although at the turn of the century the hundred largest firms in British manufacturing controlled about 15 per cent of total net output, their share increased to approximately 50 per cent by the mid-1970s.[4] There has also been a growing concentration of ownership; by the late 1960s, the hundred largest firms owned 75 per cent of the net assets held by publicly-quoted companies.[5] Thus, the twentieth century has seen the concentration of manufacturing assets into fewer industrial conglomerates and, as Hannah has argued, the principal cause has not

Table 2.1: Changes in the British Occupational Structure, 1911–71

	Major occupational groups as a percentage of total occupied population 1911–71							Growth indices of major occupational groups, 1911–71 (1911 = 100)						
	1911	1921	1931	1951	1961	1966	1971	1911	1921	1931	1951	1961	1966	1971
1 Employers and proprietors	6.7	6.8	6.7	5.0	4.8	3.4	2.6	100	107	114	91	93	68	50
2 White-collar workers	18.7	21.2	23.0	30.9	35.9	38.3	42.7	100	119	141	202	247	276	303
(a) Managers and administrators	3.4	3.6	3.7	5.5	5.4	6.1	8.6	100	112	122	197	201	240	330
(b) Higher professionals	1.0	1.0	1.1	1.9	3.0	3.4	3.8	100	107	130	236	390	451	504
(c) Lower professionals and technicians	3.1	3.5	3.5	4.7	6.0	6.5	7.7	100	121	130	189	253	286	336
(d) Foremen and inspectors	1.3	1.4	1.5	2.6	2.9	3.0	3.0	100	118	136	249	287	311	311
(e) Clerks	4.5	6.5	6.7	10.4	12.7	13.2	14.0	100	151	169	281	360	392	410
(f) Salesmen and shop assistants	5.4	5.1	6.5	5.7	5.9	6.1	5.6	100	99	139	129	141	153	138
3 Manual workers	74.6	72.0	70.3	64.2	59.3	58.3	54.7	100	102	108	106	102	105	98
(a) Skilled	30.5	28.8	26.7	24.9	25.3	23.7		100	99	100	100	107	104	
(b) Semi-skilled	34.4	29.0	28.7	27.2	25.4	26.1		100	89	96	97	95	102	
(c) Unskilled	9.6	14.2	14.8	12.0	8.6	8.5		100	155	176	153	115	119	
4 Total occupied population	100.0	100.0	100.0	100.0	100.0	100.0	100.0	100	105	115	123	129	135	133

Source: R. Brown, 'Work' in P. Abrams (ed.), *Work, Urbanism and Inequality*, London 1978, Table 2.8.

been independent business growth but rather mergers, takeovers and amalgamations. Consequently, the number of small businesses has fallen:

> Parallel to this movement towards larger enterprises, small firms continued their almost uninterrupted decline. Between 1958 and 1963, for example, the share in net output of manufacturing firms with less than 200 employees declined from 20 per cent of the total to only 16 per cent, and the demise of more than half of the small companies was reported to be due to acquisition by larger rivals.[6]

Even where small firms retain legal independence they have often become technically subordinated to the needs of larger businesses. As Friedman has pointed out, many have grown to be dependent upon the requirements of larger enterprises which subcontract to them the production of limited 'runs' and specialist goods and services.[7]

The decline in the small firm sector of the British economy has attracted much attention over recent years. The Bolton Report indicated that the share of small manufacturing firms in employment and output declined 'substantially and almost continuously' from the mid-1920s onwards.[8] Thus, between 1935 and 1963 employment in small manufacturing enterprises fell from 38 per cent to 20 per cent of the total and output from 35 per cent to 16 per cent.[9] The Report concluded that up to the mid-1960s 'the contribution of small firms to economic activity was declining in most industries' and, further, that this trend was continuing.[10] However, recent evidence suggests that this long-term decline has stopped. Between 1963 and 1973, for example, employment in small manufacturing enterprises remained at 21 per cent of the total whilst output only fell marginally from 18 to 17 per cent.[11] This led the Wilson Report to claim that 'the contribution of small firms appears to have stabilised in recent years'.[12] Whether or not recent government policies designed to encourage the formation of small businesses will have any lasting effect in rejuvenating the small firm sector is, as yet, uncertain.

It is, then, little wonder that observers have coined the term 'corporate economy' since, clearly, a few very large companies control the 'commanding heights' of both the national economy and the international economic system.[13] This has led Scott to argue that:

> The top 100 British firms and the top 500 American firms comprise the high-profit sector of the economy and dominate a periphery of

relatively small firms operating in restricted low-profit markets.[14]

He further claims that the largest firms are mainly multi-product companies which have grown through the takeover of businesses within related areas. The growing concentration of production under the control of a diminishing number of large corporations is, then, indisputable. Nevertheless, it is important to take account of the *differential* impact of this trend upon various sectors of the economy. The move towards capital concentration and large-scale organisation is far from uniform. Some branches of the economy are characterised by high levels of industrial concentration such that organisational structures and the material conditions of production are determined by a few giant corporations. In these 'advanced' sectors of the economy, fixed capital expenditure is extremely high. The dominance of a handful of highly-capitalised multinational companies in petrochemical manufacture is well known, but a similar situation exists in other industrial spheres. In 1973, for example, the five largest enterprises in both tobacco and sugar processing accounted for virtually *all* employment, output and capital expenditure in those industries.[15] Such 'monopoly' concentration, however, does not extend to every sector of manufacturing. The five largest companies in the furniture and upholstery industry, by contrast, were responsible for only 11 per cent of employment, 14 per cent of output and 24 per cent of capital expenditure.[16] Utton has summarised these variations as follows:

> Generally speaking those sectors of industry associated with very large capital requirements appear amongst the most heavily concentrated, such as chemicals and allied trades, electrical engineering and electrical goods, vehicles and iron and steel and non-ferrous metals. On the other hand, sectors usually associated with smaller firms tend to rank low in terms of concentration, e.g., cotton, woollen and worsted; clothing and footwear.[17]

The relevance of these comments is confirmed in Tables 2.2 and 2.3 which indicate the levels of employment and output accounted for by manufacturing firms of different sizes. These figures, taken from the Wilson Report, assume that small firms are those with less than 200 employees. Whereas the electrical engineering, vehicle manufacture and chemical industries are characterised by the predominance of large corporations, there is an overwhelming predominance of small businesses within those sectors that produce highly specialised 'short-

Table 2.2: Employment in UK Manufacturing Industry According to Size of Firm in 1973 (thousands)

Industry order	Firms 1–99 employees	Firms 100–199 employees	Total small firms	Total all firms	Small firms as % of total
Food, drink and tobacco	75.8	33.3	109.1	797.2	13.7
Coal and petroleum products	2.4	0.9	3.3	37.2	8.9
Chemical and allied industries	32.0	15.3	47.3	389.4	12.1
Metal manufacture	37.8	20.7	58.5	497.9	11.7
Mechanical engineering	171.5	63.2	234.7	910.5	25.8
Instrument engineering	25.9	11.3	37.2	149.3	24.9
Electrical engineering	45.7	23.8	69.5	773.6	9.0
Shipbuilding and marine engineering	14.5	5.7	20.2	181.6	11.1
Vehicles	31.8	17.9	49.7	793.1	6.3
Metal goods not elsewhere specified	166.1	49.7	215.8	543.5	39.7
Textiles	71.9	45.4	117.3	584.3	20.1
Leather, leather goods and fur	21.8	4.8	26.6	43.2	61.6
Clothing and footwear	117.1	46.4	163.5	440.4	37.1
Bricks, pottery, glass, cement, etc.	39.3	16.2	55.5	283.6	19.6
Timber, furniture, etc.	123.6	36.6	160.2	276.7	57.9
Paper, printing and publishing	127.7	42.2	169.9	576.1	29.5
Other manufacturing industries	66.1	27.0	93.1	338.7	27.5
All manufacturing industries	1,108.6	396.9	1,505.5	7,268.3	20.7

Source: *The Financing of Small Firms*, (The Wilson Report), Cmmnd 7503, Table 2.5.

Table 2.3: Net Output in UK Manufacturing Industry According to Size of Firm in 1973 (£ million)

Industry order	Firms 1–99 employees	Firms 100–199 employees	Total small firms	Total all firms	Small as % of total
Food, drink and tobacco	257.1	126.1	383.2	3,431.3	11.2
Coal and petroleum products	13.8	6.6	20.4	430.0	4.7
Chemical and allied industries	152.2	76.7	228.9	2,377.4	9.6
Metal manufacture	113.7	70.3	184.0	1,887.2	9.7
Mechanical engineering	508.7	197.4	706.1	3,070.8	23.0
Instrument engineering	67.5	33.0	100.5	413.8	24.3
Electrical engineering	119.0	67.3	186.3	2,332.1	8.0
Shipbuilding and marine engineering	34.7	16.9	51.6	463.0	11.1
Vehicles	87.2	49.2	136.4	2,597.4	5.3
Metal goods not elsewhere specified	455.7	144.7	600.4	1,601.5	37.5
Textiles	164.6	104.9	269.5	1,645.4	16.4
Leather, leather goods and fur	53.3	12.2	65.5	107.9	60.7
Clothing and footwear	201.6	81.7	283.3	811.4	34.9
Bricks, pottery, glass, cement, etc.	141.1	55.9	197.0	1,134.1	17.4
Timber, furniture, etc.	411.5	127.5	539.0	1,015.4	53.1
Paper, printing and publishing	392.9	137.3	530.2	2,176.5	24.4
Other manufacturing industries	183.2	81.9	265.1	1,104.6	24.0
All manufacturing industries	3,161.3	1,180.1	4,341.4	25,377.0	17.1

Source: *The Financing of Small Firms*, (The Wilson Report), Cmmnd 7503, Table 2.6.

run' commodities; for example, the manufacture of leather goods, furniture, clothing and various metal products.

What accounts for this variation? Boswell has given a detailed answer; he suggests that small firms are evident in the following sectors:

> First, they are still numerous and important in such traditional industries as cotton, wool, hosiery and footwear, and also printing and publishing. In the textile industries in particular they form large clusters in such old industrial regions as Lancashire, the West Riding of Yorkshire and parts of the East Midlands. Second, there has been a continued influx of small firms into the vast engineering and metal-working industries, often providing components or subcontracting services to larger concerns, with strong concentrations, for example, around the motor industry in the West Midlands, but generally pretty widely dispersed. These are the specialist servants or myriad small dependants of our major industries. Third, there has also been a continued influx into those sectors which have long favoured the small entrepreneur: consumer goods trades with low costs and high labour content, products with strong elements of fashion and specialization, like furniture and clothing. Finally, modern technology has spawned a new generation of small firms in such areas as plastics, scientific instruments and electronics, again widely dispersed geographically, although typically on the new trading estates and in revival or boom areas. Thus, small firms are important in sectors traditional, craft-based or new, in fields both heavy and light, in both producer and consumer goods industries, and in all parts of the country.[18]

It seems, then, that there are four major factors which explain the persistence of small businesses in manufacturing. First, there are 'traditional' industrial sectors which may be regarded as the legacy of an earlier stage of industrialisation. These are characterised by the persistence of 'entrepreneurship' which, coupled with the perpetuation of craft skills, encourages the formation of small-scale enterprises. In the printing industry, for instance, there is a history of craftsmen either starting their own enterprises or acquiring those of retiring employers. Elsewhere, occupational inheritence in the textile and hosiery industries, for example, has often led to the preservation of traditional family businesses. Industries such as these tend to be characterised by technological systems which enable employees to retain the skills necessary to become small employers. As Boswell suggests:

Historically, in this country some industries have been more receptive than others to working-class founders of small firms. Men of humble origin found it easier to set up business in sectors where technological and capital requirements were low ... In a craft-based, low-capital sector like hosiery most of the fathers of men who founded firms were manual workers – in stark contrast, say, to the more capital intensive and also much more upper class atmosphere of steel.[19]

Secondly, the growth of mass-production, assembly-line technology has encouraged the formation of small firms through subcontracting the manufacture of various specialist components.[20] Such small businesses tend to be heavily dependent for their survival upon one or a few large customers; indeed, they are often little more than subsidiaries. The Bolton Report, in summarising the findings of one of its surveys, gives many examples of this dependent relationship:

A large London department store indicated that virtually all its turnover of women's fashions and half its sales of top quality clothing were supplied by small firms. Of the suppliers to the furnishing accessory divisions of the same store, 85 per cent were small firms. One of the largest diversified manufacturing companies had 950 suppliers of which 40 per cent were small firms. A tractor manufacturer replied that 60 per cent of the parts and components entering its main plant came from small firms. A large rubber company estimated that 35–40 per cent of its total purchases were from small firms ... One of the 'Big Four' motor manufacturers had 1,200 suppliers of which 13 per cent were small firms accounting for 3½ per cent of total purchases, although small–medium sized companies, just outside the Committee's terms of reference, accounted for very much more. A division of one major aerospace company had 76 suppliers in the United Kingdom manufacturing parts and components under sub-contract, and of these 43 per cent were small firms; of its 104 material suppliers 12 per cent were small firms. Most of the large companies praised small firms for their low prices, speed, flexibility and service and one company claimed that it could not operate without them.[21]

Thirdly, there are sectors of manufacturing that remain labour-intensive. These are obviously ideal 'sites' for the formation and persistence of small firms, if only because of the low level of capital required for starting a business. Usually, as Boswell suggests, they tend to cater for specialist needs and changing fashions; typically, they are heavily dependent upon skilled labour rather than sophisticated machinery. In clothing and footwear manufacture, for example, wages and salaries account for 58 per cent of total costs while in the chemical industry, they represent less than 35 per cent.[22] Labour-intensive small firms, dependent as they are upon skilled labour, tend to be flexible in their productive techniques so that changes in demand can be swiftly met with little capital outlay. At the same time, changes in fashion can create markets which skilled employees may perceive as new business opportunities, and this can encourage them to start their own enterprises. The labour-intensive sectors of manufacturing, then, are often characterised by high rates of business turnover because of fluctuations in consumer fashion.

Finally, there are sectors where technological change has enabled small enterprises to emerge with new systems of production.[23] The use of plastics rather than steel, for example, has allowed the small-scale manufacture of commodities using relatively cheap equipment. Recent advances in computer and microchip technology have drastically reduced the cost of labour-saving devices so that many small businesses can afford to lease or purchase desk accounting and other data processing equipment. Such changes have encouraged the geographical decentralisation of manufacturing and the growth of small units of production. Often, technological innovations pioneered within large organisations have led to the formation of 'spin-off' businesses by ex-employee managers and technicians.[24] Some of these enterprises compete in the same markets as their larger counterparts; others, however, concentrate upon specialist products which are supplied to only one or two large customers. The manufacture of various scientific precision instruments is, for example, typically subcontracted by larger corporations to smaller businesses.

These differing circumstances, then, account for variations in the level of concentration found within manufacturing industry. As such, they explain the persistence of small businesses despite the overall trend towards large, highly-capitalised corporations. Such variations in industrial concentration are, however, far more striking *outside* the manufacturing sector. As Table 2.4 shows, small firms in manufacturing account for 20 per cent of all employment but this represents the low end of a continuum which rises to 49 per cent in retail trades and 82 per cent in 'miscellaneous services'. Similarly, whereas small manufacturers account for only 16 per cent of total output, the contribution of small enterprises rises to 29 per cent in the motor trades and 73 per cent in hotel and catering.

Table 2.4: The Relative Importance of Small Firms in Different Industries, 1963

| | Small firms as percentage of all firms | | |
Economic sector	Numbers employed	Net output	Number of firms
Miscellaneous services	82	68	99
Hotel and catering trades	75	73	96
Retail trades	49	32	96
Road transport	36	26	85
Building and construction	33	27	92
Motor trades	32	29	87
Wholesale trades	25	11	77
Manufacturing	20	16	94
Mining/quarrying	20	20	77
Total: all groups	31	21	93

Source: *Report of the Committee of Inquiry on Small Firms*, (The Bolton Report), Cmmnd 4811, Table 3.1.

The importance of small firms, then, varies considerably between different areas of the economy. In general, as the Bolton Report indicates:

> Small firms have a relatively greater share of the labour-intensive service trades than they do of manufacturing and mining, while in road transport and construction they occupy an intermediate position.[25]

Although The Bolton Report uses a flexible measure of 'smallness' for different economic sectors, it stresses that *all* small firms are distinguished by three key features:

> Firstly, in economic terms, a small firm is one that has a relatively small share of its market. Secondly, an essential characteristic of a small firm is that it is managed by its owners or part-owners in a personalised way, and not through the medium of a formalised management structure. Thirdly, it is also independent in the sense that it does not form part of a larger enterprise and that the owner-managers should be free from outside control in taking their principal decisions.[26]

Certain sectors of the economy — most notably agriculture and professional and financial services — are, however, excluded from the Bolton Report yet these are also areas where small-scale enterprises have a significant share of the market. Indeed, the importance of these and other 'service' sectors as the bases for small business formation is illustrated in Table 2.5 which shows the industrial distribution of the self-employed between 1961 and 1975.

If small businesses are to be found in those sectors of the economy which require low levels of fixed capital investment and are labour-intensive, this is reflected in patterns of ownership. The Bolton Report found that in manufacturing, proprietors' capital accounted for roughly 60 per cent of the total assets of small firms; in non-manufacturing sectors the respective figure ranged between 50 and 65 per cent. However, closer inspection discloses differences between economic sectors; only one-fifth of small manufacturing firms were wholly-owned by *one person* whilst in retailing, sole proprietorship was overwhelmingly predominant.[27] Similarly, as would be expected, the extent of *family* ownership varies; a survey commissioned by the Bolton Report, and summarised in Table 2.6, indicates it is extensive in the wholesale and retail trades, but relatively low in small manufacturing.

It is clear, then, that not all sectors of the economy are characterised by the exclusive domination of large-scale, publicly-owned conglomerates. There are still areas of industrial activity where small firms are predominant and, even in those characterised by large corporations, small-scale enterprises continue to fulfil important economic functions. Thus, we should not overemphasise the ownership and control of Big Business; there remain a diversity of economic spheres within which small businesses are important. This is reflected in the nature of the employment relationship which varies between different enterprises and sectors of the economy. As we shall now discuss, this has implications for the formation of small businesses.

Many observers have stressed the increasing uniformity of work as it is experienced by most white-collar and industrial employees.[28] Within the context of large-scale bureaucratic structures, work tasks previously performed by owner-managers and entrepreneurs have become subdivided, routinised and allocated to a wide range of positions. The growth of the modern corporation has fragmented the work tasks of industrial workers, bringing about a process of 'de-skilling' which has reduced the extent to which responsibility and discretion can be exercised in the workplace.[29] The ideas of F. W. Taylor and 'scientific

Table 2.5: The Self-employed as Proportion of Employment by Industry, 1961 to 1975

Industry	1961		1966		1971		1975	
	Men	Women	Men	Women	Men	Women	Men	Women
Agriculture, forestry, fishing	35.6	15.7	31.3	18.1	42.6	23.0	41.4	23.5
Manufacturing	1.3	0.8	1.2	1.3	1.8	0.9	1.9	0.9
Construction	10.9	1.4	12.4	2.3	22.0	2.4	24.2	2.0
Transport and communication	3.0	0.8	3.1	0.8	4.9	1.2	5.7	0.7
Distributive trades	21.9	10.2	18.6	9.1	21.6	9.7	19.2	8.5
Insurance, banking, finance, business services	6.3	2.3	5.2	2.3	6.7	3.0	6.7	2.4
Professional and scientific services	16.8	1.9	13.3	1.8	13.5	1.7	13.0	1.6
Miscellaneous services	20.9	7.8	17.4	8.5	21.7	10.7	18.5	9.2
Total	8.6	4.1	7.9	4.2	9.9	4.3	9.9	3.9

Source: *Royal Commission on the Distribution of Income and Wealth*, Report No. 8, Cmnd 7679, Table 2.15.

Table 2.6: **Percentage of Small Firms Which Are Family-owned**

	Manufacture	Construction	Wholesale distribution	Motor trade	Retail trade
Wholly owned by members of the same family	38	44	69	49	68
Other forms of ownership	62	56	31	51	32

Source: *Report of the Committee of Inquiry on Small Firms*, (The Bolton Report), Cmnd 4811, Table 2.4.

management' in general, embody many of the principles which, together with technological change, are said to have brought about this 'de-skilling'.[30] Braverman has shown how such principles can give management almost complete control over workers' activities by removing their potential to exercise discretion and take decisions. He quotes Taylor thus, 'all possible brain work should be removed from the shop (floor) and centred in the planning or layout department'. Similarly, management 'specifies not only what is to be done, but how it is to be done and the exact time allowed for doing it'.[31] The application of these principles has led to the detailed delineation of work tasks and the growth of unskilled and semi-skilled work. Many observers have argued that this process has affected not only the majority of manual occupations in manufacturing industry but also white-collar occupations in retailing, banking, commerce and the service sector generally.[32] Consequently, the occupational structure is seen to be increasingly polarised between a declining minority of positions that have vested within them authority, autonomy and expertise and a growing mass of manual and non-manual occupations which are routinised and 'de-skilled'.

As a result, the experience of work is said to have altered significantly for the majority of employees. It is no longer 'satisfying' or 'creative' since it offers little opportunity for the independent exercise of skill, discretion and judgement.[33] Instead, work is an unrewarding and essentially *alienating* experience, devoid of interest or variation. To an increasing extent it is regarded as a 'chore' which has to be endured in order to satisfy other needs outside of work. The resulting low levels of employee involvement has contributed to the view that workers cannot be *trusted* to perform in accordance with the objectives of higher management. Consequently, there are pressures to make both manual and non-manual work even more closely prescribed and regulated in order to reduce levels of individual discretion to a minimum. This is the downward spiral of the 'low trust – low discretion' syndrome described by Fox, the end result of which is the imposition of more rigorous supervisory systems and the increasingly precise stipulation of work tasks within large-scale organisations.[34]

Despite these overall trends there is, within certain sectors of the economy, the persistence of skills that enable employees to start their own small-scale enterprises. Although one of the major tasks of management is to direct and control the work process, the most appropriate strategy for achieving this will vary according to a range of social and technical factors.[35] The extent to which workers in particular industries conform to different types of supervision and control will, for example, strongly influence managerial strategies.[36] Similarly, the technical conditions of production will determine the level of mechanisation and the extent to which work tasks can be broken down into highly routinised operations. In view of these considerations, it is questionable whether the application of 'scientific management' is always the most appropriate strategy for increasing production and profitability. Friedman has argued, for example, that the attempt to regulate work performance through a detailed division of labour can, under certain circumstances, lead to a reduction in productivity.[37] Thus, workers may resist managerial attempts to increase control by developing counter-strategies of either a collective or individual kind. Factories characterised by large-scale assembly-line production, for example, tend to have higher rates of absenteeism, labour turnover and industrial conflict.[38] In response to this, management has sometimes adopted a policy of 'responsible autonomy' rather than 'direct control' such that workers are given some leeway to adapt to changing circumstances as they arise in the process of production.[39] Occupational tasks are, then, structured in a manner that enables workers to enjoy a greater degree of autonomy and discretion; recent developments towards 'job enlargement', 'job enrichment' and 'team work' may be interpreted in these terms.[40] But whether the strategy of 'responsible autonomy' or 'direct control' is adopted will be largely contingent upon the particular character of the workforce. Friedman argues that the former is adopted for 'central' workers, whose labour is expensive and difficult to replace, whilst the latter is more appropriate for 'peripheral' employees, whose labour can be easily and cheaply substituted by others.[41] Consequently, various groups of white-collar, technical and skilled manual workers continue to enjoy 'responsible autonomy' while most semi- and unskilled operatives are subject to more rigorous control procedures as exercised through the mechanisation of work tasks, the division of labour and close supervision. In some occupational groups, then, workers are able to exercise judgement, responsibility and discretion; they are, to use Fox's terms, *trusted* to get on with their work. Within the general parameters stipulated by management, they retain certain skills and technical competences which are, to some extent, *independent* of the particular form of organisation imposed by management. They are, then, less dependent than others upon their employers.

In general, those in craft-based occupations and 'technical' or 'professional' employment have proved best able to resist managerial attempts to 'de-skill' their work.[42] Some groups of craftworkers, for example, through apprenticeship systems and strong trade unions, have retained a degree of work autonomy. Consequently, they have been able to defer, if not entirely prevent, the introduction of new technological systems and to resist the imposition of close supervision.[43] Other skilled workers have developed systems of shopfloor organisation which allow them to preserve areas of job autonomy and to delay the restructuring and mechanisation of work tasks.[44] As such, their labour may be said to be only *formally* subordinated to capital and this fundamentally affects the employment relationship, as the Brighton Labour Process Group has pointed out:

> When the labour process is only formally subordinated to capital there is the production of surplus value and its appropriation, but the objective and subjective conditions of labour are such as to provide a material basis for continual resistance to the imposition of valorisation as the unique objective of the production process. Real control of production is not yet firmly in the hands of capital. There is still a relationship between labour and the conditions of labour within production which provide labour with a degree of control and hence with a lever with which to enforce its class objectives which may, of course, be different from those of the fully developed proletarian labour of the mature capitalist mode of production. They may be objectives of artisanal labour, craft prerogatives over recruitment into the trades and over the content and performance of work, and so on. This . . . was general in the historical period in which simple co-operation was still the dominant form of the social organisation of the labour process; but it survives to some extent in social formations in which the mature capitalist mode of production is dominant (for example, in parts of the construction industry).[45]

The 'oppositional' tactics traditionally adopted by skilled manual workers have increasingly been implemented by technical and professional employees and the growth of white-collar unionism is but one manifestation of this trend.[46] Trade unionism represents, perhaps, the most common channel for *collective* employee organisation and action. However, employees can also react *individually* to changes that threaten their workplace autonomy. One such response is to leave one employer and join another where conditions may allow the personal retention of skills. Another response is, however, to establish an independent business which will grant freedom from any externally-imposed division of labour. In this sense, skill can be used as an important form of 'start-up' capital, particularly in labour-intensive sectors of the economy where fixed capital investment is low. Thus, skilled craftsmen in traditional industries as well as technically-qualified personnel in more modern 'light' industries possess expertise which can be used as a basis for small business formation. That many do, in fact, take up the option of self-employment is clearly demonstrated in Table 2.7.

Leaving aside the special category of farmers and fishermen, Table 2.7 illustrates the tendency for small business proprietors to be found in professional, technical and craft-based occupations.[47] They are strongly evident, for example, in the construction, painting, decorating, leather, wood and textile trades, but are rarely found within heavy industry. In other words, small businesses tend to be located in the labour- rather than capital-intensive sectors of the economy.[48] This suggests that, where initial capital costs are low, they may represent a means whereby individuals are able to retain control of their work and be free from managerial/employer interference.

If large-scale, highly capitalised business enterprises are associated with complex bureaucratic structures, small businesses are less reliant upon formalised, impersonal control and more dependent upon the delegation of tasks to skilled craft and technical workers.[49] Small firm employees are, then, often given considerable work autonomy within what is often a *high trust* relationship.[50] This, in turn, enables them to develop the capacity for responsibility and decision-making which can be conducive to their 'experimenting' through the formation of their own small-scale enterprises. This is the 'small firm dynamic' within which small business proprietors, in the absence of bureaucratically-organised managerial systems, extend autonomy to skilled employees. As a result, they acquire many of the competences necessary to start their own businesses.[51]

Thus, with the exception of small firms in areas of 'high technology'

Table 2.7: Distribution of Male Self-employed by Occupation, 1971

Occupation	Employees in employment '000s	Self-employed '000s	Number in employment '000s	Self-employed as a % of number in employment %
All economically active	13,560	1,471	15,031	9.8
Farmers, foresters, fishermen	378	246	623	39.4
Miners and quarrymen	233	–	234	0.2
Gas, coke and chemical makers	122	–	122	0.2
Glass and ceramic makers	60	1	61	1.8
Furnace, forge, foundry, rolling mill workers	148	3	152	2.1
Electrical and electronic workers	488	27	515	5.2
Engineering and allied workers	2,307	98	2,405	4.1
Woodworkers	335	63	398	15.8
Leather workers	49	7	55	12.2
Textile workers	134	2	135	1.4
Clothing workers	63	13	75	16.6
Food, drink and tobacco workers	217	34	250	13.4
Paper and printing workers	208	6	214	2.9
Makers of other products	187	11	198	5.4
Construction workers	364	154	517	29.7
Painters and decorators	198	62	260	23.9
Drivers of stationary engines, cranes, etc.	288	3	291	1.0
Labourers	942	22	964	2.3
Transport and communications	1,141	68	1,209	5.6
Warehousemen, storekeepers, etc.	477	–	478	0.2
Clerical workers	1,035	7	1,043	0.7
Sales workers	833	313	1,147	27.3
Service, sports, recreation	717	148	865	17.1
Administrators, managers	830	–	830	–
Professional, technical workers	1,472	180	1,651	10.9
Armed forces	240	–	240	–
Inadequately described	95	4	100	4.3

Note: The total number in employment (column 3) is rounded to the nearest thousand.
Source: *Royal Commission on the Distribution of Income and Wealth, Report No. 8*, Cmnd 7679, Table 2.13.

we would expect the proprietors of small businesses, compared to the executives of larger enterprises, to be 'academically' under-qualified. A recent study shows that 40 per cent of the chief executives of the 500 largest companies in Britain had university degrees and that of the remainder, 20 per cent were qualified chartered accountants.[52] By contrast, within the small firm sector there is a greater emphasis upon 'trade-based' skills and learning 'on the job'. This point is borne out in Table 2.8 which shows the educational qualifications of small business executives within the sectors of the economy covered by the Bolton Report.[53] These data confirm the absence of careers based upon the acquisition of 'academic' meritocratic qualifications within the small firm sector. Thus, small businesses continue to provide a context within which individuals, through the possession of practical work skills, are able to experience upward mobility.

Table 2.8: Educational Qualifications of Chief Executives in Small Firms

| | Percentage of all Small Firms | | | | |
Educational qualifications	Manufacture	Construction	Wholesale	Motor trade	Retail trades
No higher education	71	57	78	64	82
Degree	10	9	7	–	–
Accounting	8	6	4	4	1
Professional or trade	10	26	8	32	15
Management	1	3	2	–	1
Other	–	–	1	–	1

Source: *Report of the Committee of Inquiry on Small Firms,* (The Bolton Report), (Cmnd 4811), Table 2.8.

Such, then, are the circumstances that enable the reproduction of the entrepreneurial middle class within an economy which is over-whelmingly dominated by the ownership and control of large corporations. But if, so far, we have outlined the *general* technological and economic circumstances conducive to the persistence of small firms and, hence, the entrepreneurial middle class, we have not yet considered the *specific* conditions under which this may occur. We do so by reference to a *critical case* – the building industry – which is the subject of our next chapter.[54]

Notes

1. For a general discussion of these trends, see, for example, J. Westergaard and H. Resler, *Class in a Capitalist Society*, Harmondsworth, 1976 (especially Chapter Two) and J. Scott, *Corporations, Classes and Capitalism*, London, 1979.

2. See F. Bechhofer, B. Elliott and D. McCrone, 'Structure, Consciousness and Action', *British Journal of Sociology*, vol. 29, 1978 and R. Brown, 'Work' in P. Abrams (ed.), *Work, Urbanism and Inequality*, London, 1978.

3. See, for example, the historical data presented in the *Report of the Committee of Inquiry on Small Firms*, (The Bolton Report), Cmnd 4811, London, 1971; *Royal Commission on the Distribution of Income and Wealth, Report No. 8*, Cmnd 7679, London, 1979; N. Buxton and D. Mackay, *British Employment Statistics*, Oxford, 1977; G. Routh, *Occupation and Pay in Great Britain 1906– 79* (2nd edn), London, 1980.

4. L. Hannah and J. Kay, *Concentration in Modern Industry*, London, 1977, p. 1.

5. L. Hannah, *The Rise of the Corporate Economy*, London, 1975, Table 10.1.

6. Ibid., p. 166.

7. A. Friedman, *Industry and Labour*, London, 1977.

8. *Report of the Committee of Inquiry on Small Firms*, (The Bolton Report), p. 67.

9. Ibid., Tables 5.1 and 5.2.

10. Ibid., p. 67.

11. *The Financing of Small Firms*, (The Wilson Report), Cmnd 7503, London, 1979, Tables 2.2 and 2.3. The discrepancy between the 1963 figures is due to the different business registers drawn upon by the Bolton and Wilson Reports.

12. Ibid., p. 45.

13. See, for example, J. K. Galbraith, *The New Industrial State*, Harmondsworth, 1972; Scott, *Corporations, Classes and Capitalism*; R. Jessop, 'The Transformation of the State in Post-war Britain' in R. Scase (ed.), *The State in Western Europe*, London, 1980.

14. Scott, *Corporations, Classes and Capitalism*, p. 16.

15. *Report on the Census of Production, (Summary Tables) 1973*, Table 13.

16. Ibid.

17. M. A. Utton, *Industrial Concentration*, Harmondsworth, 1970, p. 75.

18. J. Boswell, *The Rise and Decline of Small Firms*, London, 1973, p. 17.

19. Ibid., p. 45.

20. Friedman, *Industry and Labour*.

21. *Report of the Committee of Inquiry on Small Firms*, (The Bolton Report), pp. 31–2.

22. *Report on the Census of Production, (Summary Tables) 1975*, Table 5.

23. *Report on the Committee of Inquiry on Small Firms*, (The Bolton Report), pp. 76–7.

24. In the recent recession there has been a tendency for some groups of managers to buy up ailing companies which previously employed them.

25. *Report of the Committee of Inquiry on Small Firms*, (The Bolton Report), p. 34.

26. Ibid., p. 1.

27. M. Tamari, *A Postal Questionnaire Survey of Small Firms*, Research Report No. 16 (commissioned by the Bolton Committee), London, 1971, Table 6; Merrett Cyriax Associates, *Dynamics of Small Firms*, Research Report No. 12 (commissioned by the Bolton Committee), London, 1971, Table 2.6.

28. For a general-based discussion see A. Fox, *Beyond Contract*, London, 1974a and for a case-study T. Nichols and H. Beynon, *Living with Capitalism*, London, 1977.

29. See H. Braverman, *Labor and Monopoly Capital*, New York, 1974.

30. See F. W. Taylor, *Scientific Management*, New York, 1947.

31. Cited in Braverman, *Labor and Monopoly Capital*, pp. 113, 118.

32. See, for example, R. Crompton and J. Gubbay, *Economy and Class Structure*, London, 1977; P. D. Anthony, *The Ideology of Work*, London, 1977; G. Salaman, *Work Organisations*, London, 1979.

33. Evidence of this contemporary disenchantment with work is available in M. Weir (ed.), *Job Satisfaction*, Glasgow, 1976 and Special Task Force to the Secretary of Health, Education and Welfare, *Work in America*, Cambridge, Mass., 1973.

34. Fox, *Beyond Contract*.

35. For early studies using the so-called 'contingency approach' see J. Woodward, *Industrial Organisation*, Oxford, 1965; T. Burns and G. M. Stalker, *The Management of Innovation*, London, 1961.

36. The classic case study is A. W. Gouldner, *Patterns of Industrial Bureaucracy*, London, 1964.

37. Friedman, *Industry and Labour*.

38. See, for example, E. Chinoy, *Automobile Workers and the American Dream*, New York, 1955; C. R. Walker and R. H. Guest, *The Man on the Assembly Line*, New Haven, Conn., 1957; Woodward, Industrial Organisation. For a concise review of various forms of industrial conflict, see R. Hyman, *Strikes*, London, 1972.

39. See the discussion in Friedman, *Industry and Labour*.

40. For a review of recent experiments see P. Warr and T. Wall, *Work and Wellbeing*, Harmondsworth, 1975; Weir, *Job Satisfaction*.

41. Friedman, *Industry and Labour*.

42. For occupational examples, see A. Zimbalist (ed.), *Case Studies on the Labor Process*, New York, 1979 and T. Johnson, 'The Professions in the Class Structure' in R. Scase (ed.), *Industrial Society: Class, Cleavage and Control*, London, 1977.

43. An historical analysis is provided by T. Elger, 'Valorisation and Deskilling', *Capital and Class*, No. 7, 1979.

44. For contemporary discussions see E. Batstone, I. Boraston and S. Frenkel, *Shop Stewards in Action*, Oxford 1977 and W. Brown, R. Ebsworth and M. Terry, 'Factors Shaping Shop Steward Organisation in Britain', *British Journal of Industrial Relations*', vol. 16, 1978.

45. Brighton Labour Process Group, 'The Capitalist Labour Process', *Capital and Class*, no. 1, 1977, p. 37.

46. A recent analysis is provided by R. Crompton, 'Trade Unionism and the Insurance Clerk', *Sociology*, vol. 13, 1979.

47. Although self-employment is high in farming, fisheries and forestry the influence of inheritance is particularly strong and, given the need for sizeable sums of startup capital, this is not a popular contemporary avenue for new businesses.

48. See *Report of the Committee of Inquiry on Small Firms*, (The Bolton Report), Chapter Three.

49. See, for example, Woodward, *Industrial Organisation*, and G. K. Ingham, *Size of Industrial Organisation and Worker Behaviour*, Cambridge, 1970.

50. See Fox, *Beyond Contract*.

51. Supporting evidence of this dynamic is available in a recent review of research by G. Bannock and A. Doran, *Small Firms in Cities*, (Economics Advisory Group Ltd for Shell UK Ltd), 1978.

52. *Report of the Committee of Inquiry on Small Firms*, (The Bolton Report), p. 9.

53. Merrett Cyriax Associates, *Dynamics of Small Firms.*

54. The decision to undertake a single case-study within one industry was based upon the view that, given limited resources, an *intensive* enquiry was more likely to reveal the *processes* underlying the reproduction of small-scale capital and the entrepreneurial middle class. In our opinion, the building industry brings together most clearly the characteristic features conducive to the formation, growth and persistence of small, independent businesses. It is, therefore a *critical* rather than *typical* case which illustrates, nevertheless, a process that operates, to varying degrees, in other sectors of the economy. The specific attributes of building are considered in more detail in Chapter 3.

3 THE FORMATION AND GROWTH OF SMALL BUSINESSES: THE CASE OF THE BUILDING INDUSTRY

In the last chapter we identified those parts of the economy within which small businesses are likely to emerge. In general, sectors characterised by skilled labour rather than capital-intensive production tend to be more favourable for business formation. Typically, a refined division of labour will not have developed nor will 'academic' meritocratic qualifications be regarded as necessary prerequisites for proprietors and executives. Instead, 'experience', often gained in other small firms, is seen as a more appropriate training. The commodities produced tend not to be standardised and are characteristically sold in markets which are subject to considerable fluctuation according to consumer preference and fashion. For all these reasons, there is likely to be a tradition of small businesses and self-made proprietors which, in itself, creates an industrial subculture that serves to encourage the further formation and growth of small-scale enterprises.

We have argued elsewhere that it is the personal services sector of the economy that most aptly illustrates these processes.[1] It is here that the small firm and the 'informal' economy continue to thrive; indeed, the two are inextricably linked. Thus, the 'informal' economy often represents the first milieu within which individuals test the market, acquire basic business expertise and accumulate funds that can be used for the subsequent establishment of 'legitimate' businesses. Personal services, however, incorporate a wide variety of economic activity which includes wholesaling, retailing, hotels, catering, construction and building, motor trades, road haulage and professional services. Whilst these different trades share many important characteristics there are nevertheless variations between them which can make generalisations difficult. Firms tend to be larger in wholesaling, for example, than in retailing; the skills required to be a self-employed car mechanic are of a very different kind to those needed by an independent newsagent; the market served by a watch-repairer is different, in most respects, from that of a publican and so on. Because of these factors, some sectors of the personal services bring together, more than others, the characteristics that emerged from our discussion in Chapter 2. Of these, general building – better than any other single sector – illustrates the economic and social processes most favourable to the formation and growth of small-scale business units. In this sense it represents a *critical* rather than exceptional case because it highlights – in the clearest possible manner – processes which operate in many other small business sectors of the contemporary capitalist economy. This is not to deny that general building, like any other, has certain distinctive features. Nevertheless, concentrating upon small businesses within one particular industry allows the intensive study of the factors which account for the continued reproduction of the entrepreneurial middle class. General building, as we hope to demonstrate in this chapter, possesses *par excellence* those features which are most conducive to the formation, growth and persistence of small, independently-owned private businesses.

Within urban industrial economies the building and construction industry fulfils an important role. Houses and hotels, factories and offices, roads and bridges are the physical testimony of its impact. Furthermore, society is dependent on the industry for the maintenance of this stock and its expansion. The products of construction, therefore, range from the repaired gatepost and replaced window frame to major motorways and shopping centres. In the mid 1970s it employed approximately 1.7 million persons, or about six per cent of the total labour force.[2] As Hillebrandt has pointed out, the repair and maintenance sector *alone* has a labour force larger than that employed in either agriculture, coal-mining or shipbuilding.[3] In terms of net output, the industry accounts for roughly six per cent of gross domestic product; a figure which matches, for example, the combined output of the chemical and vehicle industries.[4] Building and construction also represents an important centre of investment as well as of production and employment; in any given year it normally accounts for no less than one-half of all gross fixed capital formation.[5] The industry, then, cannot be regarded as an economic 'backwater'; unlike some other sectors of the economy which are conducive to the reproduction of the entrepreneurial middle class it cannot be dismissed as a declining legacy of an earlier industrial era.

The vast majority of firms in the building and construction industry are small, privately-owned general builders, and it is this sector which we have concentrated upon in our research. The overwhelming predominance of small firms within the industry is illustrated in Table 3.1. Thus, in 1976, 92 per cent of all private contractors in the building and construction industry employed less than 25 workers. Together, these firms accounted for almost one-quarter of the value of all work

Table 3.1: Distribution of Private Contractors by Numbers Employed and Value of Work Done, 1976

Numbers employed	Numbers of private contractors	Percentage	Percentage of work done
0–1	26,953	32	1.4
2–24	50,391	60	22.6
25–114	5,213	6	21.6
115–1199	1,119	1	34.7
1200+	63	1	20.7
Total	83,739	100	100

Source: Department of the Environment, *Private Contractors' Construction Census, 1976*, Tables 1 and 6.

completed. By contrast only one per cent (63) of all contractors employed over 1200 persons, although they accounted for almost 21 per cent of all work done. The type of work undertaken by these larger enterprises – the construction of power stations, steelworks, motorways and so on – differs significantly from the small-scale installation, repair and maintenence work that constitutes the basis of the small builder's business. In this sense, large firms tend to be 'civil engineers' whilst small businesses tend to be general builders; to a considerable extent they serve different markets and utilise distinctive technologies. Nevertheless, the two sectors cannot be entirely divorced since both make a significant contribution to the construction of housing.[6] Indeed, it is this continuity that enables a non-bureaucratic, skill-based pattern of rapid, upward social mobility to persist. On the basis of little capital but with trade skills, it is possible to start a general building business and then to develop it into a large-scale enterprise within a relatively short period of time.

This point is confirmed by ownership patterns within the industry. In 1970, for example, 139 publicly-quoted companies were wholly or partially engaged in building and construction work.[7] This represented a minute proportion (0.2 per cent) of the total number of firms in the industry. By contrast, the vast majority of all building and construction businesses were *privately owned*.[8] This suggests that the limited resources of private companies are still sufficient to meet the necessary levels of capital investment. Indeed, in 1970, the gross value of capital stock per head employed was lower in building and construction than in any other major industrial grouping in Britain.[9] As the Bolton Report has indicated, 44 per cent of all small building firms (that is those with less than 25 employees) are wholly-owned by members of the same family.[10] Even within the small proportion of larger publicly-quoted companies the original founding families often continue to exercise a considerable degree of control. Hillebrandt notes, for example, that a study of 'some ten of the largest companies shows that in most of them the founder's family is on the board, usually as chairman or managing director'.[11]

Approximately 90 per cent of private firms in the building and construction industry are classified as *'general builders'*.[12] Together, they account for 51 per cent of *all* employment and 45 per cent of the value of all work in building and construction.[13] These figures suggest that the overwhelming majority of general builders are also *small* builders. Indeed The Bolton Report found that 91 per cent of all general builders employed less than 25 workers.[14] Table 3.2 indicates the spread of work undertaken by general builders in comparison with firms in other sectors of the industry.

Table 3.2: Type of Work Undertaken by Main Sectors in Building and Construction

Sector	New housing (%)	Other new work (%)	Repair and maintenance (%)	Total
General builders	48	26	26	100
Building and civil engineering	30	64	6	100
Civil engineers	8	82	10	100

Source: Department of the Environment, *Private Contractors' Construction Census, 1976*, Table 41.

The importance of housing and repair and maintenance work for general builders is not surprising. This is precisely the type of activity which can be independently undertaken by small-scale, locally-based, private firms which lack the capital resources necessary for the large-scale construction of, for example, office blocks, roads or bridges. Indeed, a special investigation commissioned by the Bolton Report showed that small firms with under 25 employees carried out 48 per cent of all repair and maintenance work and 42 per cent of all new private housing.[15] As a general rule, the smaller the enterprise the more important is small-scale alteration, repair and maintenance work. This is brought out in Table 3.3.

Repair and maintenance continues to be heavily dependent upon traditional building methods and craft skills. Within the building and

Table 3.3: Type of Work Done by Private Contractors, 1976

Numbers employed by contractor	Percentage of work			
	New housing	Other new work	Repair and maintenance	Total
0−1	25	10	65	100
2−24	32	25	43	100
25−114	34	44	22	100
115−1199	29	59	12	100
1200+	22	72	7	100

Source: Department of the Environment, *Private Contractors' Construction Census, 1976*, Table 39.

construction industry as a whole, over 80 per cent of total expenditure is devoted to wages and salaries and almost 60 per cent of those employed are skilled manual workers.[16] The skilled workers employed by general builders are not typically tied to expensive machine technology; indeed, they are normally dependent upon manually-operated tools. Consequently, as Table 3.4 shows, the 'traditional' skills of carpentry, bricklaying, painting, plumbing and plastering are far more significant for general builders than for other types of construction businesses. Thus, those enterprises specialising in civil engineering tend to be more dependent upon 'mechanical equipment operators' (that is, operators of excavators, motorised scrapers, trenching machines, plant machanics, etc.) and so-called 'crafts' which often involve the use of heavy machinery (e.g. concreters, demolishers, excavation heading drivers, well-drillers etc.).

Overall, the proportion of manual operatives employed by the main sectors in building and construction is roughly the same — 70 per cent — but the skill distribution varies as does the ratio between salaried and manual employees.[17] Since general builders tend to be small, family-controlled businesses heavily reliant upon craft labour, the proportion of their non-productive white-collar employees is less than in the other sectors. The need for administrative, technical and clerical staff is less in these enterprises because many significant areas of decision making are delegated to skilled operatives 'on the job' or else they are the responsibility of the proprietors who are frequently directly involved in the production process. These features are illustrated in Table 3.5 which shows that less than one-fifth of those employed by general builders are classified as 'white collar'.

The need to make many important decisions at the point of production arises from the fact that general building, as a work process,

Table 3.4: Employment of Operatives in Main Sectors of the Building and Construction Industry (per cent)

Sector	Carpenters and joiners	Bricklayers	Plasterers	Painters	Plumbers	Mech. equip. ops.	Other craft	All others and labourers	Total
General builders	24	19	3	9	9	2	3	31	100
Building and civil engineering	18	10	1	3	2	8	18	40	100
Civil engineering	4	1	—	—	—	15	32	46	100
All trades	20	13	2	6	3	6	14	36	100

Source: Department of the Environment, *Private Contractors' Construction Census, 1976*, Table 22.

Table 3.5: Distribution of Employment in Main Sectors of the Building and Construction Industry, 1976

	Type of labour (per cent)			
Sector	Working proprietors	Administrative, professional, technical, clerical	Manual operatives	Total
General builders	11	19	70	100
Builders and civil engineers	1	28	71	100
Civil engineers	2	26	72	100

Source: Department of the Environment, *Private Contractors' Construction Census, 1976*, Table 35.

has a number of distinctive features compared with many other branches of the economy. As Hilton, for example, has stated:

> A building site is unlike any other industrial place of production. A complicated series of operations has to be married to a flow of materials and labour, and often on sites which may themselves present special problems. Nor is the direct control over labour and production processes vested in a single management as would be the situation in a factory. There may be anything from one to a dozen or more autonomous building firms involved on one site, and they will take their place in the production queue to carry out work which has been sub-contracted to them. Their relationship with the main contractor can vary from one of amity to the extreme where a great deal of resentment exists.[18]

Further, as Higgin and Jessop have suggested:

> roles in the building industry are in a state of considerable confusion. The implications of this for the experience of any individual in the building team are, firstly, he finds that there is no settled and stable definition of what his job actually is, and secondly nobody else can be clear about exactly what he does and what he is responsible for.[19]

If, then, the work process within many sectors of manufacturing has become highly routinised, there are persisting ambiguities and uncertainties in general building.

One of the factors which accounts for this is the specialist nature of the product. Most firms within the industry produce 'one-off' jobs, whether it is a speculative housing project or small-scale maintenance and repair work. This, in itself, reduces the extent to which there can be rigidly-defined work tasks and stable decision-making structures. In fact, the nature of the commodity demands operating flexibility and adaptability.[20] Thus, foremen, supervisors, craftsmen and others involved in the execution of tasks 'on the job' have to make decisions of the kind that would be usually vested within clearly-defined management structures in industrial manufacturing plants. These constitute inherent areas of uncertainty which, as Crozier has shown, are important sources of worker autonomy that defy managerial attempts to extend its control.[21] This is reinforced by the existence of strong craft ideologies which emphasise the functional autonomy of skills. Consequently, the general building process requires co-operation between groups of 'semi-autonomous' craft workers. This has been emphasised by Stinchcombe in his discussion of the building industry in the United States.[22] He claims that, 'the construction industry depends upon a highly professionalised manual labour force', which, he says, 'serves the same functions as bureaucratic administration in mass production industries, and is more rational than bureaucratic administration in the face of economic and technical constraints on construction projects'.[23] He argues that while bureaucratic administrative systems are more efficient in manufacturing, they are uneconomic in general building because of instabilities in volume and product mix, and in the geographical distribution of work. In other words, 'craftsmanship' is more economic for the purposes of stipulating acceptable levels of output, codes of conduct and the achievement of production goals. Indeed, craftworkers in general building are the epitome of what Erik Wright describes as 'semi-autonomous' employees. As he states:

> Today there are still categories of employees who have a certain degree of control over their own immediate conditions of work, over their immediate labour process. In such instances the labour process has not been completely proletarianised . . . In their immediate work environment, they maintain the work process of the independent artisan while still being employed by capital as wage labourers. They control *how* they do their work, and have at least some control over what they produce . . . More generally, many white-collar technical employees and certain highly skilled craftsmen have at least a limited form of this autonomy in their immediate labour process.[24]

This 'semi-autonomy' of craftworkers in general building is further strengthened by the fact that technological innovations have not, in general, brought about large-scale de-skilling. Indeed, experiments in 'industrialised' housing which were seen as a means to increase productivity have been far from successful. As Stone has argued, 'industrialised building systems find it extremely difficult to compete in terms of cost with traditional building; at best they are comparable with the costs of traditional building'.[25] Furthermore, she claims that:

> Traditional methods appear to be more flexible and can more easily meet fluctuations in demand than industrial system building. Long contracts are required for system building because of the way costs rise if factories operate at a low level of output – a high proportion of factory costs are fixed, since often neither the labour force nor the overheads can be reduced easily when output falls below the optimum.[26]

Thus, with market fluctuations, it is difficult to introduce the widespread use of 'industrialised' building systems within which it would be possible to increase the productivity of labour through the large-scale mechanisation of work tasks, the development of a detailed division of labour, and an increase in the level of supervisory control. In other words, a work process in which there is the *real* subordination of labour to capital.[27] Such a process would then replace more 'traditional' forms of building which, according to Stone:

> usually implies a loose form of organisation in which the operations follow a recognised order and in which both the order and the work in each operation is well understood by the skilled craftsmen and is implied by the design *without any need for detailed instructions.*[28] (our italics)

Rather than the widespread adoption of 'industrialised' building systems, technological change has more often involved the use of prefabricated components and the mechanisation of operatives' tools.[29] It is through these means that productivity has been increased; there is the extended use of cement mixers, mobile cranes, excavators, tractors, compressors, etc. However, the use of mechanical power remains low compared with manufacturing such that general building remains highly labour-intensive. In fact, it is difficult to see how many work tasks can be further mechanised. As Stone has suggested:

It is difficult to visualise any mechanical plant which could assist bricklayers; mechanical hand-tools can be used to assist the carpenter and possibly the plumber; such tools reduce the physical work but generally do little directly to increase productivity.[30]

Despite this, mechanisation has reduced the need for labour, particularly in the movement of components on sites, in excavation works and in the use of prefabricated components. According to a government study:

In recent years there has been an increased use of plasterboard instead of plaster; ready-made kitchen units; pre-hung doors and pre-glazed windows; prefabricated roof trusses, floors and staircases; electric harnesses; pre-formed plumbing kits; and aluminium windows which require no painting. Such changes . . . have contributed to a reduction since the last war of some 50 per cent in site labour required to build a conventional brick house.[31]

Although this has reduced the amount of labour required, the report suggests that no fundamental process of de-skilling has occurred. There has been a reduction in the *volume* of work undertaken by bricklayers, plasterers, plumbers and electricians, but the *content* of these jobs has remained more or less the same. The assembly of prefabricated components requires, for example, fewer bricklayers and plasterers, but for those remaining, the tasks are fairly unaltered. At the same time, the use of prefabricated components has not reduced the amount of labour required of such craftsmen as painters, carpenters, roofers and glaziers.[32]

It appears, then, that the work process in general building is fairly resistent to de-skilling.[33] Mechanisation and the increasing use of prefabricated components has not, on the whole, lead to the breakdown and subdivision of work tasks. Further, as various studies have shown, technological innovations have not strengthened the intensity of supervisory control over workers; many skilled employees have been able to retain varying degrees of work autonomy.[34] If, further, it has been difficult to remove 'areas of uncertainty' from the work process, this has been reinforced by the variable market situation of most general building firms. This is due to at least three major factors.

In the first place, many firms obtain a substantial part of their work through submitting tenders for contracts. Since contracts tend to be fairly short-term, work procedures cannot be routinised to the same extent as in manufacturing. At the same time, most firms undertake a number of concurrent contracts which means that there is considerable mobility of labour between sites as specific work tasks are completed. This, then, further reduces the possibilities for establishing precisely defined work procedures and supervisory systems. Secondly, the market uncertainty of general building firms is reinforced by the state which uses the industry as an economic regulator. Because of its importance in the economy – both in terms of the size of its labour force and its contribution to gross capital formation – the state has tended to use building and construction generally as a means of regulating the aggregate level of demand in the economy. This has affected the formation and growth of firms and the demand for building labour. Finally, the market situation of building firms fluctuates because of the seasonal nature of various work activities; many exterior finishing tasks can only be performed under favourable weather conditions. While such conditions are, on the whole, irrelevant in manufacturing because they are unlikely to affect the flow of production, in the building process they are a factor which always has to be taken into account. Consequently, they have important implications for the organisation of the work process and constitute a further source of uncertainty with which proprietors, managers and workers have to cope.

This, then, concludes our short survey of the general building sector. From this it is clear there are a number of factors conducive to the formation of small businesses. In the first place, the industry constitutes an environment that encourages employees to start their own businesses because the required level of initial capital outlay is low. Even in the retail trade, which is often regarded as the sector in which businesses can be easily started, greater capital investment is needed in order to acquire stock and obtain leases.[35] Building workers, on the other hand, can decide to 'start on their own' with virtually no capital except, possibly, their tools (which they often already possess) and sufficient savings to cover the initial period of trading. Indeed, it is even possible that during this period finance may be 'indirectly' provided by the state since workers may register as unemployed during the first few weeks while undertaking small-scale jobs for clients.[36] Alternatively, they may receive redundancy payments from employers which similarly serve as a source of startup capital.[37] It is only at a later stage, when they perceive that full-time self-employment offers satisfactory economic returns that problems of finance are confronted, and they may then be forced to buy larger quantities of materials and to obtain credit facilities.

If the formation of business units is encouraged by the low level of capital required, this is reinforced by the *nature* of the market. There is a greater degree of competition between businesses in this branch of the economy compared with many others, despite the existence of monopolies in the production of certain building materials and prefabricated components, and the occasional practice of price 'agreements' among the largest companies within the industry.[38] But the nature of the market is such that it is difficult to envisage how there could be a monopoly in the provision of building, maintenance and repair services of the sort found in the production of many standardised consumer commodities and in 'heavy' capital-intensive industries. In other words, the very *nature* of the industry's products preserves, in a fairly permanent manner, opportunities for the formation of small businesses. There are always roof tiles to be replaced, fences to be repaired, walls to be painted, gates to be replaced and so on, such that it is highly unlikely that all sectors of the industry will ever be characterised by a high level of monopoly. Thus, the nature of the market virtually guarantees the continuous reproduction of small business units since only labour and rudimentary tools are required to undertake small-scale repair and maintenance, which can then form the basis for longer-term capital accumulation.

From this discussion it is also clear that attempts to convert the *formal* into *real* subordination of labour have been far from successful. Although there has been some mechanisation of the building process, particularly in the use of power tools, the movement of materials on site and the use of prefabricated components, this has not brought about a fundamental de-skilling of craft jobs. Consequently, workers have been able to retain a considerable degree of autonomy in the execution of their tasks. This, a feature of many craft-based technological systems, provides a context within which workers can consider the possibilities of starting their own businesses.[39] In an industry in which little initial capital is required, craftworkers possess skills which exist *independent* of the technological process owned and controlled by employers. Further, in the execution of their tasks, craftworkers may notice little difference between themselves, the self-employed and small employers whom they may be working alongside on a particular work site. To become self-employed, then, is seen to be a realistic possibility.

The persistence of worker autonomy is further reinforced by the high rate of mobility within the industry.[40] Workers are continually required to move from one site to the next by virtue of the inherent features of the building process. Consequently, craftworkers, with their skills and tools, are often constantly searching for the best paid jobs available on different work sites. This not only reinforces their notions of craft 'independence' but also leads to an emphasis upon 'self-reliance' in the labour market. This is clear from Sykes' study of navvies in the construction industry in which he found that workers tended to be highly mobile, moving from one employer to the next in order to maximise earnings.[41] According to him, this cultivated a strong ethos of individualism such that workers had only limited attachments to both employers *and* working colleagues. Consequently, any norms of collective solidarity that did develop were of a temporary kind and limited to specific work sites. In general building, where similar circumstances of mobility prevail to encourage 'self-reliance', this is conducive to many workers considering the possibilities of setting up their own small businesses.

Taken together, the structural features of the general building process foster an ideological fabric that encourages the formation of small-scale enterprises. As we have stated, workers enjoy a certain degree of autonomy in the execution of their tasks which, together with the nature of the building process, leads them to subscribe to ideas of individualism and self-reliance. These features sustain notions of entrepreneurship if only because on sites, craft employees will often be working alongside or for subcontractors who were once themselves, employees. Such personal contacts are likely to encourage workers to consider the possibilities of 'starting on their own'. As Bannock and Doran have suggested:

> It seems plausible that employment in small firms is much more relevant to a preparation for setting up a small business than employment in a large firm. In small firms, employees gain experience over a wider variety of tasks and have better opportunities to work with and get to know the owner manager of the firm. It is relatively easy for an employee to become aware of the whole environment facing a small business since communications are informal and relatively easy.[42]

Further, most managers and directors in general building, unlike their counterparts in many other branches of the national economy, are former craftsmen. Even in the larger firms, there is little direct entry of trainees into managerial and supervisory positions from educational institutions; on the contrary, there is considerable recruitment from manual operatives.[43] Many of the owners of the largest firms have either inherited their businesses from men who, as craftsmen, started their own businesses, or independently founded them.[44] The low level of initial capital required and the high proportion of small firms in the industry reaffirms the availability of these opportunities. Indeed, this is important for the manner in which worker dissatisfaction may be expressed. If craftworkers become resentful of their position as employees they can decide to 'try it on their own'; with their skills and craft tools, they have – under favourable market circumstances – the necessary requirements. By comparison, this opportunity is not available to workers in many other branches of the national economy.

To conclude, general building possesses the necessary characteristics for it to be regarded as a *critical* case wherein the dynamics of business formation and growth can be studied. We have, therefore, selected a range of business proprietors that enable us to examine attitudes and behaviour symptomatic of different categories within the entrepreneurial middle class. The details of our data-collecting procedure are described in the methodological appendix but, briefly, interviews were conducted with a total of 90 general building proprietors, some of their wives and 10 of the senior managers during 1979. The businesses were based in the south of England and varied from self-employed craftworkers at one extreme to well-established family firms employing up to 1200 people at the other. Twenty-five interviews were conducted with men in each of our four categories. In addition, interviews were conducted with some wives in order to explore more fully the role of the family and the interconnections between the 'domestic' and 'business' spheres. The *self-employed* used no additional labour other than their own (and unpaid family help). The *small employers* had an average of six permanent employees, but on occasions they also used labour-only subcontractors. These two groups fall within the 0–1 and 2–24 employees categories of the private contractors' census (see Table 3.1 above) which covers 92 per cent of all employers in the industry. The *owner-controllers* and *owner-directors* employed between 25 and 1200 workers and therefore, together, are drawn from the remaining eight per cent of private building contractors. Despite their manifest differences all these enterprises were private concerns independently controlled by their owners.[45] There was, of course, some variation in the extent to which particular enterprises specialised in certain trades. Nevertheless, all the businesses undertook, in differing quantities, general building work for private and public customers;

there were, therefore, no specialist, labour-only subcontractors in our study. We turn, now, to consider each of the four categories of proprietors in some detail in order to *illustrate* the processes conducive to the formation and growth of small businesses and, hence, to the reproduction of the entrepreneurial middle class in the modern economy. Although, then, these proprietors are chosen from a specific industrial sector, their experiences highlight the dynamics of a more general pattern.

Notes

1. R. Scase and R. Goffee, *The Real World of the Small Business Owner*, London, 1980.

2. Department of Employment, *Yearbook, 1975*.

3. P. M. Hillebrandt, *Economic Theory and the Construction Industry*, London, 1974, p. 10.

4. See J. D. Sugden, 'The Place of Construction in the Economy' in D. A. Turin (ed.), *Aspects of the Economics of Construction*, London, 1975. Definitions which include the value of materials and supplies purchased from other industries suggest that the contribution to gross domestic product is nearly twelve per cent. See Hillebrandt, *Economic Theory and the Construction Industry*, p. 10.

5. Hillebrandt, *Economic Theory and the Construction Industry*, pp. 10–11.

6. See, for example, National Economic Development Office, *How Flexible is Construction?*, London, 1978 and P. M. Hillebrandt, *Small Firms in the Construction Industry*, Research Report No. 10 (commissioned by The Bolton Committee), London, 1971.

7. R. A. Burgess *et al.*, (eds.), *The Construction Industry Handbook*, Lancaster, 1973, p. 77.

8. Ibid.

9. Sugden, 'The Place of Construction in the Economy', Table 1.1.

10. *Report of the Committee of Inquiry on Small Firms*, (The Bolton Report), Cmnd 4811, London, 1971, Table 2.4.

11. Hillebrandt, *Economic Theory and the Construction Industry*, p. 90.

12. This calculation excludes 'specialist trade' firms. See Department of the Environment, *Private Contractors' Construction Census 1976*, Table 8.

13. Ibid, Tables 7 and 14. Again the calculation excludes 'specialist trade' firms.

14. Hillebrandt, *Small Firms in the Construction Industry*, Table 7.

15. Ibid., Table 4.

16. *Report on the Census of Production, (Summary Tables 1975)*, Table 5 and Economic Activity Tables, *Census of Great Britain, 1971*.

17. See Department of the Environment, *Private Contractors' Construction Census, 1976*.

18. W. S. Hilton, *Industrial Relations in Construction*, London, 1968, p. 13.

19. G. Higgin and N. Jessop, *Communications in the Building Industry*, London, 1965, p. 51.

20. For a first-hand discussion of the managerial problems which this poses see C. Foster, *Building with Men*, London, 1969.

21. M. Crozier, *The Bureaucratic Phenomenon*, London, 1964.

22. A. Stinchcombe, 'Bureaucratic and Craft Administration of Production: A Comparative Study', *Administrative Science Quarterly*, vol. 4, 1959.

23. Ibid., p. 261.

24. E. O. Wright, *Class, Crisis and the State*, London, 1978, pp. 80–1.

25. P. A. Stone, *Building Economy*, London, 1966, p. 71. See also the discussion by J. F. Eden, 'Mechanisation' in D. A. Turin (ed.), *Aspects of the Economics of Construction.*

26. Stone, *Building Economy*, p. 79.

27. See the discussion in Chapter 2.

28. Stone, *Building Economy*, p. 52.

29. Ibid., Part Two; Hillebrandt, *Economic Theory and the Construction Industry.*

30. Stone, *Building Economy*, p. 91.

31. National Economic Development Office, *How Flexible is Construction?*, p. 27.

32. Ibid., Chapter Six.

33. We acknowledge, however, the growth of 'factory-based' component production 'off-site' under conditions where a detailed division of labour and close supervision are more likely to prevail.

34. See, for example, Tavistock Institute of Human Relations, *Interdependence and Uncertainty: A Study of the Building Industry*, London, 1966 and Hilton, *Industrial Relations in Construction.*

35. See F. Bechhofer, B. Elliott, M. Rushforth and R. Bland, 'Small Shop-keepers: Matters of Money and Meaning', *Sociological Review*, vol. 22, 1974b.

36. See, for example, R. E. Pahl, 'Employment, Work and the Domestic Division of Labour', *International Journal of Urban and Regional Research*, vol. 4, 1980.

37. Examples are discussed in Scase and Goffee, *The Real World of the Small Business Owner.*

38. Evidence of such agreements is presented in Direct Labour Collective, *Building with Direct Labour*, London, 1978.

39. See the discussion in Chapter 2.

40. A recent survey of carpenters and bricklayers found:

> in addition to movement between other occupations and industries . . .
> very significant movement within construction carpentry/joinery; between
> firms, between firms and public authorities, between bench and site . . .
> between shuttering and other carpentry on site. For brick-layers, there is
> considerable movement between contractors and also between employment
> and self-employment.

National Economic Development Office, *How Flexible is Construction?*, p. 42.

41. A. J. Sykes, 'Navvies: Their Work Attitudes' and 'Navvies: Their Social Relations', *Sociology*, vol. 3, 1969a, b.

42. G. Bannock and A. Doran, *Small Firms in Cities*, (Economics Advisory Group Ltd for Shell UK Ltd), 1978, p. 17.

43. See Hillebrandt, *Economic Theory and the Construction Industry.*

44. For an illustrative example see the biography of Frank Taylor (of Taylor Woodrow) described in A. Jenkins, *On Site, 1921–71*, London, 1971.

45. There are, of course, instances where very large companies are nevertheless actively managed in a personal way by their owners. We would include such owners within the entrepreneurial middle class. It is only when *both* control and ownership extend substantially beyond the confines of the proprietor and his family that membership of the class is threatened. In our own sample, enterprises which had limited legal liability were normally close companies. Close companies are free from control by other non-close companies and are directly managed by a maximum of five 'participators' who own the business. Whilst each 'participator'

may, in fact, be more than one individual and can include loan creditors, close companies are the typical legal form for incorporated, independent, owner-controlled family businesses. For further information see M. Chesterman, *Small Businesses*, London, 1977, Chapter 3 and *Report of the Committee of Inquiry on Small Firms*, (The Bolton Report), pp. 4–7, 203–5. Further details concerning the ownership of larger enterprises in the sample are included in Chapter 7.

4 THE SELF-EMPLOYED

There are few studies of the self-employed.[1] They are typically regarded as a 'residual' category and as the declining legacy of an earlier economic epoch. As a result, the processes whereby employees *become* self-employed have rarely been described. Further, the manner in which social, technological and industrial changes continue to provide opportunities for self-employment have been neglected. As we discussed in Chapter 2 the possibilities vary between different industrial sectors and they are more likely to be found in areas where the *formal* subordination of labour to capital prevails. Most estimates suggest that between four and five per cent of the total working population of Britain are self-employed.[2] We are, then, discussing a very small proportion of the labour force although, of course, such figures only refer to the *registered* self-employed; they do not include those who, in various ways, produce saleable commodities and services which are exchanged within the 'black economy'.[3]

Of all self-employed men, 18 per cent are to be found in the building and construction industry.[4] Further, within this industry, 16 per cent are self-employed compared with an average of six per cent for men in all other sectors of the economy.[5] Indeed, during the 1960s and 1970s, there was a rapid growth in the numbers classified as self-employed in building and construction – from 169,000 in 1961 to a peak of 435,000 in 1973 – an increase of 157 per cent.[6] Much of this was due to the development of 'labour-only' subcontracting in response to the fiscal advantages of self-employment.[7] Nevertheless, for reasons discussed in the last chapter, self-employment in the building and construction industry has always been high in Britain and most other industrial countries. Even in the United States, where 'industrialised' building systems are relatively well-developed, there remains a high proportion of self-employed craftsmen.[8]

What are the factors which lead to self-employment? There are, of course, financial reasons but these are often inextricably connected with various social and psychological factors. As the literature suggests, an important motive is the quest for personal autonomy. For many, self-employment promises freedom from the constraints of supervisory control. This is emphasised by Chinoy in his study of automobile workers in the United States,[9] and by Bechhofer and his associates in their research into shopkeepers in Britain.[10] They suggest that the overriding attraction of self-employment is *independence*; indeed, the strength of this appeal is sufficient to compensate for long and often arduous working hours. This is further reflected in their general attitudes and styles of life. According to the investigators, the shopkeepers' outright ownership of houses and consumer durables reflects 'a general constellation of beliefs in which maintaining your independence is important and actually owning, rather than simply having the use of objects, is a part of this'.[11] These sentiments are linked to notions of self-reliance, personal responsibility and success through one's own efforts. In an earlier study Goldthorpe and Lockwood found that a significant proportion of 'affluent workers' in their sample had either made an attempt to start their own businesses or considered the matter seriously. They suggest that workers sought:

> a form of work which would offer a relatively high level of *both* economic *and* inherent rewards; and in the latter respect the main attraction in having one's own business was, of course, that of being independent and autonomous – of 'working for yourself' and of 'being your own boss'.[12]

Such findings have been confirmed by studies in the United States where ideologies that emphasise *autonomy* and *freedom* are strongly expressed. The 'American Dream' stresses the possibilities of individual opportunity either through upward mobility within bureaucratically-structured organisations or by becoming self-employed. According to Mackenzie, this has been:

> the goal of the majority of aspiring workers, especially those working in factories. To these men, a business of one's own has been regarded as offering prestige, independence, and above all, freedom from the constraints of a particular work-situation.[13]

If Chinoy found that automobile workers wanted to set up their own business to *escape* the alienation and control of their everyday work, Mackenzie found that other reasons prevailed. More specifically, 'several craftsmen sought a business of their own because they saw this as the way to improve their standards of workmanship and thus the intrinsic benefits from the quality of the work they produced'.[14] This, together with the desire to increase their earnings, was the major appeal of starting a business. In other words, self-employment was seen less as an escape from control by others than as a positive means whereby craft skills could be more fully exercised. The search for *autonomy* and *independence*, then, conceals a diversity of personal motives and expectations. Consequently, it is necessary to search for the deeper meanings that such ideas have for those who start their own businesses.

In our study we interviewed 25 male self-employed sole proprietors, together with some of their wives.[15] Of the men, 18 had previously been employed as skilled manual workers, five as semi-skilled workers and two as lower-grade non-manual employees. Of their fathers, five had been skilled manual employees, six were self-employed while the remainder were from a variety of lower-grade, non-manual backgrounds. These sole proprietors were, therefore, overwhelmingly working-class both in terms of their fathers' and their own previous occupational experiences. What, then, were their motives for starting their own businesses?

In general, their decisions were related to various 'negative' experiences associated with their previous employee role; they did not express a strong prior commitment to notions of personal advancement through self-employment. Of the 25 respondents, seven had been forced to leave their previous occupations through illness, redundancy and unemployment, while a further 14 had given up previous jobs because of dissatisfaction with certain aspects of their employment situation. Of those forced out of a job, starting a business was an alternative to unemployment. This is illustrated in the following:

> I came down from Southampton and I couldn't get a job. I signed on the dole and I got my six weeks' money but I couldn't get a job, so I thought 'Sod it – I'll go self employed'. I just went plastering – just local, small stuff. Of course you don't need a lot a work to keep one guy going.   (112)

> As it happened, I was made redundant from a construction company . . . We had no children then, and we were living in a rented cottage with no responsibilities. We had £180 redundancy money in our pockets, which was a lot of money then, so we decided to have a go. And really, I've never looked back since then.   (115)

Many respondents had decided to become self-employed because of a wish to exercise greater control over their immediate work tasks. Indeed, their decisions may be seen as the outcome of an essential tension which confronts many craftsmen in modern capitalist enterprises. This is invariably related to perceived threats to their working autonomy, and the growing encroachment of managerial control over the exercise of their skills. The Bolton Report found evidence of these attitudes among craftsmen in *all* sectors of the economy:

> If the independent craftsmen felt he could take employment in a large organisation which offered him the same satisfaction and scope for developing his skills . . . there would be little problem. Many craftsmen, however, would not willingly give up their independence. If forced to do so by circumstances their creativity . . . would suffer. Independence is in itself an attraction, as it is to other small businessmen. There is in addition a distrust of industry. The director of the Crafts Council stated: 'there is a very considerable degree of satisfaction to be gained from independence. Because you are to that extent a free man. You can work when you want to work, and you need not work when you do not want to. The craftsman has been afraid. He has felt that industry was swallowing him up and would not allow him any freedom or any creative ability.'[16]

Such sentiments were strongly evident in our own study:

> Well, the thing was, at my old firm you had to be there at 7.30 on the dot. And then you were told where to go, what to do, and how to do it — more or less. That's the gist of it. You were just a number. In the end I got a horrible job — I got really browned off. So I said, 'All right, I'll leave on Friday'. (103)

> In a big firm you are just a number really. You've got to clock in, in the morning and there's timekeepers to make sure that you don't skip out of the gate and up to the pub at dinner time. Timekeepers come into the canteen as well. If they catch anyone going in five minutes early, they dock you quarter of an hour. But being self-employed there's a lot of advantages. You needn't get up at a certain time — you can start work when you please. (122)

> When you work for yourself, you are a little bit more free to plan your work and be able to take a day off or to work at the weekend. You can just plan your work accordingly, that's the real main advantage of being on your own. (106)

Self-employment, then, offers the opportunity to escape from highly-routinised work tasks and close control by others. If the academically-qualified can achieve some working autonomy within professional employment, the chances for manual workers are much less. Hence, the attractions of self-employment for workers in a wide range of industrial settings. However, it is often easier for those employed in building to realise this ambition because of the social and technological characteristics of the industry. These were spelt out, in straightforward terms, by one of our respondents:

> You can more or less start on you own with very little capital. All you need is a van and a few tools in the back and the possibility of one or two jobs that you've got lined up . . . In the building industry there's still a high proportion of skilled workers and you can more or less use your skill as capital if you see what I mean. There's a lot of industry these days where skilled labour is tending to die out.   (115)

There are, of course, economic motives for self-employment but these often reflect a resentment of working for others. Many respondents were reluctant to allow employers to benefit from their labour; by becoming self-employed they were able to retain these profits for themselves. As one of the respondents explained:

> The major disadvantage of working for somebody is that you've got to do as you're told within reason. You've got to accept somebody's orders and authority. You've got far greater freedom as your own boss. But it's not just the freedom. To work for somebody else you always feel that somebody's got their hand in your pocket. That you are not getting your just dues.   (102)

The reasons for becoming self-employed influenced the way respondents operated their businesses. Since self-employment was primarily an escape from supervisory control, it is not surprising that few regarded it as the initial stage in a longer-term process of capital accumulation. Although a number may expand their businesses and become employers, this was not typically an explicit intention. Essentially, the respondents regarded themselves as craftsmen rather than *businessmen*; in this sense their orientations to work resembled the alleged 'ideals' of craftsmanship rather than profit-making and long-term business growth. The 'image' of the craftsman, as portrayed in the literature, is illustrated in C. Wright Mills' description:

Craftsmanship as a fully idealized model of work gratification involves six major features: there is no ulterior motive in work other than the product being made and the processes of its creation. The details of daily work are meaningful because they are not detached in the worker's mind from the product of the work. The worker is free to control his own working action. The craftsman is thus able to learn from his work; and to use and develop his capacities and skills in its prosecution. There is no split of work and play, or work and culture. The craftsman's way of livelihood determines and infuses his entire mode of living.[17]

Similarly, Lockwood and Goldthorpe outline the characteristics of the ideal-type craftsman as follows:

The craftsman works with tools which, if not his own property, are his at least in a psychological sense; over a lengthy period of apprenticeship he has mastered their use and made them extensions of his hands, and even, one might say, of his personality. The craftsman's task is either one which is complete in itself, such as the making of a specific article – a gun, a shoe, a wheel – or, if not, forms part of a collective task – say, the building of a ship – in which the relationship of his contribution to the whole can be clearly seen. In carrying out his work the craftsman is able to proceed largely according to his own pace and plan. He requires no external assistance nor external supervision; he is his own taskmaster. The craftsman thus in various ways derives gratification directly from his work activity – from the initial devising of his task, from the continual joining of design and action and from the ultimate creative achievement. His work is his chief form of self expression, the mainspring of his entire way of life. His leisure, for example, is not a refuge from his work but an adjunct to it, a time of recreation in the full sense of the word.[18]

Although the *ability* to pursue independently intrinsic job satisfaction through craft self-employment cannot be disputed, a rather one-sided picture emerges from these accounts. The autonomy of self-employed craftsmen has been overemphasised to the neglect of the constraints upon the production and sale of their goods and services. In fact, their capacity to enjoy autonomy is severely curtailed by competition in the petty commodity sector of the market. These conditions directly determine the extent to which the craftsman 'is free to control his own working action' and 'proceed largely according to his own pace and plan'. Because they operate within a capitalist economy, they are subject to two major limitations upon the performance of their skills. First, customers largely determine the conditions under which work is performed – both in 'time' and 'quality'. Secondly, competition sets the parameters within which goods and services are sold. This is reinforced by market fluctuations; a sudden fall in customer demand can limit the extent to which craftsmen are able to profit from the exercise of their skills. Thus, although the self-employed may be removed from the close supervision of employers they are none the less, subject to the scrutiny of customers and the fluctuations of market forces. They are, then, *indirectly* controlled by others and thereby often *forced to* behave as businessmen. As the Bolton Report states:

> If he is to make an adequate living from his work the independent craftsman must also be competent as a businessman, for in many ways he is running a small business much like any other. This means that records and accounts have to be kept if only for tax purposes, and that his goods have to be sold, sometimes against stiff competition both from other craftsmen and from mass-produced articles . . . Most small businessmen strongly resent having to spend time on paperwork and administration, but for the craftsmen the annoyance is even greater, because he is unlikely to regard himself as a businessman at all, and may well have chosen his way of life precisely to avoid the stresses and routines of business.[19]

Many of these points were illustrated by our respondents. When asked about their personal objectives, they attached considerable importance to earning a living as well as to enjoying job satisfaction and independence. In this sense, self-employment represented the *least disagreeable* way of 'getting by' in a modern economy.

> Basically, the business is a way of making money. It's my living. And it's a better living than I would normally get if I was employed. (120)

> If you're working for somebody there wouldn't be the job satisfaction you can get doing it for yourself. Job satisfaction is the main thing . . . as long as you make a living. I've got a family and a wife to support but as long as I can support them that's all I want . . . I'm

content with the work and I feel no need to expand . . . You've just
got to find that happy medium.   (115)

It's a way of making money. And you've got a bit of freedom to a
certain extent. There's nobody going to say you're five minutes late
or that you can't have half a day off.   (104)

I'm in self-employment really, I suppose, to make enough money to
support my family. I don't think I'd be doing what I'm doing if I had
independent means!   (116)

It's a way of keeping myself in a job more than anything else . . .
You don't set out to make money, you set out to make a living and
enough profit so your capital isn't diminishing.   (117)

Such opinions confirm Kurt Mayer's summary of evidence in the
United States. He concludes that generally 'small businesses remain
small. In the overwhelming number of cases business ownership means
little more than an alternative mode of making a living.'[20] Even those
strongly committed to their *craft* recognise they are constrained by the
demands of their customers. In this sense, customers replace employers
as a source of external supervision and control:

A lot of people say you haven't a boss but you have. The clients are
the bosses. They're the ones that more or less rule you. Well, you're
free — you can turn around and say 'I won't come in tomorrow' and
nothing's said . . . but you've just got to work a bit harder when you
come back.   (103)

People do reject estimates — often because they can't afford it.
There's one woman down the road, I gave her a price but she's had
it done by someone else. Mine would have been a better job . . . but
they find somebody who's a handyman or a retired pensioner rather
than a skilled joiner, and they'll do it cheap.   (124)

For these reasons the 'independence' of the self-employed has been
too heavily stressed. They may be removed from controls inherent
within the employment relationship, but they are subject to the
dictates of market forces. Some of these points were emphasised by the
respondents:

It's often all down to price. If you can do a job ten pounds cheaper than somebody else, then in a lot of cases that is the difference between getting or losing the job . . . People are much more price conscious than they used to be.   (123)

Sometimes the margin can be 12½ per cent and sometimes you drop it down to 5 per cent if you think the job is too expensive . . . It depends on the work I suppose . . . Over the years I've collected quite a few regular customers and so, to a certain extent, you're not in competition with anyone else. You know that they want you to do the job, but by the same token you mustn't jump the price up because you know you are going to get the job. You've got to be fair otherwise you'll lose the customer.   (118)

There's people like myself who take a bit more pride in their work and don't charge a great deal for it – sort of middle of the road. But there's quite a lot of people who do that and so you've got a certain amount of competition . . . There's always someone trying to cut you down on price.   (106)

I still have enough pride in my work to do what I consider a reasonable job. My work could be improved but the financial restraints don't allow me to. That's probably why I don't make as much money as I could . . . The price obviously depends on how bad I want the job, although I've usually got enough work in hand. (116)

Self-employed craftsmen, then, operate in a market within which an acceptable level of living can only be achieved by their making a profit on work activities; unless, of course, they are subsidised by the income of other family members. However, since the market is characterised by considerable uncertainties, one of the major problems confronting them is the need to develop strategies which allow some protection. The most usual way is to establish a 'book' of regular customers. Thus, *social* obligations are created which cement the *economic* relationship between craftsmen and customers. These affect the pricing of jobs if only because estimating is heavily dependent upon the craftsman's personal judgement and experience. In addition, however, it can be influenced by the needs of particular customers which often represent a more important consideration than the cost of materials, overheads and labour.

I never charge old age pensioners, there's no use. I'm not a businessman, I'm not hard enough when it comes to the money . . . This is
why I'll never be successful. There's loads of other things I do as
well. I do lots of spare time jobs with no pay at all. I've just built an
extension for my mate in my spare time . . . I'm too soft.   (108)

Old ladies . . . We don't charge them as much as we would charge
somebody else. If we thought they couldn't afford it I'd perhaps do
three days' work and charge them for two to keep the price down.
(106)

As a result of these practices, the self-employed often have to
'balance the books' by 'overcharging' other clients; in particular,
profit-making enterprises. Most of the respondents used entirely
different methods of economic calculation in pricing work for these
customers since this was removed from the context of social obligation
and profit maximisation was given a higher priority:

Pricing depends on the job. If I'm coming to a customer, some guy
in a house, I mean I can't charge him what I charge a factory. It
would be sort of £50 to £60 a day . . . it's an entirely different
method of pricing.   (112)

Clearly, the maintenance of a network of regular customers enables
craftsmen to protect themselves from the rigours of the market by
obtaining a fairly stable flow of work and a reasonably predictable
level of income. It also acts as a constraint upon the employment of
labour, and hence business growth, because the customer relationship
is founded upon personal obligation. If employees are hired this can
prejudice the whole basis upon which the trading relationship is
established and, therefore, the self-employed's market situation.

People that I do work for obviously get a personal service – they
get the actual man. They phone up for Mr Hains and they get Mr
Hains to come round and do the job. They don't get a workman
that they've never seen in their lives. You see they develop a personal
relationship with you and it carries on from there . . . Once you
employ people you employ trouble . . . The biggest job I do is about
£2,000 . . . I don't really want to be tied up too long on one job. If
you do that you lose all your regular customers. It's far better, in my
opinion, to have a circle of customers and from each customer

you've got, say, a week's work a year. Then you've got a continuous
run of jobs and the money keeps coming in.   (121)

Basically, I've built up a lot of customers — mainly old age pensioners
and school teachers — people like that, who want a room done at a
time. A room decorated here, and a room decorated there. If I spend
more than ten weeks away from these people, then I lose them, you
see.   (114)

'Social' obligations, then, are economically-structured; they enable
craftsmen to protect themselves from market forces. Further, the trust
upon which the relationship with customers is established, protects the
craftsmen against the risk of non-payment for their services; it is a
hedge against the costs incurred by undertaking work which is only
rewarded after labour has been expanded and costs incurred.

Some craftsmen work regularly for only one or two large customers.
But if this provides a 'shield' from the market, it creates a relationship
of dependence which explicitly challenges the craftsmens' notions of
autonomy. The advantages and disadvantages of this form of trading
were expressed as follows:

Most of my time is taken up working for an estate agent . . . I do all
their repairs and maintenance . . . I don't tout on the open market —
I usually refuse private work . . . All I have to do is to phone up and
say 'Look, I'm short of work', and work is produced for me . . .
Cut-throat competition is no good. All it finishes up with is
bankrupt builders and dissatisfied clients.   (102)

We've advertised recently because of our major customer wrapping
up. That was sort of £30,000 a year to us which was gone just like
that . . . It was quite a blow to us, quite a bit of money. We'd been
there since 1972 . . . I haven't got that much work on hand now.
(112)

If major clients are lost, self-employed craftsmen may be forced into
the 'open' market and money must be spent on advertising for new
customers. The financial returns of such an exercise are often low and
many of the self-employed are compelled, because of their limited
personal savings to become, once again, employees.

In fact, on the basis of the interviews, it is possible to suggest that a
majority of our respondents are prone to a process of

'proletarianisation'. Despite the various strategies which they cultivate for the purposes of coping with the market, there are several influences that put their 'autonomous' position at risk and which can force them to become wage labourers. One of the more important of these is the ageing process which erodes their single most important asset — labour power. As they become older, both the intensity and length of their working day tends to decline and they are less able to 'exploit' themselves.[21] As two of our respondents told us:

> I have to be careful what I do because I'm aware of my own limitations . . . over the next fifteen years I'm going to get tireder and probably slower. I'm fifty-two. I find I get tired after eight hours work — much more so than when I was thirty and had all that lovely useful energy.   (102)

> When you reach my age and my physical state you realise that things will deteriorate eventually. Let's not pretend that I'm going to be able to do things that I do now till I'm eighty-five because it's unlikely that I shall . . . I get one or two aches and pains — an arthritic sort of complaint — that most of us are susceptible to. And that is going to get worse. I'm a little bit concerned as to what happens then.   (116)

Consequently, there is often a tendency with age, for self-employed craftsmen to return to relatively more 'secure' jobs as employees. If independent craftsmen own capital assets as well as use their own labour, the latter is the more significant component within the 'mix'. Anything which injures the quality of labour power — accidents, injury, ill-health and ageing — severely threatens their livelihood.[22]

There is, of course, the possibility of reducing this dependence by exploiting the labour of others. However, there are forces which operate against this. First, as we have already indicated, many feel that employing labour will challenge personal relationships with customers and, hence, the economic basis upon which their businesses are established. Secondly, they are reluctant to act as 'small capitalists' because employees are seen to be potentially unreliable. This, in turn, reinforces their commitment to existing and known working practices and severely limits the possibilities for capital accumulation. These opinions were typically expressed as follows:

> Employing people is a problem. I occasionally use my brother-in-law

and I know he's all right. He's the sort of bloke you can leave, you
know. As for taking other people on, I'd have to really know them.
You can advertise for blokes but you just don't know what you're
getting.   (111)

As a one-man business, you're working for your own wage plus a
little bit of profit and you're doing a job at a reasonable cost. When
you're employing one or two men, they want a wage and then
you've got stamps and insurance . . . you'd price yourself out of the
kind of work I do. Whereas I'm conscientious, because it's my
business and I've got to make sure the job is done right, if you're
employing people it's hard to find blokes who you can rely on –
who'll do as well for the customer.   (114)

We could have been a big firm by now but it wasn't our ambition . . .
We find so much trouble when other people do the work – you're
always going back to straighten up behind them and it's just not
worth the trouble. We didn't have an intention of being big and we
don't want to be.   (110)

Despite this reluctance to employ people, it is difficult to regard the
self-employed as 'independent'; on the contrary, they are heavily
dependent upon the work of others – that is, of family members.
Although the contribution of children and of various relatives is sometimes important, it is the 'input' of wives that is crucial for the purposes
of enabling husbands to be self-employed. Despite some deliberate
attempts to exclude their wives, it was clear from the interviews that
the nature of self-employment *demands* their direct, albeit limited,
involvement.[23] As one man told us:

I'm old-fashioned – I don't think a wife should have too much
'know' in a business. They tend to look at a bill, say for £300, and
think, 'Oh Christ, where's that money coming from?' So I tend to
keep the wife very much away and she can take a message, that sort
of thing. She used to reckon up all the invoices for me, but as for
knowledge of the business, no.   (121)

Many respondents stressed how, without their wives, there would be
nobody available to answer the telephone, take messages, place orders
for materials, and so on. One man explicitly emphasised the business
advantages of being married:

Living on my own, I was never here. I used to go out and have a
couple of pints and socialise. But if people want you to do work they
need to speak to you and they just kept ringing and ringing and they
never caught me. And so it just wasn't on. Now my wife does all the
typing work . . . and people know that if they ring they're going to
get somebody. It seems to work very well. (122)

This observation captures the essence of the contribution that married
women make to their husbands' businesses. They tend to undertake
routine clerical and administrative functions of the sort that are
specified by, and subordinated to, their husbands' activities. Thus,
wives are not primarily responsible for any specific functions nor are
they expected to work regularly; instead they are required to help as
and when needed. The division of labour which often emerges was
expressed by one couple in the following exchange:

Wife: I do all the book work. Well, that's not quite true is it?
          My husband writes out his accounts and I type them up
          and do most of the VAT. We've got a friend who is an
          accountant and he checks on me to see what I've done.
Husband: You do all the final paper work really – the invoices and
          what have you. I pencil out what's required and then the
          Missus types them on headed paper. Sometimes, she will
          also do the envelope for it. (116 and 116w)

This supportive role was further illustrated by the comments of several
women:

I just answer the phone when I'm here. I keep saying he ought to
get an answering machine! I also just type out any bills or estimates.
We've got somebody who does our books – an accountant – and
that helps keep that side straight. So really, I don't think I'm much
help. I don't think I contribute much. (112w)

I started off by doing the bookkeeping and typing. An accountant
set up the books for me and I went from there . . . I also do telephone
calls for him. I try to take as much off my husband as I can by
keeping in touch with customers if he can't see them at a certain
time. (118w)

I think my husband could do the books if he had to. It's just a

matter of knowing how to set it out for the accountant . . . I went
to an accountant and he showed me how to do it when we started
the business. If I'm a bit stuck I ring him up and so far it's been all
right.   (106w)

The hours that married women devoted directly to their husbands'
businesses varied between one and eight each week. Most of their time
was devoted to the telephone which, in many respects, is the lifeline of
the self-employed. Married women were often able to perform these
tasks more competently than their husbands because they had acquired
clerical skills through earlier paid employment.

My wife has to help me because I'm not very good at filling in these
forms . . . She's better at bookwork than I am . . . She's a stock
control clerk. She's very experienced at general office work – she's
familiar with ledgers and all that sort of thing. She's good at that.
Whereas I've only got to do two hours of bookwork and I've got
myself a headache.   (102)

My husband automatically knew that I'd been a secretary and when
he thought of starting on his own he said to me, 'Well look, you
know all about office work – you're the ideal person', sort of thing.
I think perhaps if I hadn't have done office work he might not have
even considered starting on his own.   (118w)

Husband: I could not manage it myself. I can't type . . . and I'm
           inhibited about writing out things by hand . . . you've got
           to know how to spell . . . So I require my wife.
Wife: You see, I did work in an accountants as a typist and it
           gave me an extra bit of knowledge. I gained some
           experience there.   (116 and 116w)

Paid employment not only gives married women skills which they may
later use in their husbands' businesses, it is also an important source of
income during the initial period of business formation. If, at a later
stage, they are unable to retain paid employment because of the
demands of their husbands' businesses, their income is often crucial
when their husbands first become self-employed. Indeed, some of the
women who were interviewed took paid employment *because* their
husbands became self-employed, and thereby subsidised the business
during the initial period of trading and through any subsequent period
of financial difficulty.

Certainly, my wife helped the business with her earnings at the beginning. In other words, the arrangement was that she didn't call on my earnings at all. I would have 'paid' my wife the maximum under the tax allowance and that would have gone into the building society . . . or been used for buying stock.   (116)

At the time I applied for my job my husband's work was getting very low and we thought if it was low in summer, come winter he was going to find that he really hadn't got much work on. A job was advertised and I applied . . . I wanted to go back to work although I still envisaged that it would, in fact, have been some stage further in the future.   (124w)

It suits me very well to have a part-time job through the summer. I suppose if things got really bad in the trade I might have to consider going out to work to help the business . . . Obviously, when I go to work in the summer I do help to supplement different things . . . We probably have a little extra in the food line – things I wouldn't buy normally, that are more expensive. And we probably go out to eat more often too.   (125w)

As far as involvement in their husbands' businesses is concerned, wives fill essentially subordinate roles; there were virtually no instances of women participating in the more important areas of decision making. As two of them told us:

I leave everything to him. I trust my husbands' judgement and I'm no good when it comes to business. As long as I've got my housekeeping every week that's as far as my financial interests go . . . Other self-employed people we know have the same relationship as I have with my husband; the wife doesn't get involved.   (112w)

Wife: I was very reluctant about setting the business up really . . . and although we usually discuss things that affect both of us, as far as the business is concerned I don't have any real influence.

Husband: I suppose my wife is not really in a position to give an informed opinion . . . I generally work alone. There is not really much I can discuss with her to my advantage . . . I make the final decisions.   (116 and 116w)

The wives' role is not only subordinate, it is also taken-for-granted and unpaid. In pricing work and in calculating overheads, self-employed men rarely recognise the monetary value of their wives' contribution:

> Although we don't have VAT to deal with, there's an awful lot of time that goes into the business that's never accounted for, like the bookkeeping. But I don't do the bookkeeping, my wife does that. She spends several hours doing that and perhaps once a month she goes through all the paperwork that I accumulate.   (106)

It is usually only in the accounts submitted to the Inland Revenue that there is any recognition of the married women's business involvement.[24] One wife, on being asked whether she was paid for her services, answered:

> I hadn't thought I was, but when the accountant did the accounts, he said I'd been paid a weekly wage last year, but I hadn't known it! But I think it's the way they do it, it's as broad as it's long. It's just for tax purposes really − my services are worth so much a week.   (124w)

But perhaps the major role of the married women we interviewed was their responsibility for almost *all* domestic tasks. In this their position was similar to that of wives described in studies of 'traditional' working class families.[25] As one of them pointed out:

> It's not so much the work that the wife does in the business *as such.* It's the work she does to *enable* the husband to spend more time in the business. And I think quite often the wives do a lot which in another situation they'd expect their husbands to do. You know, work around the house and things which they do in order to let their husbands have more time in the business.   (124w)

Thus, married women contribute to the ongoing viability of businesses by 'freeing' their husbands from the need to undertake various domestic chores so that they can devote a greater proportion of their time to 'work' activities. If, then, women were directly involved with the business this was normally secondary to their domestic concerns:

> I sometimes sit down and have a morning to do the bookwork or I might have an evening, when the end of the month comes, to write

the cheques or something like that. But I don't stick to a strict
routine – when I've got time I sit down and do it . . . You see, my
husband dries up the tea things but that's about it. He always says
he doesn't believe in doing a lot at home. He's out at work all day
and he never does any housework or anything like that.   (125w)

Life was very tiring for the first two years of the business. We had
our daughter and my father was ill so I was helping my mother as
well. And then my daughter had a lot of ill health for years with
asthma . . . After she began to get better my mother had Parkinson's
disease and so I was helping her. So I was quite domestically tied-up
with the family . . . I tried to take as much off my husband's
shoulders as I could during those first few years.   (118w)

My husband will come in tea time and say there's some bills to do
tonight . . . so we might have about two hours of an evening typing
. . . But I'm not a women's libber! Housework is a full-time job and
it can be a pretty thankless task. But you men seem to think we are
happy in our little world – cooking and cleaning . . . It's taken for
granted . . . Although if I'm not well my husband doesn't necessarily
say, 'Get up and cook my tea, woman', he'll do it then.   (112w)

The manner in which the self-employed and their wives organise their
businesses is, to some extent, reflected in their life styles. Just as they
are not entirely committed to profit-making in their businesses, so they
do not give total priority to improving their material living standards;
instead they tend to emphasise economic stability and the need to
'get by'. This is often the original motive for self-employment; it is
seen to offer the opportunity to opt out of the 'rat race'.[26] Many of the
respondents felt that their standard of living was lower than employees
with comparable trade skills and this was often regarded as an inevitable
consequence of the one-man business:[27]

I wouldn't say I was any better off than an electrician working for a
firm really . . . With a one-man business you can only do so much
work . . . You can make a bit more money by getting a good price
on a particular job . . . But there's probably a lot more which you
don't do so well on . . . I don't see how you can make a lot of
money if you're working for a living as a one-man business . . . The
self-employed are average wage earners . . . or just about coming up
to the average if they're lucky.   (123)

A number of the married women were prepared to accept a lower living standard because it was seen as the 'cost' which had to be borne in return for their husbands' personal autonomy.

> You've got to be prepared to take the risk . . . there's a certain amount of insecurity because you never know how your money is going to come in. Sometimes, you can be in the red and sometimes things are quite good but you never know . . . You and your husband have got to live as one over this sort of thing. You've got to be prepared if things are not so good to go without . . . Odd times, I've thought that we'd be better off it he'd taken a permanent job and not worked for himself but he wouldn't be happy, I know that. He's happy being his own boss and pleasing himself. It would reflect upon the whole family if he was miserable so we just keep jogging along . . . I know he's happy that way. We're never going to make a fortune we know that. It's too small a business. It's not possible to make a lot of money . . . But it has its advantages. It's given us a little bit more freedom.   (125w)

> I've never wanted for much. I'm satisfied with what I've got . . . I don't think I'm particularly greedy . . . Perhaps that's my upbringing coming from a self-employed family, knowing times of struggle. I'm reasonably happy . . . although I have to be careful. If I want to go into London, I've got to think twice about whether I can afford the petrol. That's always on my mind; can I afford to do things? . . . I make clothes which obviously does save money . . . I know that you can't alter people. I accept that my husband is like he is . . . It just makes life easier if he is happy. I wouldn't really want him going out to work and coming home miserable. I know he's reasonably content and that helps to build my contentment . . . He would be dreadfully unhappy working for somebody.   (116w)

Few expressed any resentment about their economic circumstances. This was largely due to the absence of reference groups of the kind which can shape feelings of relative deprivation.[28] Of the 25 men that were interviewed, ten explicitly claimed they made no personal comparisons with others. In a sense, this is consistent with their motives for becoming self-employed; many wished to 'opt out'. But of the remainder, any comparisons were typically with working class occupations. The following are illustrative of these:

We have a fairly comfortable standard of living, I think. As long as
we have the basis of life and perhaps a little extra then that's as
much as we really want. I suppose you could put us in line in
earnings with something like a miner on the coalface . . . industrial
workers I suppose their standard of living would be what we would
want as well.   (106)

I'm a workman – working class. I'd compare myself to bricklayers,
painters and decorators. Anybody in the building trade really. I
don't think that by being self-employed I'm better off than a lot of
people that work directly for builders.   (114)

Having 'opted out' of employment they emphasise the attractions of a
stable rather than an *increasing* level of consumption. When asked how
they saw their future living standards, twelve felt they would either
remain the same or decline:

I never compare myself with anybody . . . I think as long as you're
happy and you've got a bit in the bank and you make a bit then you
live . . . We've carried on happily and comfortable. We don't spend a
lot on different things. We go along. That's all I want.   (119)

Basically, I think our standard of living is very good. I'm always
short of cash and we never have a holiday but we've always got
enough. I've never walked to work, put it that way! And I've always
got a cigarette and I can always give the scroungers a cup of tea.
(107)

I consider that we have a satisfactory standard of living. My wife
doesn't go short of a great deal although, obviously, she may like a
fur coat or that sort of thing. But we do go out in the evening for
meals and things like that, and that's about all we expect. We don't
expect Caribbean cruises – we're easily satisfied. I might be termed
by some people as a bit of a stick-in-the-mud in as much as I don't
want to progress too much. I'm content with my lot. I don't want to
work myself up into a frenzy to earn more money so as I could
spend it out on posh cars and things like that.   (121)

I'm quite happy – I'd like more, obviously, everybody would. But I
like to live hand-to-mouth, that's the status I feel happy in,
essentially. I haven't got any debts so therefore I'm happy. I live
quite simply.   (101)

One of the factors which accounts for these attitudes is the market situation of the self-employed. Spending has to be constrained to allow savings for emergencies; bad weather, economic recession, accidents and ill health can either limit or terminate the self-employed's earning capacity:

> What about the winter we've just had! Six weeks was virtually solid rain and then I was felting all the time. But you can't do the felting in wet weather and so I was virtually six weeks with no money at all. So the good times even out the bad. All you really want to do is go easy and steady – there's no need to rush.   (108)

> The only worry I ever get in my position is whether I get ill. I'm always frightened because with nothing coming in – if we don't go to work we don't get anything.   (107)

> If my husband was ever off ill for more than a couple of days he wouldn't get the sickness benefit . . . But I don't think the financial instability really worries us very much. We don't go getting into debt . . . Even if there wasn't the income coming in for a few weeks we wouldn't have the anxiety that we'd got a lot of HP commitments or anything, apart from the mortgage. That's the only financial commitment we've got.   (124w)

During leisure time there is a general absence of participation in clubs and associations. Thirteen of the respondents did not belong to any recreational organisations; of those that did, eight were members of either sports or gardening clubs. There was, further, little evidence of 'mutual entertaining' and social relationships outside the immediate family tended to be based upon extended kin. The respondents, then, seemed to have no aspirations for a life style within which involvement in community and formal organisations is significant.[29] If they had friends who were not family members, these tended to be manual workers who were typically encountered in relatively informal contexts:

> I belong to the British Legion, but only to play snooker . . . now I'm not in any clubs. We don't mix a lot in things like that . . . Not husband and wife clubs anyway. I don't like that type of idea. I like to go down to the pub though, to see a few of my mates.   (122)

Husband: I don't think it's affected us – being self-employed . . . We mix with the same people as we did before. We still play cards down the pub on Friday night with the same guys as we did fifteen years ago . . . lorry drivers, people like that, you know.

Wife: The trouble with small businesses is there's a lot of snobbery involved . . . Social climbing, I can't stand it! The majority of my best mates live on the council estate down there. They're terrific . . . We like to think we'll always be the same. (112 and 112w)

If the self-employed live almost exclusively by the use of their labour power and have a life style which can best be described as 'working class', it would be surprising if this were not reflected in their broader socio-political attitudes. As we have already indicated, their desire for self-employment and work autonomy can be seen as a rejection of the employee role; of being subordinated to others within a capitalist-controlled work process. But many were critical of the way in which society was more generally organised; if only because it gave inadequate social recognition and economic rewards to those who performed productive labour. By the same token, white-collar workers were regarded as making little social contribution:

Historically, a man who gets his hands dirty is at a pretty low social level . . . I've always resented the fact that someone could stand behind a counter or sit behind a desk in an immense office and hold down double the income that I could and have a social standing in the community probably double mine. In actual fact, he's purely living off someone else. He doesn't create anything; he doesn't build anything; he doesn't make anything. He doesn't really even make employment for other people, hardly. He lives on the backs of everybody else . . . It probably makes me sound a bit like a socialist, but the ability to be able to do something should count for more. (125)

I haven't got a lot of sympathy for people who earn vast salaries working in advertising agencies and things like that. I don't think that we'd lose much if they all got fired tomorrow. People working in that sort of situation, well, I call them all parasitic jobs. (124)

Such feelings were even more strongly expressed in attitudes towards those in positions of power and privilege:

> I'm not a communist, but they've got some good points. Everybody works and everybody gets a fair share . . . The rich man gets more than what the poor man does.   (113)

> There's a lot of money that goes on higher up that the deprived people know nothing about and, obviously, the rich people want to keep things the way they are. At the other extreme, I suppose, you get situations with trade unions where they're trying to change things round . . . A lot of unions are condemned because of what they do – wrongly. It's just people at each other's throats killing each other. I suppose some more because they are discontented. They want to spread it more evenly.   (116)

> Society favours the rich. It always has done. It's organised for the rich by the rich. There's only two classes in the country; those with and those without. Basically, simplifying it, two classes, the rich and the poor.   (102)

> It's them and us – there's a big divide still . . . you still get Ascot and Wimbledon. You've got the Royal Family and they carry on with all their hangers-on . . . As far as I can see, society operates to the advantage of the ones on top against the ones down below, like me – an ordinary peasant really. There's only two classes really – the haves and have-nots.   (105)

> Obviously, there are people who earn far too much money and possibly who don't get enough . . . I would say colonels and majors in the army, possibly, are getting far too much money for playing games and, so far as I know, not really doing anything important. (109)

Many self-employed craftsmen see themselves as belonging to a productive working class. Indeed, their own personal commitment to work was part-and-parcel of the priority which they gave to productive labour. This was illustrated in their opinions about 'what was wrong' with the country. Thirteen of them attributed Britain's economic difficulties to the growing proportion of unproductive office employees in the public sector; by contrast, only two referred to the 'problem' of trade unions. In fact, a number argued in support of the trade union movement and stressed its legitimate role in a capitalist society:

> I feel a lot of sympathy for trade unions. Although they are power-
> ful they usually use their power in the right way. You only hear
> about the times when people are using it unjustly. You don't hear
> about the times when a trade union is using its power to support the
> rights of its members who are injured in a factory accident and that
> sort of thing.   (124)

> You only get one side of the argument . . . If you take the wives and
> children of trade unionists, it must cover three-quarters of the
> population so I believe they should have power. You read about
> hospital workers, the porters refusing people operations . . . It may
> have happened but those people had been asking for increased wages
> for donkey's years. Under the present system you have to be ruthless
> to achieve anything. If you just bide your time and wait for them to
> give you a hand-out, you'd be waiting for the rest of your life . . .
> It's the rich that have got the money but it's us what's got the
> power, but we haven't realised it. We haven't used it yet . . . You can
> be very rich in England but if the dustmen won't work and the
> sewage workers won't work, you're soon up the creek, to put it
> mildly.   (105)

Of those respondents who were critical of trade unions, none
expressed opposition to them in principle. Rather, they were hostile
because they felt that unions did not satisfactorily reflect working class
interests – either because the leadership no longer properly represented
the aspirations of the rank-and-file or because they were 'sectionalist'
in pursuing their objectives:

> The most unfortunate thing about unions, to me, is that in most
> cases, the leading unionists always finish up with knighthoods. Well,
> a knighthood to me is an acknowledgement of service to the
> establishment and I don't think that anyone who serves their
> members would qualify for a knighthood. They serve their own
> interests . . . Most of the union leaders are not sincere people. (102)

> Trade unions are too interested in wages and not enough interested
> in working conditions. They're often too interested in their own
> narrow, sectional views. They preach socialism and when it comes to
> it, they're only interested in their own members. They'll get more,

even if at the expense of another group of workers who belong to another trade union.   (124)

Thus, 'anti-union' beliefs among the self-employed should not always be seen as a reflection of right-wing political ideology. It should be recognised that such attitudes can be indicative of more 'socialist' beliefs, albeit tainted by a degree of disillusion.[30] Of course, both themes are to be found within the self-employed but it is surprising that attention has been devoted to the former to the neglect of the latter.[31] Even by reference to a more explicit measure of right-wing beliefs, such as voting for the Conservative Party, the respondents did not adhere to the pattern which is often attributed to them. Of the 25, twelve had supported the Conservative Party in the 1979 General Election. But of these, eight had done so for various 'negative' or 'disaffected' reasons. In other words, they had voted for the Conservatives not because they embodied values to which they enthusiastically subscribed, but rather as a result of dissatisfaction with the Labour Party. There was certainly no enthusiasm for the Conservative Party of the sort Bechhofer and his associates found among Edinburgh shopkeepers.[32]

This, then, concludes our discussion of the self-employed. Our data query a number of commonly-held assumptions about their motives, attitudes and beliefs. They appear to be neither the custodians of right-wing individualism nor the purveyors of core capitalist ethics. Their 'individualism' is best understood in terms of a search for *personal autonomy* which allows the exercise of their craft, free from the constraints of the capitalist employment relationship. Of course, not *all* the self-employed are like this; our respondents' dependence upon trade skills shaped their attitudes in ways which would be unusual among many other sectors of the self-employed where, for example, 'intellectual' competence or personal property ownership may be more important. Poulantzas has brought out the importance of this distinction as follows:

> The artisans . . . by the very nature of their work and the specific permeability that it presents to working-class agents, have always displayed an objectively proletarian polarization, far more than have the small retailers. Artisan production was the cradle of revolutionary syndicalism, and its traditions of struggle are still very much alive.[33]

As stated at the beginning of this chapter, the self-employed have been neglected in social research. But within the context of an increasing level of unemployment and the concomitant expansion of the 'black' and 'informal' economies, it seems probable that their importance within modern society will grow.[34] Further, as employment in large-scale corporations becomes less appealing the attractions of self-employment may spread beyond skilled manual workers – who are particularly prone to self-employment – to highly qualified technical staff, professional employees and managers who feel that their work autonomy is being threatened by an ongoing process of bureaucratisation.[35] But although many of the self-employed 'get by' through cultivating networks of regular customers within which they trade, some do take on employees and so become entwined in a process of capital accumulation. It is to these small employers that we now turn our attention.

Notes

1. Sociological investigations have typically been confined to traditional rural-based occupations. See, for example, M. W. Williams, *The Country Craftsman*, London, 1958.

2. See, for example, data presented in the Economic Activity Tables, *Census of Great Britain, 1971* and J. McHugh, 'The Self-employed and the Small Independent Entrepreneur' in R. King and N. Nugent (eds.), *Respectable Rebels*, London, 1979.

3. It seems generally agreed that over recent years the size of the 'black economy' has increased although individual estimates vary. It has been suggested that its value could amount to as much as 7½ per cent of the gross domestic product. For recent discussions see, K. Macafee, 'A Glimpse of the Hidden Economy in the National Accounts', *Economic Trends*, March 1980 and A. Dilnot and C. N. Morris, 'What Do We Know About the Black Economy?', *Fiscal Studies*, vol. 2, 1981.

4. This figure includes 'painters and decorators' as well as 'construction workers'. See Economic Activity Tables, *Census of Great Britain, 1971*.

5. Ibid.

6. *Royal Commission on the Distribution of Income and Wealth, Report No. 8*, Cmnd 7679, London, 1979, p. 42.

7. Such advantages derived from taxation under Schedule D and, for the 1966–71 period, exemption from Selective Employment Tax.

8. See, for example, G. Mackenzie, *The Aristocracy of Labour*, Cambridge, 1973 and B. Reckmann, 'Carpentry: The Craft and Trade' in A. Zimbalist (ed.), *Case Studies on the Labor Process*, New York, 1979.

9. E. Chinoy, *Automobile Workers and the American Dream*, New York, 1955.

10. Many of the contributions by Bechhofer and his colleagues are referred to in Chapter 1 but see, in particular, F. Bechhofer, B. Elliott, M. Rushforth and R. Bland, 'The Petits Bourgeois in the Class Structure: The Case of the Small Shopkeepers' in F. Parkin (ed.), *The Social Analysis of Class Structure*, London, 1974a.

11. F. Bechhofer, B. Elliott, M. Rushforth and R. Bland, 'Small Shopkeepers: Matters of Money and Meaning', *Sociological Review*, vol. 22, 1974b, p. 476.

12. J. H. Goldthorpe, D. Lockwood, F. Bechhofer and J. Platt, *The Affluent Worker: Industrial Attitudes and Behaviour*, Cambridge, 1968, p. 133.

13. MacKenzie, *The Aristocracy of Labour*, p. 51.

14. Ibid., p. 32.

15. For further details see the methodological appendix. In the text male respondents are identified by number. For the self-employed these range from 101 to 125; for small employers 201 to 225; for owner-controllers 301 to 325 and for owner-directors 401 to 425. Quotes from wives are signified by an additional 'w'. For the self-employed, eleven wives were present at the original interviews and a further five were interviewed separately at a later date.

16. *Report of the Committee of Inquiry on Small Firms*, (The Bolton Report), Cmnd 4811, London, 1971, p. 147.

17. C. Mills, *White Collar*, London, 1951, p. 220.

18. D. Lockwood and J. H. Goldthorpe, 'The Manual Worker: Affluence, Aspirations, Assimilation', BSA Conference Paper, 1962 cited in G. MacKenzie, ' "The Affluent Worker" Study: An Evaluation and Critique' in Parkin (ed.), *The Social Analysis of Class Structure*, p. 254.

19. *Report of the Committee of Inquiry on Small Firms*, (The Bolton Report), pp. 146–7.

20. K. Mayer, 'Business Enterprise: The Traditional Symbol of Opportunity', *British Journal of Sociology*, vol. 4, 1953, p. 179.

21. In 1971, 42 per cent of all self-employed construction workers (including painters and decorators) were under 35 years of age, by comparison, for example, to 27 per cent of farmers, foresters and fishermen and 25 per cent of sales workers. This suggests that, with age, the possibility of self-employment is far less in construction because of the importance of physical condition. See Economic Activity Tables, *Census of Great Britain, 1971*.

22. For evidence of the physical risks involved in construction work see Health and Safety Executive, *Construction: Health and Safety 1976*, London, 1978 and Direct Labour Collective, *Building with Direct Labour*, London, 1978.

23. For a discussion of the differing contributions of wives within small family businesses see R. Gasson, 'Roles of Farm Women in England', unpublished paper 1980 and C. Delphy and D. Leonard, 'The Family as an Economic System', unpublished paper presented to Institutionalisation of Sex Differences Conference, University of Kent, April 1980.

24. By declaring that their wives are paid a salary, the self-employed are often able to increase expenses that can be offset against tax.

25. For a review of this literature see J. Klein, *Samples from English Culture*, London, 1965.

26. See the discussion in J. Boissevain, 'Small Entrepreneurs in Changing Europe: Towards a Research Agenda', unpublished paper presented at the European Centre for Work and Society, Utrecht, 1980.

27. Recent evidence suggests that these views have a material basis. Employees in the building industry 'tend to have greater incomes than their self-employed counterparts, and their mean earnings are also greater' according to the *Royal Commission on the Distribution of Income and Wealth, Report No. 8*, p. 190.

28. For an extended treatment of these concepts see W. G. Runciman, *Relative Deprivation and Social Justice*, London, 1966 and, more recently, R. Scase, *Social Democracy in Capitalist Society*, London, 1977.

29. In this they closely resembled the affluent manual workers of Luton. See J. H. Goldthorpe, D. Lockwood, F. Bechhofer and J. Platt, *The Affluent Worker in the Class Structure*, Cambridge, 1969, Chapter Four.

30. See, for example, J. Tomlinson, 'Socialist Politics and the Small Business' in *Politics and Power* (1), London, 1980 and R. Scase and R. Goffee, 'Traditional Petty Bourgeois Attitudes: The Case of the Self-employed Craftsmen', *Sociological Review*, vol. 29, 1981.

31. See, for example, the various contributions of Bechhofer and his colleagues. Some recognition of 'a working class pattern of attitudes and beliefs' amongst petty bourgois shopkeepers is evident, however, in Bechhofer *et al.* in Parkin (ed.), *The Social Analysis of Class Structure*, p. 121.

32. Ibid.

33. N. Poulantzas, *Classes in Contemporary Capitalism*, London, 1975, p. 330.

34. See Boissevain, 'Small Entrepreneurs in Changing Europe'.

35. For general discussions see J. Boswell, *The Rise and Decline of Small Firms*, London 1973 and P. D. Anthony, *The Ideology of Work*, London, 1977.

5 SMALL EMPLOYERS

As soon as self-employed craftsmen hire labour they are drawn into a web of social and economic obligations which compel them to rely less on their craft skills and become more involved in administration and supervision. Further, their businesses take on distinctive characteristics; for example, they must be regarded as financial units which often require credit and generate problems of cash flow. The employment of only one person has a qualitative effect of the sort that has been rarely recognised in the literature. Indeed, as we shall argue, it is the *employment relationship* rather than any other single factor which determines the nature of the enterprise and the owner's role within it.[1]

The 25 small employers that were interviewed employed, on average six workers.[2] All of them had trade backgrounds and had previously been self-employed within the building industry. In terms of their social origins, 23 of the respondents had fathers who were industrial manual workers; of these, six — at one time or another — had been self-employed, or small-scale proprietors.[3] Only two of the respondents had fathers employed in managerial occupations. The small employers were, then, similar in many respects to the self-employed in their background and, indeed, they continued to be directly involved in manual work. The crucial difference was that, during their own work careers, they had become employers of labour. Twelve of the respondents were carpenters and joiners who, in various ways, embodied many of the key features of the traditional craftsman. Indeed, their craft has proved to be the most difficult to de-skill and carpenter employees have been able to combat managerial attempts to bring about their *real* subordination. As Reckmann has shown, technological change has not fundamentally altered their work tasks:

> There have been many ostensible changes . . . from hand to power saw, from pine board to plywood. Contrary to appearances, however, these have meant little significant net change in what the carpenter must know and decide. Hand-held power tools, though certainly faster, louder, and physically easier to use, neither do different things nor act on the material via fundamentally different physical principles than the tools of the (earlier) carpenter. Similarly, the structure principles of wood construction have not changed so

as to diminish the carpenters' skills.[4]

Further, the nature of their work leads carpenters to become the co-ordinators of a number of other building tasks.[5] One of our respondents aptly summed up this role,

> You'll find that all the best builders are carpenters and joiners. Basically, a carpenter has got to know every aspect of the job, more so than a bricklayer . . . He gets tied up with the bricklayers for setting his roof out and where his door frames have got to go in, his window frames and the hole where his stairs go . . . He's got to know where the electrician's wirings have got to go in case he puts a bit of skirting on and bangs a nail straight through it. The same with the plumbers – he's got to trim his joists for heating pipes and domestic pipes. Plasterers-door frames have got to be set so much out from the wall so that when the plasterer plasters that wall he finishes flush with your door frame . . . It's basically the key trade of the building industry . . . you'll find that everything has to co-ordinate around the carpenter on site. I think this is why you'll find that the majority of guys that have got their own businesses were carpenters. (206)

If, then, the carpenters' work role inherently entails a considerable degree of co-ordination, it is to be expected that many will become foremen, managers and even employers. If they become self-employed, they are more likely, we would suggest, to subsequently become small employers than other types of craftsmen.

It is often market circumstances which first encourage the self-employed to hire labour. As workloads increase it becomes necessary to employ others in order to fulfil obligations to regular customers; in this sense, business expansion is a response to market demand rather than an active initiative. Thus, small employers do not see themselves as *positively* committed to profit-making and capital accumulation. The following reflect the attitudes of many:

> You get to the stage where you've got so much work on that you don't know how to cope so you have to have somebody. I'm much easier in my mind since I've had employees because before, if I had a problem, that was the job at a standstill. Now, things are organised so I can call one of the chaps in to tell him where I am or go to the problem.   (212)

> We got too much work you see – couldn't cope with it so I had to take somebody else on. I took another carpenter on and then another labourer and it's just gone on from there.   (204)

With the employment of labour the nature of the business changes. More specifically, the proprietor becomes involved with supervision and administration in addition to performing manual work. Furthermore, the transition from self-employment to small employer is invariably characterised by an increase in the length of the working day.[6] If the self-employed work a 'normal' week with perhaps an additional few hours for bookkeeping, small employers regularly and systematically undertake administration *most* evenings and weekends. This uncosted work is usually necessary if the small employer is to survive in the competitive market:

> It's a long week, but basically I only cost from 7.30 till 5.00. You can't bring in what you do at night time and weekends. If you do, you might as well pack up because at the end of the day, your work would be costing so much that you'd be uncompetitive.   (206)

> I still do all the office side basically because it's easier for me to do than anybody else. I know exactly what's going on within the business. But that, to me, is a side line . . . it's incidental. It's some-thing I do in the evening to pass the evening away.   (211)

> I try and work an eight hour day, the same as my blokes do, and do most of the bookkeeping in the evening if I can . . . I think if I costed all those hours and then did the same amount of hours for another employer, I would be out of pocket.   (212)

The administration of the business, then, is not 'proper' work for which customers are charged.[7] Nevertheless, small employers work a long day:

> I always work ten hours a day – well, what I call work, on site . . . I usually do paperwork for, say, about three hours, three evenings a week. So I do fifty hours a week plus nine hours paperwork, and although my employees don't work on a Saturday, I usually do. (210)

> I'm usually up at my yard at 7.00 a.m. The men get there at 7.30.

We all have half an hour for dinner. They finish at five. I finish
around about six o'clock and then I have my dinner. Then, I usually
go out and see customers or if there's some office work to do, I go
back. So, my average working day is about eleven hours – and this
is Saturday as well, and probably Sunday . . . You've got to be
prepared to give up your evenings and weekends . . . I wouldn't have
what I've got now if I hadn't. (213)

Small employers often experience considerable tension between their
roles as 'productive workers' and 'managers'; although they still regard
themselves as tradesmen, market circumstances have led them to
employ labour. This, in turn, creates administrative problems which
they resent:

I tend to forget paperwork. Then suddenly I realise that we're
getting a bit close to the limit. Then I have to send out a few
invoices which take a month or so to come in, so we're in trouble.
This is the bane of every small businessman's life; cash flow and
paperwork. Certainly, I couldn't afford or, rather, I don't want to
afford a secretary to come in and do this. If I did have a secretary it
would release me to do a lot more work. I could probably pay for a
secretary easily by increased efficiency but I haven't got into that
yet. (202)

I dislike office work the most. I find it very hard to get the final
accounts out . . . I'm not office orientated. I'm for the physical side
. . . the actual work. (213)

I like doing the actual work. I prefer it to the bookkeeping . . .
Sitting behind a desk just doesn't appeal to me really. I prefer to
work with my hands and with tools. I think you get more
satisfaction out of doing that. (212)

These comments suggest that small employers are often ill-equipped
to cope with business growth. If there is a tension between undertaking
productive manual and unproductive office work, this is heightened by
the employment of labour. The business cannot be conducted in a
'casual' and ill-planned manner; on the contrary, the flow of work has
to be planned and satisfactory cash reserves maintained in order to pay
regular employees. This requires small employers to act in a more
'calculative' and 'rational' manner than the self-employed. Despite their

dislike for paperwork they are compelled to invoice customers regularly and determine that the flow of work gives a satisfactory financial return. Unlike the self-employed, there is less reliance upon 'guesswork' and 'experience' in the determination of costs:

> You can't afford to play about . . . Each week stuff that's taken out is booked down. The lads in the workshop have a book and what they take out, they book down . . . (Then) in the building trade you have to watch stuff that comes back off the job into your yard. This is one of the big things you've got to watch out for . . . to see how that's credited . . . If it's down (in the book) then there's no messing about. So, if you take salvage off a job, lead or anything like that, you weigh it off and credit it.   (209)

> I literally price everything. Somebody brings me a plan and I work out the amount of goods, the amount of timber and everything. I literally write it all down and I cost labour-wise every part of the job — the digging of the foundations, the brick work up to the damp course, the floor — I would do all that. Now that takes quite a long time, but this, as far as I'm concerned is a proven method . . . and it's always within a few pounds.   (215)

> I went to technical school for three years on a surveying course . . . which included estimating. A lot of people in building 'guesstimate' — they just sort of go on hearsay or what they think a job is worth. All right, sometimes it pays off; sometimes they earn a lot of money . . . But if you want the job and you're pricing against other people, you've got to know what you are doing. And that's why I went to school.   (211)

Small employers often expand their businesses in order to cope with the demands of their regular customers, but this can create tensions between 'personal obligation' on the one hand and 'economic calculation' on the other. This was well illustrated in the comments of one respondent:

> You make money in the office. You don't make money on the site . . . With a fine stroke of the pen I can earn £10. It takes me two hours to make that out of a job . . . One of the biggest things we have to do is to price the job up. You've probably got a reference book you use for pricing. Then you sit back and think about that

particular job. You think, 'Well, that job should cost so much, but
to the customer it's going to benefit them a little bit more'. So okay,
you'll put a little bit of extra profit margin on. Then you get the
reverse side of the coin . . . a very old and trusted client that
possibly can't afford more than X pounds . . . An old client does get
the benefit of your expertise whereas new customers will pay what
you want and that's it.   (218)

The conflicting demands of manual work and business administration are often resolved by delegating the less important aspects of
financial management to wives. Indeed, as with the self-employed,
family labour is indispensable, but if the role of married women among
the self-employed is *supportive*, it can more appropriately be described
as *active* among small employers.[8] Whereas for the former, women
provide routine clerical services in addition to their domestic role, for
the latter they are an integral part of a division of work within the
enterprise. Thus, their contribution is assumed, predictable and long-
term; they typically commit a considerable amount of time to the
business and acquire a wide range of financial and administrative skills.
Two of the men described their wives' role as follows:

Well, my wife is very good. She does all the wages and she does all
the VAT. She does all that side of it — all my typing and letter
writing. It's important and quite honestly — apart from employing
somebody to do that side — if I had to personally do it there would
be just no free time . . . It would get the to stage where I would have
to say either I've got to expand or I'll pack it all in.   (210)

My wife covers the telephone and she does the accounts . . . the
wages, tax, VAT and all the paperwork. I only get involved in
technical correspondence and ordering and pricing . . . She types for
me as well. She does all the necessary office work but she also does
the paperwork.   (217)

In addition to this 'routine' office work, married women also help to
organise their husbands' businesses and are directly involved in day-to-
day decision making. As a result, they devote a considerable number of
hours to 'business-related' activities; among our respondents this ranged
from eight to 40 hours each week. Some of the wives described their
work in the following terms:

I do the ordinary bookkeeping . . . I do the wages, the VAT and keep account of how much we've got and how much we've paid on all the cheques . . . When we had two gangs we both used to get up about half-past seven and I'd take one lot in the car and my husband would take the other lot in the van. When he was actually working away, then I used to take them and fetch them all through the week . . . I was doing practically an eight hour day.   (218w)

I do all the bookwork and typing, then the accounts, income tax, VAT, everything . . . I've always kept an eye on everything that was going on in the office . . . We start here at 7.30 and I'm often still here at half-past six in the evening . . . Quite often I have to take home books at night to get the bills out . . . I'm set up with a typewriter and calculator at home because I have a little office room here as well . . . I also pop all over the place in the van – I've had to do that all the time . . . I used to drop the painters off in the mornings and if there's somebody stuck out on a job I sometimes go to pick them up . . . If my husband has to go away I just take over automatically . . . Firing people – I've done that too. No trouble. You just have to be firm and know what you are talking about . . . You name it, I've done it.   (207w)

I had to be here every day. I wasn't allowed to go out because people would ring up . . . I had Wednesday and Friday mornings off – other than that I was here all the time to receive goods, check them, sign for them, answer the phone and do all the paperwork . . . Even now it's a twenty-four hour job. It doesn't end when my husband comes home at night. After a meal the phone starts ringing . . . it goes on till ten o'clock. In fact, you've got to be prepared for work whatever the time of the evening.   (211w)

In view of these responsibilities, married women are often unable to develop their own 'independent' careers; indeed, several in our own study had *given up* jobs because of their indispensability to their husbands' businesses:

As well as helping with the business I had my full-time job. I don't know how I used to manage it sometimes. That's when really it came to the point where I had to give the job up. We got busier, we got bigger and I couldn't cope with so much work. So I gave up my full-time job to concentrate more on the extra office work in the business.   (218w)

It was a long day when I used to teach . . . I'd come home about
five o'clock and do my marking first, then I'd do the books for the
business. All my heavy housework and baking I used to do at
weekends . . . I did that for the first six years then I stopped
teaching completely and I've never gone back . . . Having been a
teacher and a professional, I sometimes still hanker for it.   (207w)

I worked in a factory before . . . then I was expecting our first baby
so I stopped work . . . I don't expect I shall work again . . . I don't
think my husband would like me to go anyway. I've often said that
I could get a little job now but he said, 'No, your place is here in the
home – with the telephone!'.   (212w)

The *active* involvement of married women in business administration
and financial control reinforces the 'craftsman' identity of many small
employers. By delegating to their wives they fail to acquire the
necessary administrative skills that are important for longer-term
business growth. For their part, small employers' wives do receive some
financial reward but even so, this rarely constitutes an adequate 'rate'
for their efforts.[9] As with the wives of the self-employed, therefore,
their contribution represents a form of hidden subsidy to the business.
Furthermore, because of their husbands' long working hours, married
women are often forced to bear a heavy domestic burden. Just as their
husbands assume they will contribute to the efficient operation of their
businesses, they also expect them to be single-handedly responsible for
family relationships and domestic activities. As some of the married
women explained:

I packed up working when we got married because my husband
wasn't going to have a working wife . . . These days, I still do about
sixteen hours a week bookkeeping in the business – plus the phone
. . . But my husband will only help domestically if I'm not well –
then he rallies round very well. But I wouldn't want him to all the
time. He's got more than enough to do and I try and take as much
off his shoulders as I possibly can.   (218w)

I do have a domestic routine – yes; never do it when the husband's
there. He always says, 'Don't get that bloody Hoover out while I'm
here' . . . He doesn't do anything towards the housework . . . I've just
got to be prepared, for example, to have a meal ready at all times –
it can be as late as eight or nine o'clock.   (211w)

My husband sometimes invites half the village round to our house and he expects me to feed them all − literally! He'll provide the drinks but I have to do the eats *and* cooking *and* the cleaning up afterwards . . . A few weeks ago a friend asked my husband whether he had ever stood in his life, because he's never seen him sitting up, let alone standing! It's because he comes round of an evening or Saturday afternoon when my husband is absolutely whacked out. (207w)

Often my husband comes home in the evening and has to go out again and see to his business. But the children have just got used to it now. I sometimes think he could have spent more time with them. But they've accepted that he doesn't have much time and it's usually Mum they turn to. That's how it is.   (219w)

In this sense, then, the wives of small employers fulfil two roles, each of which is crucial to the survival of their businesses. Indeed, it would be interesting to ascertain the extent to which small business failure is related to marital stress. Certainly, the ownership of such enterprises creates tensions within husband-wife relationships as one of our respondents admitted:

My husband occasionally helps at home when he has got time, but it's very rare that he has time . . . like most men, he doesn't like doing it unless he really has to . . . You've got to have a lot of patience with each other because I'm afraid tempers get a bit frayed at times. He gets problems with his work and he thinks you don't understand. You get problems with the children and he never seems to have time to discuss them and there's school and things like that. I'm afraid things get a bit rough at times. It's not all honey. There's a lot of responsibility for him and you feel sometimes as though you are taking second place to the business. Obviously, you're not, but you just get that feeling sometimes . . . You're bound to get these things crop up in businesses. It's unavoidable. You perhaps get people who owe you money and you have to get a solicitor on to it. It all tends to aggravate, you know. And it comes through to you and the family. It seems to upset all round, really. And then it dies down again and everything is all right. It's unavoidable. You get these frictions now and again. It's just one of the hazards of having your own business.   (219w)

All of this reaffirms the function of the family as an economic *productive* unit.[10] Domestic premises are used for the purposes of the business on a much more extensive scale than among the self-employed. It is often necessary to convert a room into an office, to replace the car with a van and to use the garage as a store for materials and equipment. In these ways, the business is subsidised not only by the working contribution of married women but also by domestic resources that would normally be used for family consumption:

> We use the spare bedroom for the office and we have bits and pieces at the side of the house here. We've got far more room now. That was another reason for moving — we had no room for our equipment. Here, we've got the shed in the garden and plenty of room out of sight. (218w)

> We have a very large house here. And so upstairs we have our complete living accommodation. Three bedrooms, sitting room, kitchen, bathroom and the loft. Downstairs, the business. (207w)

Although there is a dependence upon the *active* involvement of wives, the essential characteristic of these businesses is the employment of men alongside whom small employers work. Unfortunately, in the analysis of this relationship there is little guidance to be obtained from the literature. Only a small amount of research has been devoted to the nature of employer–employee relationships within enterprises where face-to-face interaction prevails rather than bureaucratic and impersonal rules.[11] There are virtually no studies of the employment relationship in small employer businesses as we have defined them in this study. Although, for example, a substantial proportion of Bechhofer and his associates' sample of shopkeepers employed staff, the investigators do not discuss in any detail the nature of the employment relationship.[12] The only systematic study is that of East Anglian farmers and farmworkers undertaken by Newby and his colleagues.[13] They investigated patterns of employer paternalism, the nature of which they define as follows:

> On the one hand its interest is to maintain a degree of hierarchical *differentiation* from those over whom it rules; on the other hand it wishes to cultivate their *identification* by defining the relationship as an organic partnership in a co-operative enterprise.[14]

However, the authors do not distinguish between the employment strategies adopted by farm proprietors of different size. This is disappointing since, as they admit, the 'size-effect' does not operate in a straightforward fashion. They point out, for example, that the smaller farmers in their sample – those with an average of 3.5 non-family workers – lack 'the wherewithal to exercise paternalism – for example, a large tied housing stock, the ability to offer various prerequisites, the time and resources to engage in home visits, charity etc'.[15] This suggests that employers' capacity to exercise paternalism is directly related to market circumstances and, possibly, to industrial and occupational cultures.[16] As Newby states in an earlier article, the ability to 'care' for employees in a paternalistic fashion:

> will itself depend upon how much room for manoeuvre the employer is given by his own source of power – the conditions of the market for his product. Except in a situation of monopoly the individual capitalist is unlikely to be able to control market conditions so that adverse circumstances external to the employer-employee relationship may threaten its stability.[17]

Market factors, then, may require alternative employer strategies even where enterprises are predominantly small and characterised by a high level of employer-employee contact. Thus, given the known variability of market conditions in different sectors of the economy, it is reasonable to expect that the employment relationship in small-scale enterprises may be subject to significant variation. If the personal services sector in general and the building industry in particular are subject to a greater degree of market fluctuation than farming, we would expect this to be reflected in strategies of employer control.

The small employers that we studied in fact adopted a strategy which can best be described as *fraternalism*.[18] In effect, they continue to see themselves as tradesmen working *with* and *alongside* their employees. In this sense their work situation bears a close resemblance to their prior experience as *employees* and it continues to influence their present behaviour as *employers*. Some of the men described their overall approach as follows:

> I try to be fair with them. I don't know if, after a few years, whether you get biased to an employer's outlook, but I try and look back over the years when I was employed and see what my reaction would have been and use that as a guide. I feel that in a small

business if you can't do it on a friendly relationship then you should go. When there's just the three of you in close proximity, if you've got to have a heavy boss-worker relationship then you might just as well not bother.   (220)

The best way to handle men is to be straight with them for a start. Be straight, and treat them as if you're work mates . . . The way I look at it is if you've been brought up in the trade, then you are a tradesman. These men treat me like I was when I was working as an ordinary tradesman. Whether I'm a boss now or not, they talk to me the same as they do to their mates.   (203)

You've got to know what you are talking about. The men have got to have confidence in you . . . If they've got any problems I go on site and they can always speak to me. They all know that they'll be treated fairly and, obviously, they know that I, being in the game all my life, know what it's all about.   (224)

If during the 'normal working day' they work alongside their employees, they also cost their own labour in the same manner.[19] It is primarily through end-of-year profits and/or the fiscal 'perks' of self-employment that they are able to benefit from their position as business proprietors:

My accountant always tells me I am paying the men too much money . . . They earn more than me − they take home more than me. Thrice as much sometimes. They always do, but that's a fact of life. Obviously, with things like the car, the van and petrol and telephones − I get my perks that way. But in actual cash, they're better off.   (214)

I pay myself a weekly wage . . . costed as an ordinary bricklayer . . . It wasn't many years ago we were still paying ourselves eleven pounds a week . . . Obviously, we draw from the bank or from the firm according to our requirements, but this probably doesn't exceed a bricklayer's wage anyway.   (207)

The reluctance to devote themselves to full-time administration is linked to the view that such work is 'unproductive'. For them to cease manual work would not only increase costs but also introduce a 'hierarchical' dimension into the employment relationship, which could generate resentment and seriously reduce the productivity of their employees. Small employers, then, cannot be seen as living off the profits created by others. Many of those we interviewed claimed they were obliged to work as competent and productive tradesmen:

> My men appreciate me in as much as they know they don't keep me. I can keep myself. So, therefore, they don't get all bolshy and they don't turn round and say, 'Look at him riding around in a big car. He's got this and he's got that.' Because they know that I do earn it. They don't support me.   (213)

> The more work you take on and the more employees you have, the more paperwork you get. You get snowed under with it. But if I'm in the office doing all the paperwork and not doing any manual work . . . my charges would have to go up a lot and I wouldn't get the work.   (219)

Although small employers maintain a close day-to-day personal contact with their employees, they frequently leave their workers to 'get on with the job'. The technical division of labour enables employees to work with a considerable degree of personal autonomy and small employers, being themselves tradesmen, realise the need to grant them the freedom to exercise their skills.[20] This, in turn, maintains a high level of job satisfaction and reinforces their employees' identification with the business. Two of the respondents described their approach in the following terms:

> I've found that if you give a man a little bit of responsibility he'll do a better job for you and he's got something to work at, hasn't he? If you were building an extension and you sent a couple of blokes round and said, 'I want the base done' and they get on and do the base and you don't tell them anything about what's going on top, they're not interested. And if a man is not interested in his work, he's not going to work so hard and let's face it, they're there to make a profit for you, aren't they?   (204)

> From the beginning, if you give men a job to do, you must explain exactly what's got to be done and let them get on with it . . . It doesn't matter how long they take . . . as long as they make a reasonable job of it and if they do, *tell them* they've made a reasonable job . . . If you treat people as though you've got a bit of

confidence in them, they probably won't let you down, whereas the ones you keep on to, have a sort of 'I don't care' attitude.   (210)

Because skilled employees are relatively expensive and must therefore be 'kept working' it is a common practice for small employers to
relegate themselves to various subsidiary tasks or service functions.[21]
This emphasises the *fraternal* nature of the employment relationship
whilst allowing small employers to periodically check on the progress
of work. More overt forms of employer control are difficult to impose
and, in any case, are likely to trigger an antagonistic response from
workers who value their autonomy. These problems of supervision
were frequently mentioned in the interviews:

I supervise them with great difficulty . . . it's almost impossible. I
can only look at the job at the end and see that it's come out
reasonably well within my expectations. If I call at the job too many
times then they obviously get the idea that I'm checking up on
them . . . then they have two hours for lunch . . . I mean, I can't
win! So I can only look at the job at the end and think, 'Well, that's
turned out within my expectations so we'll discard half a day —
they've still got the job out on time . . . I try not to push too much
and hope . . . that I get a reasonable amount . . . All I expect is a
reasonable day's work. I don't expect them to break their necks.
(220)

I want someone that I don't have to run after. I'd rather pay the
money and know that the work is going to be done right than get
someone who'd do it as a cheap Jack . . . So I need someone reliable
. . . Take the one I've got now, I know I can leave him . . . because
he'll tell me what he wants and I'm confident I can leave him. I
know it will be done. I rely on him a lot and he revels in it . . . I
find if you ask them to do something that's better than brow-
beating. I don't brow-beat. You can't say, 'You will do this, you
will do that'. I get more done for me by buttering them up as it
were, 'That's a good job', or 'Do you think that you could get that
done by Friday?' Put it in that manner and invariably you find that
it gets done.   (219)

Most people in the building trade are prickly types — they don't like
to be treated as serfs, as one might say. They like to be asked . . .
They're very independent — builders . . . You can't supervise

workers on a site like you can in a factory.   (225)

The dependence of small employers on their workers is heightened by the fact that they typically employ only six or seven men. Consequently, the poor performance – or absence – of one man can have a disproportionately large impact on productivity. This vulnerability heightens small employers' dependence upon their men working together as equals in a team which 'pulls together'. If this all-round effort is not achieved the consequences can be disastrous as one respondent explained:

> One bloke we've got is deteriorating . . . you put him on a job and it goes into debt. Every day is a headache – what can we give him today? With a bigger firm they can afford to carry him, but a small firm can't.   (201)

For their part, small employers reciprocate employee commitment by giving them special privileges. In doing so, they cultivate personal relationships which are characterised by well-established patterns of mutual obligation:

> Well, with employing a small amount of people you find that you know them all personally. I can go to any one of my fellows and say to him, 'Look, George, we're in trouble' . . . Last week one chappy was on holiday, we had one fellow go sick and another one break his thumb. That meant to say that myself and my partner were virtually the ones left in the firm. I said to the chap who's on holiday, 'We could do with you back on Monday'. 'Okay, no problem', he said. This is the sort of reaction you get. But on the reverse side of the coin, if that chap said, 'Look Governor, I need £100', I'd find him £100 and I'd let him pay me back when he could. This is it – it's a personal relationship. Let's put it this way, we're working with them eight hours a day and you're only with your spouse about another eight so this is the sort of relationship that you get.   (208)

'Fringe benefits' such as these are generally used as a means to retain good employees but in some cases they also give them the opportunity to 'experiment' on their own. Perhaps the major fringe benefit is the use of the employers' equipment and materials for the purposes of spare-time work. Small employers recognise that this is important for their workers since it represents a means by which they can supplement their earnings. This, in turn, reduces pressure for wage increases.[22] The implications of this practice are, however, far-reaching since it allows employees to 'trade' autonomously and thereby obtain experience of 'quasi'-self-employment. Judging from their comments few small employers perceived this to be a threat to their own businesses:

> This is the great thing with me, if somebody wants something — a can of paint or something because they've got a job to do — as far as I'm concerned, they can have it. If they ask for anything, nine times out of ten, they will get it . . . you get little bits and pieces over and you don't mind (letting them have it) . . . If a bloke wants to work, say the afternoon himself, then as far as I'm concerned, it's all right as long as he doesn't work on my patch.   (219)

> One chap takes the van home evenings and weekends . . . I wouldn't object if they do odd jobs. In fact, I let them have the materials. (212)

> They do work on their own . . . as long as it's not one of my customers I'm not worried . . . if they want the van for their own use, fair enough, it doesn't worry me. I mean, I don't even charge them petrol.   (210)

If these spare-time practices prove to be successful, some employees may decide to start their own businesses on a full-time basis.[23] Thus, the *fraternalism* of small employers demands the extension of fringe benefits which can eventually lead to employees becoming self-employed. Perhaps the most extreme instance of this practice is when small employers make the necessary legal arrangements for their employees to eventually take over the ownership of their businesses.[24] The assets involved in such a transfer may not be particularly extensive but the implications for the employment relationship are significant. Two small employers described such transference schemes:

> We've got a limited company in the offing and we are going to pass the business over to the lads. We'll be in an advisory capacity or, perhaps, I shall be doing a bit of work for them. As long as I can earn a bit of money.   (225)

I made two of my blokes into directors . . . I hope that in perhaps
ten years' time I can consider getting out of it altogether . . . The
reason I made it a company and two of my fellow employees into
directors is that they've both got children and eventually they should
have sufficient capital to buy me out. If not, they've got shares and
I will climb into the background and still take an income from it.
(211)

Clearly, the bond between small employers and their employees
extends beyond the 'cash-nexus'. A working relationship is established
which allows employees considerable job satisfaction and provides
them with the personal skills and assets necessary for them to 'go it
alone' should they so wish. Because small employers put considerable
'trust' in their workers and expect them to behave in a responsible and
conscientious manner, they are careful in their recruitment procedures.[25]
Workers are expected to meet criteria of acceptability, as *employees*
who can be relied upon to do a 'reasonable day's work' and as *people*
who will be able to establish satisfactory relationships with customers.[26]
Thus, employers' perceptions of customers' preferences often determine the personal qualities of the workers they are prepared to employ.

I've got to have someone that I can leave on the job to keep my
customers happy. Someone who will look after my interests and
generally see to it that we keep the customers happy.   (219)

I try to find somebody who has got a reasonable personality because
when you are going into private houses and dealing personally with
mostly women you feel you've got some responsibility to send
somebody who is a bit respectable looking . . . Customers are
entitled to expect something for what they pay for . . . so it's a
question of finding someone who can handle these situations. (220)

You'd want him (a new employee) on a trial period to see that the
type of work he does is really neat. I think also the appearance of
him is important, neat and tidy, a pleasant sort of chap. Somebody
who could deal with customers – talk to customers as well as I can,
really.   (212)

Careful recruitment further enables small employers partially to
relinquish the responsibilities of supervision and control. In effect,
notions of customer obligation operate as a form of employee control

since workers feel it is their 'duty' to complete a reasonable and fair-priced job. 'Unreasonable' and 'expensive' work has to be paid for, it seems, by the customer rather than the employer. One small employer described the particular technique he used to exploit this relationship:

> My men are working for a private person and they have got to satisfy that person. That is why I'll never have a job number; the time is always booked to Mr and Mrs So-and-so. If you book it to a job number, any amount of time can go on a number. When they're charging an hour's time, they're charging Mrs So-and-so and she's to pay it. I like them to realise that.   (209)

The heavy emphasis upon the 'personality' of workers partly accounts for small employer claims that there is a general shortage of suitable, skilled labour. But 'suitable' in this sense normally refers to general personal characteristics as well as to technical competence. Hence, many small employers in our study were reluctant to recruit from Job Centres on the grounds that those available may not be 'reliable', 'conscientious' or 'trustworthy'.

> (My workers) are all skilled men in their own right . . . If they were to leave I could never replace them. I would just have to go back to being a one-man band . . . Tradesmen are so hard to get . . . I do private work and when they go into people's homes I don't mean they've got to touch their forelock or call them sir, but they've got to be a little bit respectful . . . you want a person who's got a bit of respect for people . . . You cannot take somebody off the Labour Exchange or Job Centre and bring them in . . . I think a lot of them are virtually unemployable.   (213)

If, by virtue of their recruitment and work practices, small employers establish personal relationships with their employees, this rarely extends into non-work life. Contact outside work is limited if only because of the long working day consisting as it does of 'productive' manual work and 'non-productive' administration in the evenings and at weekends.[27] Two small employers summed up their spare-time activities in the following manner:

> Our leisure time is normally taken up with running the business and the day is filled quite comfortably without joining any clubs. (217)

I haven't got any free time . . . I've got bits and pieces to do.
Occasionally, I might nip up the local and have a jar. I get up there
at ten and they close at eleven. But just an hour away from booking
at times, you feel you need it.   (223)

One of the wives put her point of view in strong terms:

I would like to see my husband not work so hard . . . I can't
remember when he's had a free Sunday or a free Saturday for a very
long time. When you take the staff home on a Friday they're
finished. They don't know how lucky they are . . . They've got
peace of mind Saturday and Sunday which we haven't got still . . .
We are so busy trying to make a go of it that you don't think of
leisure time so much . . . So we don't make a habit of seeing any of
the customers . . . and we don't got out with the employees.
(218w)

In the limited leisure time which is available, some small employers
meet their workers on an informal basis. This is typified by having an
occasional drink with their employees, either at home or in the pub:

Some of the chaps who work for me started at school the same day
as me and I go out and have a drink with them on Friday or
Saturday night, the same as I did before I took over the business.
That doesn't worry me as long as I enjoy someone's company.
(210)

If the men are doing a very dirty job or a late job on a Saturday or
Sunday we take them home and give them a drink and what have
you . . . I make them a meal as well — it might be breakfast, lunch or
evening meal. But we always make something — make sure they
have something to eat. I think they do appreciate it . . . My husband
looks after them. Although it's an employer-employee relationship,
he's one of the lads . . . you know what I mean? He's one of the boys
and this helps an awful lot . . . When I'm here it's just the same. I'm
just another employee as far as anybody else is concerned . ... there's
no barrier.   (207w)

These, then, are the central features of the *fraternal* strategy. The
dependence of small employers upon 'indispensable' workers, the
nature of the work tasks and the unstable and competitive conditions

of the market compel the structuring of *fraternalism* between
employers and employees. Indeed, given the conditions under which
these businesses operate, *fraternalism* represents the only feasible means
by which these proprietors can control and manage labour. Small
employers, then, define the relationship with their employees as 'an
organic partnership in a co-operative enterprise'.[28] However,
hierarchical differentiation, which represents the other key element in
Newby's definition of paternalism, is largely absent. *Fraternalism*
represents a means whereby small employers can overcome the tension
deriving from their role as *both* employers *and* workers. Although they
may own various physical assets, their businesses are primarily
dependent upon theirs' and others' *labour*. Small farmers may also
work alongside their employees but, we would suggest, the larger
capital assets which they possess − often through inheritance −
fundamentally affects the relationship with employees in two major
ways.[29] First, it makes the contribution of their own manaul labour
to the success of the business relatively less important than that of the
productive assets which they own. Secondly, it ensures a difference in
material wealth between themselves and their employees which makes
the exercise of paternalistic authority a more appropriate form of
managerial control.

As with paternalism, however, *fraternalism* has its own contradictions which lead to strain, conflict and perpetual 'redefinition'. In a
variety of ways the employment of labour demands that small
employers behave in a reasonably 'rational' and 'calculative' manner.
In order to retain their employees they must ensure a regular flow of
work, possess sufficient assets for cash flow purposes, adopt reliable
bookkeeping systems and negotiate credit with banks. These market
pressures conflict with their self-identity as tradesmen. Consequently,
they are frequently torn between their role as employer and as
productive worker. Recent attempts to 'formalise' and 'regulate'
employment relationships have heightened this conflict. The legislative
measures of the mid-1970s, for example, assume that the participants in
the employment relationship are *either* employers *or* employees.[30]
They fail to recognise the dual role of small employers and the nature
of employment relationships within these enterprises. As one of our
respondents stated:

> The paperwork and the rules these days are really colossal for a small
> businessman. The rules were made looking at big businesses . . . but
> when you are running your own business you don't get round to

doing it . . . It's also more difficult in a small business because you're in a more personal relationship and there's more friction if you reprimand somebody than there is in a big firm.   (220)

Small employers object to this legislation because it restricts their prerogatives as employers and also challenges the fraternal relationship with their employees.[31] This, in turn, damages the operating efficiency of their enterprises and ability to maximise profits. There are, then, forces which inevitably compel small employers to exercise their authority as business proprietors. This necessarily differentiates them from their employees despite the operation of *fraternal* strategies. Small employers cope with these tensions largely by reference to the *risks* which they have incurred in establishing their businesses. The instabilities of the market are as evident to employees as they are to small employers; indeed, many now working for others will have experimented with their own businesses in the past. It is this which mitigates tensions in the employment relationship; dissatisfied workers can, with a minimum of capital, set up on their own and trade largely on their skills.[32] Once established, they too can employ others and, if successful, can legitimate their material benefits and workplace authority by reference to risks taken in an unstable market. Some may even 'break through' to a size of enterprise which removes them entirely from direct involvement in manual work and makes the fraternal strategy less appropriate. Many more, we suspect, revert to working entirely on their own or, indeed, become once again, employees.

There are, then, tensions in the *fraternal* relationship. It would be surprising if these were not reflected in the more general attitudes and beliefs of small employers if only because they are 'torn' between the two roles of employer and productive worker. These conflicting influences were most clearly evident in their views about the class structure and their own position within it, the nature and contribution of productive work and the role of the state in society.

Self-assignment to class may be regarded as a crude measure of how individuals see their position in society.[33] However, among our respondents, no coherent pattern emerged such that it is difficult to summarise their social imagery. Whereas some stressed their attachment to the 'working class' others emphasised their 'middle class' self-identification.[34] The variety of their responses, as reflected in the following quotations, illustrate the difficulty of detecting any systematic patterns. Typical of the 'working class' attitudes were the following:

I'd have to put myself as working class. Given the level of income and my background, and if you divide society into these things, then the fact remains that I work and I still work with my hands, so I'm working class.   (220)

I'm very low on the tree . . . I'm still working class in a sense, but just a little bit up from the bottom of the working class. That's what I would say.   (209)

I suppose I'd say we were working class . . . better off working class. Perhaps a little bit better off than we were when we was on a council estate, put it that way . . . We built this (the business) ourselves. We got nothing in our laps . . . We had no money when we started, but we gradually got a bit and we built up from there.   (204)

On the other hand, the respondents who saw themselves as 'middle class' gave opinions of the following kind:

I suppose you could put us in the category of the average man – middle class, like a civil servant on, for arguments sake, £8,000 a year, owning his own home and car . . . So average middle class. The average self-employed guy has a comfortable standard of living. (206)

I'm middle class, I suppose . . . just above the average . . . just above the working class. You want something out of life. You want to enjoy yourself – save a few pounds for when you retire and enjoy yourself again, that's it.   (201)

I'm middle class. There's a lower class which, no matter what you give them, they'll never alter. They couldn't mix, but I reckon I could mix with the highest and the lowest. So, I'm in-between sort of thing . . . I'm of a working family – my parents were working class and I didn't have any money to start with . . . yet as I say, I could have a Rolls-Royce if I wanted to – but I don't want a Rolls-Royce, I'm content.   (205)

I'm middle class because I've been in a position to be able to join a golf club and I've bought my own home – although a working man owns his own house today. But I can have more time off if I want – well, a working man could do that but he won't get paid for it. (224)

The small employers quoted above regarded themselves as 'middle class' primarily by reference to their patterns of consumption and life styles. However, it is clear that these respondents were making comparisons with the working class rather than with managerial and professional employees; they differentiated themselves from the former rather than identified with the latter.[35] This is to be expected in view of their personal experiences, occupational careers and everyday working relationships with employees. But, on the whole, small employers feel uncertain about their social location. The source of such doubts were well described by one of the respondents:

> We can't all be equal . . . Take me, now I'm willing to take a chance by going out and tendering for jobs that I'm going to make money on instead of just offering my labour for sale. But none of my men would want to do this; they are happy as they are . . . being employed. They know what I do out of hours and they wouldn't want to do it. So, therefore, by virtue of me being willing to become a businessman/employer you could say that I'm a class above them . . . You can't put self-employed people in the same context as employees because, as I see it, we are a different breed of people. We fall by ourselves whereas employees fall or rise by their employers . . . But I'm a wholly convinced capitalist, put it that way. There's bad things about it and there's good things about it. Take me, I provide employment for five people, whereas I could have been content to have worked for somebody. In my own little way I'm a capitalist, and yet I think I'm a socialist, if that's a possibility . . . The worker is sometimes exploited . . . I think that the worker has to be compensated for his labour.   (213)

This account expresses a common dilemma for small employers — they empathise with *both* employers and employees. However, there are several issues about which they have strong craft and often, working class attitudes. These are an outcome of their prior experience as employees and are reflected in their attitudes towards the social contribution of productive labour.

As with the self-employed, small employers stress the value of productive work and, hence, the functional importance of manual employees. This is to be expected in view of their negative attitudes towards administrative obligations and the way in which they relegate these to their 'spare-time'. Many of our respondents were resentful, for example, of the low earnings received by skilled tradesmen and the high incomes of 'unproductive' non-manual workers.

> Some of the young boys in the office jobs, they get good money for the hours they actually work as against a tradesman who is working physically hard and still has to know a lot about his trade. That's where the poor old farm workers are very poorly done by. We've got friends who are farm workers and they are very skilled people . . . yet their money is very poor. Now to me, that is wrong because they are skilled tradesmen. There's very few people that could do the work they do.   (222)

> There's a lot of waste of time with paperwork. Whereas you could produce more from the point of view of production, and production after all, is money. It's not the paperwork. All right, the pen is probably mightier than the sword but I feel if you do away with the paperwork you'll get a lot more production.   (216)

The low value which small employers place upon 'unproductive' white-collar work largely explains their generally negative attitudes towards the state. Indeed, we found little evidence to support the assertion that they regard the state as 'neutral' and above class interests. According to Poulantzas, for example, small employers see the state as a means by which the values of individualism may be protected from the combined threat of organised labour and big business; it is, then, an independent arbitrator which preserves the 'freedom' of small businesses despite the growth of collectivism.[36] But among our respondents, by contrast, the state was regarded as a source of oppression administered by unproductive bureaucrats whose interests are alien to their own. Thus, some stressed its entirely 'self-interested' nature, whilst others associated it with forces undermining the economic viability of small businesses.[37] In this latter view the state was seen as part of a package which incorporated the Labour Party, the trade unions and other powerfully organised elements within the corporatist economy. The particular group(s), however, with which the state was most closely associated varied; some small employers stressed its allegiance to the wealthy and powerful:

> I would say that the structure of the state is very self-perpetuating. The decisions that they come to obviously help run the country – that is their function. But I also think that they tend to ensure their own life so that the Treasury will continue to pass Acts that enable

the Treasury to exist . . . I don't think it necessarily helps the lower or middle class. I think, perhaps, it does lean towards the upper class – the money structure in the city. If you are a stockbroker it probably helps you quite considerably.   (202)

Others saw the state as the representative of organised labour. In this view, employment protection, unemployment benefits and social welfare expenditure were generally regarded as detrimental to the interests of small employers because they reduce the 'will to work' and shift the balance of power in favour of employees.

In a nutshell . . . it's been made too easy for those that don't want to work. They can get money and they can get social security . . . it doesn't seem right that they can get money like that whereas we are working ourselves to death.   (221)

A lot of taxes are mainly socialist inspired. They are always hitting at the profits of companies and it's the wrong way of thinking really . . . In fact, business has stagnated over the last few years and there hasn't been any reinvestment because they have been penalised profit-wise. You wouldn't mind if you knew where the profits were going but the profits are going to support a sort of welfare state – you know, a lot of it is, in fact, wasted.   (217)

They've made it far easier for the employee to be protected by the government bureaucracy – more than they have changed it whereby the employee should stand on his own feet and not have the protection of the government.   (213)

With redundancy and unfair dismissal, you're guilty until you're proved innocent with the tribunals. This is all wrong.. . . They made tax laws so that you couldn't employ people . . . I don't like them at all. They may be good for the workmen but they certainly aren't for me personally.   (225)

With all the social security and unemployment benefit it's so easy now if somebody doesn't like a job for them to just walk off it and not bother to get another one for six months . . . It's so easy for somebody not to work, you can still enjoy life and have a very comfortable existence.   (202)

All our respondents were agreed, however, that state expenditure had 'got out of hand', that its involvement in the economy was excessive and that its regulative functions were detrimental to productivity.

There's too many civil servants. The forms I get from government departments – some of the questions they ask me are totally irrelevant. I have one form that asks, 'How many houses did you decorate last month?' Now what's that got to do with the economy of Britain? It's just employing somebody for nothing . . . We all pay tax . . . and they should be spent on social services rather than propping up industry, like shipbuilding, which we're just keeping for the sake of keeping men in work. Yet if they took less tax, you'd probably get businessmen taking on more people. If I didn't pay as much tax I could take on one more person quite easily.   (210)

I think all government bodies tend to be very inefficient over staff because there is no end product and nobody is going to account at the end of the year and say, 'We've gone bankrupt'. There's no final figure, no final end to it all. It will just be written over into next year . . . it becomes more and more inefficient and although it's the age of vast organisations, I feel they must be terribly inefficient. (202)

Among the small employers we interviewed, then, there are a number of conceptions of the state which do not square with the description offered by Poulantzas. On the contrary, the state is seen to represent social forces which are primarily alien to their own interests as employers. But these views need to be interpreted by reference to the value which they place upon productive work and their ambivalent class self-placement. In general, small employers may be regarded as tradesmen who, because of market demand, are *forced* to employ workers. This is reflected in the way they organise their businesses and in their more general attitudes and beliefs. Their position as small employers is challenged by a number of contradictions; the dependence upon their own and others' labour – as well as their working-class origins – 'pulls' them towards the working class while, as employers, they are 'drawn' to the middle class. Furthermore, their location within the entrepreneurial middle class is often tenuous. Some revert to self-employment while others expand the scale of their enterprises, withdraw from 'productive' work and become 'full-time' owner-controllers. It is to these we now direct our attention.

Notes

1. The employment relationship is, of course, particularly important for small firms in *labour*-intensive sectors of the economy.

2. Eight of their wives were present at the original interview and made contributions to the discussion. In addition, five wives were subsequently interviewed separately. Extracts from their accounts are signified in the text by a 'w'.

3. Typically, these six fathers had begun their careers as employees, 'experimented' with self-employment and small-scale proprietorship in middle age and then reverted to employee status in later life. Their occupational biographies represent an empirical illustration of the proletarianisation process which occurs with ageing. See the discussion in Chapter 4.

4. B. Reckman, 'Carpentry: The Craft and Trade', in A. Zimbalist (ed.), *Case Studies on the Labor Process*, New York, 1979, p. 96.

5. For a discussion of the central role of carpentry/joinery in building and the tendency for general foremen and supervisors to be drawn from this trade see C. Foster, *Building with Men*, London, 1969, p. 202.

6. Many studies have stressed the long working hours of small employers. See, for example, F. Bechhofer, B. Elliott, M. Rushforth and R. Bland, 'Small Shopkeepers: Matters of Money and Meaning', *Sociological Review*, vol. 22, 1974b and D. Bertaux and I. Bertaux-Wiame, 'Artisanal Bakery in France: How it Lives and Why it Survives' in F. Bechhofer and B. Elliott (eds.), *The Petite Bourgeoisie*, London, 1981.

7. Only physical exertion through industrial labour represented 'real' work for our respondents.

8. These concepts are derived from the analysis by R. Gasson, 'Roles of Farm Women in England', unpublished paper, 1980.

9. The business earnings of wives rarely exceeded the maximum payable without tax liabilities. This varies according to individual circumstances but for our respondents the sum was approximatley £1500 per annum.

10. For comparable evidence in other economic sectors see Bertaux and Bertaux-Wiame, 'Artisanal Bakery in France' and H. Newby, C. Bell, D. Rose and P. Saunders, *Property, Paternalism and Power*, London, 1978.

11. See, however, G. K. Ingham, *Size of Industrial Organisation and Worker Behaviour*, Cambridge, 1970; E. Batstone, 'Deference and the Ethos of Small-town Capitalism' in M. Bulmer (ed.), *Working Class Images of Society*, London, 1975; H. Newby, 'Paternalism and Capitalism' in R. Scase (ed.), *Industrial Society: Class, Cleavage and Control*, London, 1977.

12. See, for example, Bechhofer *et al.*, 'Small Shopkeepers: Matters of Money and Meaning'. Other publications from this research are cited in Chapter 1.

13. Newby *et al.*, *Property, Paternalism and Power*.

14. Ibid., p. 29.

15. Ibid., p. 172.

16. For a discussion of this point see J. Curran and J. Stanworth, 'Worker Involvement and Social Relations in the Small Firm', *Sociological Review*, vol. 27, 1979b and 'Self-selection and the Small Firm Worker – A Critique and an Alternative View', *Sociology,* vol. 13, 1979a.

17. Newby, 'Paternalism and Capitalism', p. 71.

18. We initially labelled this strategy 'egalitarianism'. However, after discussion with members of the SSRC Social Stratification Research Seminar (in particular, Garry Runciman and Mike Rose) we have altered this to 'fraternalism' – a term that, perhaps, better recognises the imbalance of power which, in the final analysis, exists between employer and employee.

19. Labour-time devoted to administration was largely uncosted by our respondents.

20. See the discussion of building tasks in Chapter 3.

21. In building, such tasks might involve, for example, mixing concrete, fetching appropriate tools, collecting materials and so on.

22. In this sense, small employers encourage their employees to operate in the 'black' economy.

23. The practice of 'moonlighting' has recently been described as 'one of the single biggest spurs to setting up one's own business'. P. Stothard, 'Trapped — Why Our Small Businesses are Still Struggling', *Sunday Times*, 10 February 1980. For further evidence see R. Scase and R. Goffee, *The Real World of the Small Business Owner*, London, 1980.

24. For evidence of a similar practice amongst small-scale French bakers, see Bertaux and Bertaux-Wiame, 'Artisanal Bakery in France'.

25. We use this term, following Fox, to refer not to personal 'liking' or 'disliking' but to the trust relationship which emerges where work roles are not rigidly defined and formally-prescribed measures of work performance are unnecessary. See A. Fox, *Beyond Contract*, London, 1974a.

26. The importance of personal attributes in employee recruitment is discussed in Newby *et al.*, *Property, Paternalism and Power*, Chapter 4.

27. This severely limits the ability of small employers to regularly engage in any type of 'formal' recreational activity; membership of clubs and associations amongst the respondents was low.

28. Cf. note 14.

29. For evidence concerning the material assets owned by small farmers see Newby *et al.*, *Property, Paternalism and Power*.

30. We refer specifically to the provisions contained in the Trade Union and Labour Relations Acts of 1974 and 1976 and The Employment Protection Act of 1975.

31. For a survey of small employer attitudes towards this legislation see R. Clifton and C. Tatton-Brown, *Impact of Employment Legislation on Small Firms*, Research Paper No. 6, Department of Employment, 1979. The 1980 Employment Act has exempted small businesses from some of the requirements stipulated under earlier legislation.

32. We are surprised that this individualistic expression of worker resentment has not received more attention. It has implications for employment relationships in general and the meaning of 'independence' for small business owners in particular. See the discussion in Chapter 4.

33. For a discussion of the methodological difficulties involved in research on class self-placement see J. H. Goldthorpe, D. Lockwood, F. Bechhofer and J. Platt, *The Affluent Worker in the Class Structure*, Cambridge, 1969; R. Scase, *Social Democracy in Capitalist Society*, London, 1977; Newby *et al.*, *Property, Paternalism and Power*.

34. These terms are introduced here as used by our respondents.

35. For the small employers we interviewed, the term 'working class' typically referred to industrial manual workers.

36. N. Poulantzas, *Classes in Contemporary Capitalism*, London, 1975, p. 296.

37. For evidence of these attitudes amongst small business owners more generally, see R. King and N. Nugent (eds.), *Respectable Rebels*, London, 1979. Present government strategy assumes that government 'interference' is generally detrimental to small business formation and growth.

6 OWNER-CONTROLLERS

Whereas small employers work alongside their employees, owner-controllers are solely concerned with management and supervision. They are, therefore, more reliant upon financial and administrative expertise than trade skills and, because of their lack of *direct* involvement in the work process, are more likely consciously to adopt systems of employee control. This affects, in a qualitative sense, the nature of the employment relationship and creates a set of attitudes and beliefs which are quite distinct from those of the self-employed and small employers. In general, owner-controllers, because of their *exclusive* function as employers, do not display the ambiguous and often contradictary attitudes of small employers; in fact, their views reflect many of those symptomatic of competitive capitalism. Indeed, our category of owner-controller closely resembles the classic entrepreneur – a figure which has captured the popular imagination and become the personal embodiment of many cherished capitalist values.[1] Wright Mills has described the entrepreneur's role in nineteenth-century USA as follows:

> In the classic image . . . He was the active owner of what he had created and then managed. Nothing about the operation of his going concern failed to draw his alert attention or receive his loving care. In his role as employer, he provided opportunity for the best of the area where he lived to learn from working under him; they might themselves save a portion of their wages, multiply this by a small private speculation, borrow more on their character, and start up on their own. Even as he had done before them, his employees could also become captains of industry.[2]

Such beliefs and values continue as powerful ideological influences within present-day Western societies. In fact, the attraction of these ideas has grown in recent years, underlining Wright Mills' cogent observation:

> As an economic fact, the old independent entrepreneur lives in a small island in a big new world; yet, as an ideological figment and a political force he has persisted as if he inhabited an entire continent.

He has become the man through whom the ideology of utopian capitalism is still attractively presented to many of our contemporaries . . . It has become the grab-bag of defenders and apologists, and so little is it challenged that in the minds of many it seems the very latest model of reality.[3]

Wright Mills could have been describing a number of the owner-controllers we interviewed. They subscribed to a set of beliefs which in many ways are comparable to those widespread in the United States. In our own study we interviewed 25 respondents who were exclusively concerned with the management and supervision of employees. Their businesses were not sufficiently large to warrant the delegation of managerial functions to other administrative and white-collar employees; by definition, all owner-controllers manage their enterprises single-handedly. However, it is possible to detect three distinct 'routes' to entrepreneurship, each of which reflects a more general pattern in society. While, in our research, there were 'self-made' founder-owners, there were others who had inherited businesses and, further, those who had acquired them from their previous employers. Since their experiences in becoming owner-controllers were different, and related to contrasting social and economic processes, it is useful to briefly describe these.

The twelve *founder-owners* had manual working-class backgrounds in terms of their fathers' occupations. Of these, eight had began their working lives as carpenters before becoming self-employed and, later small employers; they were, then, genuinely 'self-made'. The remainder were 'technically' more qualified; they had invested their capital in businesses of a size which immediately required them to concentrate solely upon management and administration. All four had managerial experience before starting their own businesses; their major problem had not been the acquisition of supervisory skills but access to start-up capital. The following accounts illustrate the experiences of the 'self-made' *founder-owners* who had expanded their businesses through the investment of their *labour* rather than *capital*.[4]

I originally started in 1957. Previously, I'd been out to Canada to get some experience and then I came back and started the business as a carpenter subcontractor. From 1957 until 1960 I gradually built up until I employed about four men. Then I found I had sufficient capital to build the first house which I proceeded to do. I lived in it for six months and then I sold it and went into partnership with a bricklayer who owned some land. He had the land and no capital and I had the capital from the proceeds of selling the house. We then proceeded over the next three years, building an average of twelve houses a year . . . (later) I started to build myself . . . and its just gone from one thing to the other.   (305)

After the war I started in a very small way in business on my own . . . At first I was working for myself in the evenings and at weekends. I was building up quite a substantial number of private customers so I eventually decided to go one hundred per cent on my own . . . I was working extremely long hours, seven days a week . . . I began to build up a labour force of my own. As time went by I could see that this was really my field . . . I went on from there buying larger pieces of land and eventually finished up building several hundred houses and being invited to tender for local authority work . . . At this moment we've got in front of us at least a three year programme . . . so we're now well and truly set.   (317)

I was never educated into running a business in any way prior to starting up and whatever I've learnt, good or bad, has been through working . . . (Originally) there was myself and another carpenter . . . and bricklayer who I did my apprenticeship with . . . We were doing mainly subcontract work for various other builders. Obviously, we're not talking about starting up in business and all putting a couple of hundred or thousand in. We're literally talking about starting up in business with the first week's wages. That's paid in the bank and then you draw out a little and hope to have a little bit in . . . We used to take a job each and when the bank loans got a bit low or when the suppliers started to squawk for money then we all dashed around and had an evening working out bills. In the back of our minds we thought that any time not spent on the job was a complete waste of time. To coin a term, it was head down, arse up . . . We never have been out to get rich quick . . . We've grown with the firm rather than it being some sort of monster that's grown away from us.   (310)

I built this house in my spare time. It took about four months and we lived there for about eight years, and then we sold it . . . Then I bought a plot from the council for about four hundred quid and built a bungalow, again in my spare time . . . In all, I did three in my spare time . . . Within a year, I stopped using the tools because I thought, 'I'm getting nowhere fast. I'm flogging my guts out working on site and I should be somewhere else, I should be lining up the next bit of land to do the next job and here I am banging away with a hammer. It's costing me money working on site.' So, as soon as I could I packed up the tools . . . I didn't have an education. I never had my qualifications . . . so I could hardly go and work for the civil service or even a big national firm. Take estimating, I never had the methods – I wouldn't have known the maths, so it was only me that would employ me.   (304)

These *founder-owners*, then, had started on their own in a similar manner to many of the self-employed and small employers; they, too, had often undertaken work in their spare time prior to trading independently. Further, many originally had no long-term ambitions of business growth and their subsequent expansion was primarily a response to market circumstances. The major investment had been their own manual labour but now, because of the growth in scale of their enterprises, they had been forced to become full-time managers.

The 'route' of the remaining four *founder-owners* was rather different. As technically-qualified specialists they had acquired considerable experience in various supervisory and managerial positions with large employers.[5] Having made the decision to start on their own, this prior work experience encouraged them to concentrate immediately solely upon the management of *others*. The following comments are illustrative of this:

I started off as a management trainee with a national company . . . then I went to another firm in London as an assistant contracts manager . . . I was on block release as well and I got the Institute of Builders exams . . . I didn't get the sort of interest I wanted out of the job at all. I'm one of those people who find it very difficult to work under other people, if I'm truthful. It's not something I do very well, put it that way. And that, amongst other things, is what made me start on my own . . . I set up in 1974 . . . with far too little capital. In fact, with virtually nothing . . . I did anything I could get hold of at that stage by subcontracting a lot . . . After two or three years we were employing about fourteen.   (309)

I didn't think that I could get on higher than when I was working for somebody else. I was the area manager and supervised design and site work. I couldn't afford to buy shares in the company or anything like that. The only way I could do it was to accumulate a certain amount and start on my own . . . I suppose when you work for another firm you are always frustrated to an extent and you feel that the directors are having a better time than you are . . . (At the start) we didn't have our own works. I was purely on design and negotiating contracts and subletting the actual construction of much of the work to other firms.   (314)

The reason why I started on my own was because I found that being employed in industry I was abused a lot. I found that you were working your balls off and in fact, in a lot of cases you weren't recognised for it. I used to work . . . on a minuscule commission and someone else was reaping all the benefit from it. And I thought, 'Well, this is jolly silly – why don't I damn well do it myself'. That's, to my mind, why I did it initially.   (307)

Clearly, for these *founder-owners* an important reason for starting their own businesses was to be released from the control of others and to benefit from the rewards of their own efforts. As with the self-employed, work autonomy was a crucial factor in their decision. However, it was more difficult for them to 'experiment' in business because of their lack of trade skills and so they were forced to start by employing several workers in order to effectively utilise their own managerial and technical competences. In this sense, the initial risks were greater than those incurred by the self-employed and small employers. This, however, was less of a problem for the eight *family inheritors*. Of these, seven had undergone a period of formal training and acquired various technical qualifications. They had then worked as operatives in their fathers' and, occasionally, other businesses in order to obtain the necessary practical experience. This had enabled them to grasp the 'realities' of business life and to understand at first hand the strategies that they would later need in order to exercise effective managerial control.[6] As a result, *family inheritors* were often confronted with fewer managerial problems than the less technically-qualified founder-owners. As one of the respondents recalled:

` During the first period of my career I was just labouring on the site for the first eighteen months. I can remember being under a brick-layer who gave me a general idea for a week or two, but I virtually worked with all the trades. It was very useful. I had done some of that sort of work before – painting and so on. That was particularly helpful, I think, in order to understand the feelings among workers on the site, and what have you. Then, in the second period I worked for the estimators and in the third period I was thrown into the deep end under the contracts side, being responsible for one of the contracts.   (312)

Since taking over from their fathers, some of the *family inheritors* had expanded their businesses whilst others had either kept them at a similar level of trading or had contracted. These differences are reflected in the following accounts:

My father was doing about ten houses a year and the odd alteration as well . . . The turnover was about £80,000 . . . I joined the company in 1960 and from then on we started to opt out of the private sector and go totally into the public sector . . . and we approached a bank for finance and went slowly but surely from there . . . The contracts we're doing now are in the region of £800,000 and our turnover is around £2 million a year.   (306)

My father started the business about thirty years ago . . . and slowly progressed in size up until about seven or eight years ago when we were running at about seventy employees. He died three years ago and the current size . . . is just over sixty . . . I had intended to expand some years back but things haven't been very good for expansion over the last five years and we've been marking time. We are at a difficult size to expand because you've got to do several things at once. You've got to have the work there, you've got to have the right people to be responsible and all the other problems. To me, I'm not out for having a great George Wimpey company because there would be just more problems . . . Quite honestly, there seemed no advantage in expanding. You know, what are you in the world for? To make a decent living and live in a pleasant way, that's what it's always seemed to me.   (319)

I joined the firm in 1936 . . . Since then we have not expanded a lot . . . Some firms have expanded and taken on many directors. Some have expanded and then disappeared entirely . . . In 1928 we employed 120; today we employ thirty-eight . . . I think that one might say we haven't been ambitious enough. But, as I say, we're still here.   (324)

In addition to the founder-owner and the *family inheritors* there was a further group of five *employee benefactors*. Their presence is a reflection of the problem that often confronts small business proprietors who either have no offspring or, alternatively, children with no inclination to carry on the business. In these circumstances, employees are often explicitly recruited and then trained to take over the business.[7] After the proprietor's death, they typically become responsible for its management while ownership is subdivided between them and surviving family members. Sometimes, owner-controllers will 'bring in' a manager immediately prior to retirement, as in the following example:

> Basically, since the war this hasn't been much of a company . . . It's dropped back . . . It's a family business . . . the owner, who's now seventy, basically has all the shares and his wife owns one, sort of thing . . . The business has only remained here because it was here . . . it couldn't have been formed in today's competitive environment . . . The company will have to change. It will go out of business if it doesn't . . . I am, hopefully, in the process of buying the owners out . . . So I'm taking over a company which has been run down and trying to pick it up and do something with it. I'm interested in looking to the future and making it grow.   (311)

These, then, are the three major paths whereby our respondents became owner-controllers. Despite such variations there were few differences in the ways in which they organised and managed their businesses. Unlike the small employers, they are responsible for enterprises which are largely separate from domestic relationships. Whereas the former usually operate businesses from their homes, the latter typically own specific premises. There is a clear distinction between work and home which, in turn, separates the owner-controllers' occupational role from other social and domestic activities. Indeed, compared with small employers, their working hours are shorter if only because administrative tasks are conducted during the course of a 'normal' day; they regard administration as *necessary productive work*. Owner-controllers, therefore, do not tend to see themselves as craftsmen but as rational and efficient managers. Further, because they regard their businesses as distinct economic units, their wives are rarely involved. In contrast to the active involvement of the wives of small employers, those of owner-controllers normally fulfil a solely domestic role.

Owner-controllers have, then, very different work roles to small employers. They own substantial business assets and operate within markets in which there are fewer opportunities to shield themselves against competition by the cultivation of extensive networks of regular customers. There are also the ongoing problems of cash flow and the negotiation of credit facilities. Furthermore, as *employers* they must be acquainted with a range of labour legislation, tax regulations and social security requirements. The dominance of a 'business' or 'entrepreneurial' identity was apparent in the comments of the following respondents:

> I tend to sit above everybody and make sure they do the work rather than me. That doesn't mean to say I'm not working but it means that I don't bog myself down with any one thing . . . So I don't have any single major activity . . . I do something of everything. (308)

> The thing that gives me the biggest thrill of the lot is planning a new project and designing it. There's no doubt about that. The other thing that gives me tremendous satisfaction is completing a good business deal.   (305)

> I like negotiating – I quite enjoy the business side of it. I like getting the planning of a new site all done. I suppose I find the actual building a little bit tedious because I feel that my job has more or less been done when the whole thing is set up.   (304)

> I'm just a person who sits here watching everybody else and doing nothing; I certainly appear to do nothing. It's very difficult to pin down what I do. My principle responsibilities are making sure that we've got enough work, trying to make sure we always cost properly . . . and build to time and if we don't, why not?   (309)

> I like getting the figures in front of me and seeing what they mean. I like producing budgets. I like doing graphs of what my turnover is and who my debtors are and making decisions from that.   (303)

Such views are in sharp contrast to those of the self-employed and small employers. The market *forces* owner-controllers to behave in a more rational-calculative fashion, as several of our respondents stressed:

> You are in competition every time and there's always the fear that one day you are going to end up with no work. I mean, I would

never recommend my children to go into it because if you want
sleepless nights it's the business to be in.   (306)

It very seldom goes on anything other than price . . . We're in
competition with most of the local companies really . . . and it's
always a matter of price, I would say. It's not a question of liking
one firm above another − it's purely a matter of who produces the
lowest figure.   (323)

If you're in competition with a larger firm . . . they're sometimes
prepared to cut prices to get in. We found that on a recent job when
a big firm was prepared to go in for a very cheap price in order to
secure a job and get a foot in the door. They have the size and they
are often very competitive in terms of time . . . On the other hand,
small firms, we find, can be more competitive − probably because
they haven't got the same overheads . . . But generally speaking, it's
all in terms of price − if we can put in the lowest competitive tender.
For every job that comes along we prepare a tender separately −
according to the market itself and also our own current situation.
(312)

If the scale of the owner-controllers' activities prevents them from
trading within a network of regular customers, they are also vulnerable
to competition from larger enterprises which, in certain circumstances,
may undercut them.[8] Indeed, during period of economic recession,
owner-controllers are often at greatest risk since they may lack the
trade skills of the self-employed and small employers but do not have
the capital resources of larger companies.[9] This, together with their
market vulnerability, forces them to negotiate extensive credit facilities.
These and problems of cash flow were often discussed in the interviews:

Some people, as far as payment of accounts is concerned . . . adopt
the attitude that 'Next year will do' or 'You've got a good name,
plenty of money, we'll pay you when we think'. We've got a job at
the moment . . . where the excuse is the computer − the computer
is blamed for an awful lot of things. That seems to be why we can't
get paid from local authorities and larger companies . . . We've
projected cash flows until they come out of our ears and we never
get paid on time . . . the whole trouble with the industry is that we
produce a product on somebody else's land and then people use it.
It's not like buying a box of matches over the counter − you put

your money down there . . . So the pendulum swing of the overdraft facilities is quite big. We can be at nil balance one week and, say, thirty thousand pounds overdrawn the next week . . . The role of the bank is crucial in this industry.   (316)

When I started doing work for public authorities I found that it was impossible . . . to keep up with the cash flow, which was my biggest problem of all. In other words, submitting accounts when they should have been submitted. I was, maybe, as far as six months behind because of pressures of other work . . . (Now) I'm constantly going back looking at work in progress to see what the outstanding figure is . . . Sometimes it's exceedingly difficult to ascertain . . . that side of it can very quickly get out of hand . . . You've got to watch it constantly . . . because the work in progress can get so high in four weeks that it can damage your cash flow for three or four months.   (317)

Sometimes owner-controllers try to avoid these problems by negotiating long-term contracts. This, however, does not entirely resolve the difficulties since they can then become excessively dependent upon a limited number of customers. Thus, an alternative means of coping with market risk is to diversify.[10] Whatever the strategy, they must acquire various legal and financial skills since the relatively small size of their enterprises prevents them from hiring experts on a regular, full-time basis. This means that they often rely heavily upon 'outside' technical help, as three of the respondents explained:

In 1971 I went on one of the Training Board's one week schemes for small businesses which was quite educational. I think a lot could be learned from these but, of course, the snag is that you've got to try to run a business single-handed . . . As regards actually asking for advice . . . I reached one particular stage where . . . I didn't have things under my thumb . . . I couldn't control my labour force, or know what they were doing. So we employed a consultant and went into costing the work and that was, quite frankly, way above my head. But again we learned a lot and, indeed, if there was some way in the future that we could employ outside help, then I'd do it again.   (310)

I'm only here today because of advice from the Building Advisory Service and I make no bones about it . . . It's made me very aware of

costs — the costs of running a job and running a business. It's given
me discipline. I know I have to make a certain return on my jobs . . .
If you can't put the price of your job up you have to put your costs
down in order to maintain the margin. So the discipline has come
from me. It's only the man at the top who can discipline anything
and everybody takes their cue from him.   (320)

I take advice from anywhere I can possibly get hold of it. From the
accountant . . . and I've been on courses . . . I went on two one-
week courses recently — one on the management of small building
firms and the other on finance. Both of them were very helpful.
(309)

There are, however, limits in the extent to which managerial skills
can be acquired through technical advice. Because owner-controllers'
enterprises are relatively small-scale, work relationships tend to be
personal and *informal*; indeed, many proprietors adopt a strategy of
fraternalism. But whereas for small employers, fraternalism is the
outcome of a structure of working relationships within which employer
and employee work alongside each other in a functional division of
labour, for owner-controllers it is more of a deliberate strategy,
explicitly designed to obtain employee loyalty within a hierarchical
employment relationship which emerges as a result of their own non-
involvement in manual labour. By creating a normative framework
within which employees can work in a relatively autonomous manner,
they can fully utilise their employees' skills and, thereby, maximise
profits. Such a strategy poses few problems for *founder-owners* who
have, themselves, previously been employed as tradesmen; they know
from experience the difficulties involved 'on site' and the best way to
'handle' workers. *Family inheritors*, too, have worked 'on the tools' and
acquired the necessary competence for fostering a fraternal relationship.
The nature of this managerial style is illustrated in the following:

I ask them to do it rather than tell them . . . under normal circumstances I let them think they're running their own little business
section. I say, 'I *suggest* you do it that way' rather than 'you *will* do
that' . . . and ironically they come back and say, 'I don't agree — I
think we'd be better off to do it like this'.   (301)

I think that management should be involved in all the problems of
the job equally with the men. And if they've got a problem they

know I'm not just a bloke that sits in the office . . . All my training and experience is outside on the job. So they know if they've got a problem they can ask me and I may have a better idea of getting over it. I've been in the business over twenty years – I ought to have some idea. (304)

We get the best out of the men by treating them as equals. In other words, we don't try to bear down on them too heavily. But we make it quite plain we expect a fair day's work. We get them involved in the business. We tend to discuss everything with them. Other industries don't, but we do. We'll say, 'We've purchased this land, we're building such a style of house – what do you think?' 'What's your opinion?' And this automatically makes them involved and interested. They feel as though they are part of the firm; if they see bad workmanship, they will point it out to us because they're proud of the firm they work for and want to continue to see a decent product. (305)

We try to bring the men in on decisions. We don't just tell them what to do. We have the drawings out and explain how to approach it from an estimating point of view and see if they have any comments . . . They regard this as part of the job. (315)

I believe one should not lose contact with the people who are out on the ground – it's as simple as that. Take today as an example; before I came into this office I was round on one of my sites to speak to the agent, the carpenters, the painters and what have you, to let them know I'm there and I'm interested in what they are doing . . . When a labourer is sweeping up a house it's just a chore to him, but I emphasise that the work he is doing can sell the house . . . It's as simple as that. Every job is important until the final handover of the house. (321)

Given, then, the *formal* rather than the *real* subordination of labour within the building industry, fraternalism represents the most rational managerial strategy for owner-controllers. In the interviews, many of them emphasised the 'independence' of tradesmen and the difficulty of imposing, for instance, piece-rate systems and other techniques of *direct* managerial control. Such a course could often lead to poor quality workmanship, employee dissatisfaction and high labour turnover, as several respondents pointed out:

Bonuses involve a hell of a lot of paper work and I've experienced endless arguments over them. I did introduce them to a limited degree. I'd say to some of the fellows, 'I'll give you ten or twenty pounds extra if you do it within a certain time'. But there's always arguments about whether they've done it in the time or not and whether it's finished. They'll say they've finished it and, of course, it's either badly or inadequately done or there are certain parts they haven't done.   (309)

I had the tools for thirty-odd years and I know most of the problems . . . But you can't measure work strictly – no way could we operate a bonus system . . . Most of our estimating is not that a man will lay X number of bricks an hour. I mean, we'll look at it and say 'there's a bricklayer and a labourer going to be there for three days' . . . It's purely down to experience.   (313)

There's some right rough diamonds in building . . . but we find that when they come to work, providing you show them respect, they'll show you respect and you have no bother with them at all . . . If you start shouting and ordering them about and say, after a few weeks, you didn't need them, you're just as likely to get a brick on your head, or something like that . . . You've got to handle them properly.   (305)

The trouble with a large number of workers in the building industry is that they're often unreasonable to the extent that if they don't like what you want them to do, they won't stay and argue about it, they'll just go. They're not interested – they won't waste their time listening.   (309)

Unlike small employers, owner-controllers cannot directly supervise all their employees at the same time since work is typically spread between different sites. To a considerable extent they have *no alternative* but to *trust* their employees to work 'adequately' according to a rate determined on the basis of experience. The relationship of employer-employee obligation which often emerges contrasts strongly with the norms and codes regulating employee performance in many other work contexts. Such variations in the *trust* relationship have recently been discussed by Fox.[11] He suggests that the *discretionary* content of work tasks varies and that this leads to differences in *trust* relationships. Work roles which embody a low discretionary element demand that the occupant be trained, indoctrinated, or educated in appropriate ways . . . the requirement is that he adhere to the prescribed procedures and instructions laid down for him in the form of specific external controls.[12]

By contrast, the performance of high discretion work roles requires

not trained obedience to specific external controls, but the exercise of wisdom, judgement, expertise. The control comes from within – it is, in the literal sense, self-control. The occupant of the role must himself choose, judge, feel, sense, consider, conclude what would be the best thing to do in the circumstances, the best way of going about what he is doing.[13]

Those employed in low discretion jobs are not *trusted* to produce, of their own choice, a 'satisfactory' work performance. Their work tasks are specifically defined and closely supervised through standardised routines and procedures. A failure to achieve objectives is assumed to result from a lack of voluntary commitment and employer-employee conflict is, to some extent, accepted as inevitable.[14] By contrast, those engaged in high discretion work tasks are 'deemed to have commitment to, and "moral involvement" in . . . "organisation" goals and values'.[15] Close supervision and regulation is therefore considered unnecessary because individuals are *trusted* to exercise their own self-discipline. Work activities are co-ordinated by mutual consultation and 'task failure' is assumed to result not from wilful neglect but, instead, from unintended error of judgement. Many routine, manual and non-manual occupations are characterised by a 'low discretion/low trust' spiral where

specific short-term reciprocations . . . leave little scope for long-term diffuse obligations,. . . there is no development of mutual bonds of support expressive of reciprocated trust; only the calculated wariness and suspicion expressive of reciprocated distrust.[16]

However, the nature of some manual work still requires the exercise of discretion; craftsmen, in particular, have retained some control over the execution of their work tasks since this is often a *necessity* if work is to be satisfactorily completed. As Blauner points out, 'the very definition of traditional skill implies control over tools, materials and pace of work' so that work discipline 'in craft industries is . . . essentially self-discipline'.[17] Indeed, this neatly describes the nature of the employment relationship between tradesmen and owner-controllers in the building industry. Unlike assembly-line operatives, tradesmen can exercise considerable control over their work tasks and owner-controllers, operating on several sites, can only maximise operating efficiency by cultivating a *high trust* relationship with them. As we have already indicated, they recognise that their workers are 'independent', and that they must be 'handled' carefully and 'consulted' about the tasks at hand.

However, it would be incorrect to assume that such a relationship exists between owner-controllers and *all* their employees. On the contrary, it is normally limited to 'central' tradesmen who are considered to possess essential skills.[18] These men tend to be older and to have worked for their employers for lengthy periods of time.[19] During economic recessions their employment is relatively secure whilst 'peripheral' workers are made redundant. In fact, for many employers, these 'central' workers are seen to be *the* labour force to the extent that they sometimes undertake short-term non-profitable contracts in order to keep them employed. It is to such employees that fringe benefits are extended and *fraternal* strategies directed. 'Peripheral' workers, on the other hand – because they are largely unskilled – can be easily dismissed and replaced. According to Freidman, peripheral workers:

(1) Perform work which can easily be carried out by the remaining workers.
(2) Perform work which is not necessary for the output which top managers desire to be produced after demand has fallen, (i.e. work at jobs which are duplicated).
(3) Perform work for which replacement workers are readily available when top managers want them.
(4) Will not cause disruption among the remaining workers when laid off because of lack of solidarity with them.
(5) Do not contribute to the maintenance of managerial authority.[20]

Whereas a strategy of 'responsible autonomy' is typically adopted for 'central' workers, 'peripheral' workers are often employed on a 'labour-only' subcontracted basis. This obviously enables owner-controllers to avoid many of their obligations as *employers*. In an industry where direct control through personal supervision is difficult and expensive, subcontracting enables them to abdicate from the costs

and responsibilities of direct employment. Thus, instead of increasing
managerial control over the work process, subcontracting represents a
way of avoiding such responsibilities. By subletting work, owner-
controllers are, in effect, buying labour in a fixed quantity rather than
attempting to directly control variable and unpredictable labour-
power.[21] Just as raw materials, for example, are purchased in certain
specific amounts so, too, labour is bought 'as a definite quantity of
work, completed and embodied in the product'.[22] Thus, in an
uncertain market, risks are reduced by paying a fixed price per unit for
subcontracted labour; payment is made only when a given quantity of
work has been completed. This contrasts sharply with the conditions
under which labour is normally employed; typically it is the length of
employment which is fixed with output and productivity variable. Thus,
under circumstances where particular technical, task and market
factors restrict the extent to which direct control can be exercised
over the work process, subcontracting represents a 'rational' employer
response. It enables owner-controllers, for example, to expand swiftly
or contract their businesses according to the vagaries of the market.
This is particularly important in general building since market conditions
tend to be highly unstable and, indeed, the state uses the industry as an
instrument of economic regulation. The logic of labour-only subcontracting is clearly spelt out in a recent report:

> The number of workers required will vary over the life of one
> contract. Workers will be hired only when necessary and
> subsequently laid off when their task is finished, unless the contrac-
> tor has more work for them on another job. Casual employment
> enables employers to avoid redundancy pay under the Employment
> Protection Act, and therefore, less than two years of continual
> employment has become the norm. Workers' rights are severely
> limited. Claims for unfair dismissal, for instance, are difficult to
> make. Effective unionisation, and the benefits this brings, is
> difficult to achieve.[23]

Subcontracting, then, enables an *employment relationship* to be
replaced by a *market relationship*. Permanent 'central' employees enjoy
legally-stipulated social rights and obligations which are represented in
employment protection, health and social insurance. However, these
state-imposed regulations can often be avoided for 'peripheral' workers
through subcontracting; in highly volatile market circumstances, such a
strategy constitutes a *rational* response to an *irrational* environment.

The following quotations illustrate the distinction which many owner-controllers made between 'central' and 'peripheral' workers and the associated advantages and disadvantages of the subcontracting system.

Some of the subcontractors . . . all they are interested in is making a lot of money and their name isn't really bound up in the overall contract . . . So there isn't the same interest as there is with your own direct labour. Scarce as it may be these days, employees still take an interest in the job. The chap who's getting paid by the hour takes a bit of interest in the way he's doing it . . . He will make a decent job. On the other hand, the advantage with a subcontractor is that he's got a price to do the job; you know what price you're going to pay him for it and, provided he doesn't make a mess of it so you've got to spend more money making it good, you at least know what your profit margin is on each particular part of the work . . . Also you haven't got to continue to employ a subcontractor once the work is finished – but you've got to find him again when you need another job done! As regards direct employees, we don't only look as to whether we're making a profit or not . . . they might not be making us any money but at least they get essential parts of the work done as the contract progresses.   (326)

If you go to a subcontractor and ask him for a price . . . the risk to me is not nil but it's very small. Also . . . these people have got the incentive that they are working for themselves . . . If you was to put your own carpenters on the roof, it would most probably take them twice as long as what it would if you put somebody on a price to do it . . . But there are certain jobs in building where it would be almost impossible to set incentive schemes for your own direct employees. The labour I employ direct tends to be a chap between the age of say, forty-five and retirement. They've had a lot of experience in building. I would term them 'plodders' – and that's not being disrespectful to them. They do a damn good job and you can put in apprentices with these people . . . You need them on certain jobs where skill is required more . . . With the direct employees we've got, they are not supervised full-time. There's a certain amount of trust in the chaps that I employ. What some companies would have supervisors normally do, they do this themselves. For example, on time sheets they record any variations and how long it's taken them to do various elements . . . I believe

there are certain things that an apprentice tradesman should accept
as his own responsibility without being told about it . . . They look
after themselves . . . and this only makes the job more interesting as
far as they are concerned . . . they get more involved and are more
a part of the company.   (303)

These accounts emphasise the extent to which employees are given
considerable discretion within the context of a high *trust* relationship.
By contrast, subcontractors – although often more productive – are
seen to be less *trust*worthy and less likely to produce good quality
work. Nevertheless, they reduce the need for managerial and supervisory
staff and curtail attempts by the state to protect the rights of
employees. These points were made by several owner-controllers:

We've reduced our direct labour . . . We must employ a certain core
of direct labour because it's impossible to run a company with all
subcontractors . . . The government has forced us to do it because of
industrial tribunals and things like this. You can't sack a man even
if you find them doing things they shouldn't. We're not allowed to
say anything – it's really diabolical. So we're no longer in charge of
our own labour.   (317)

Subcontracting has a distinct advantage in that you are working to a
fixed price, whereas if you've got direct labour you've got to put a
hell of a lot more work into getting them to work to a target . . .
Then there are more of the administrative problems that go along
with direct labour . . . all the extra work and money that goes into
things like holiday pay . . . It's just too much 'aggro' to get involved
with . . . Plus there's a possibility that sooner or later you're going
to get some bugger who's going to take you to unfair dismissal.
(309)

If you subcontract, there aren't so many levies to be paid to the
government for employing staff – PAYE, national insurance, all
those things which have drastically gone up. It costs a bomb just to
employ a person to arrive at the gate on a Monday morning now.
Then they don't always want overtime because they're the sort of
person who aren't going to be pushed. Whereas the labour-only
subcontractor is trying to earn money and he likes to work long
hours and perhaps, Saturdays and Sundays. So there's a difference
there.   (319)

Severe fluctuations in the level of trading, often exacerbated by state attempts to regulate the economy, directly encourage owner-controllers to make use of subcontracted labour since it can be engaged and shed according to work demands. Two of the respondents made the following observations:

> We do, at times, find it hard to keep a continuation of work. We might get held up in sales or messed about by the government and then we can't start something else so we work it so that we can keep our own employees fully employed. The advantage with subcontractors − though it costs us more − is that we don't have to buy them throughout the year. Or find their holiday pay, social security or anything else. They are to be used and you use them . . . We do have some direct employees for quality control. They do the main essential work . . . and cope with any emergency.   (305)

> Ideally, I'd like to employ all our own labour but it's the nature of the business that we can't guarantee ten thousand pounds worth of work every week . . . If the weather suddenly holds up or the market changes then . . . a nicely planned programme is disrupted . . . Then, say a client wanted something redesigned . . . You may have to rush round and find outside contractors . . . Next week you've got nothing so your own men are just tidying up.   (314)

Subcontracting, then, enables owner-controllers to cope with variable market circumstances and to relinquish many of what are normally regarded as employer responsibilities. Nevertheless, they *are* employers who are not *directly* involved in manual labour and this is reflected in their wider attitudes and perspectives. In general, they do not seem to be riddled with contradictions in the manner of the small employers. They are firmly committed to notions of individualism and stress the value of self-help, hard work, and personal success.[24] Society, they claim, *should* be organised as a race in which all individuals can freely compete. As one of the respondents stated:

> If you've got the will to do it you'll do it. I'm a great believer in mind over matter. I used to do a lot of sport and you can see the winner of any race, it's his *mind* that's winning the race. His mind's telling his body it's got to do it . . . whereas anyone whose body rules their mind, says pack up. And it's just the same with running a business really. If you've got to do something, you must do it. (322)

The fact that these conditions are no longer seen to prevail was the basis for considerable disenchantment:

> I think people in general have lost the will to work. The incentives, for some reason, have disappeared. It really is all about the will to work and the will to want to get on. So many people are content to get as much as they can from the company they are working for in the shortest possible period of time. And they can get it without really wanting to put in more time and effort. They want to put less time in and less effort and they want to get paid more for it.　　(302)

However, this respondent went on to suggest that the building industry is an exception to the general rule:

> This industry is where perhaps you get the greatest movement between classes. The self-made man sets up on his own and he really is basically uneducated and yet he can become very wealthy. In fact, there are probably more self-made men in the top class of earnings and living standards than there are people with inherited fortunes . . . The opportunity is open to everybody providing they want to work.　　(302)

Individuals, then, and *not* society, should be responsible for their own material wellbeing; through hard work and personal self-sacrifice a high standard of living can be achieved. This was succintly put by one owner-controller:

> I'm satisfied with the return I get from the business. If I'm not it's up to me, isn't it? That's the whole point of being on your own − there's nobody I can go to and say 'I want more money'. That's it, isn't it? I mean, if I want more money I've got to go out and get it and earn it. So any small business man when he says he's not getting enough, what he's really saying is that he's not doing something right.　　(304)

Such attitudes are to be expected among those who are daily exposed to the market and have to organise labour for the purposes of profit. In contrast to most managerial employees, owner-controllers have no predictable career hierarchy within which they can progress on the basis of age, qualification, preformance and experience. Instead, their economic rewards are unpredictable and subject to considerable fluctuation. Consequently, by virtue of owning and controlling their enterprises, they accept as normal the need for risk, self-reliance and personal independence. This, in turn, affects the character of their personal beliefs and life styles. We found that very few of them participated in clubs and associations or were engaged in patterns of mutual home entertainment. Their styles of life were, on the whole, 'privatised' and 'home-centred'.[25] As two of them told us:

> I don't belong to any clubs or associations although, obviously, it would be to my advantage. I don't want to live with my business twenty-four hours a day – you do, in a sense, inevitably, but there's no need to add to it. That's my personal view.   (323)

> You need a break at the end of the day . . . I'm not one for going around and taking people out for the sake that it's going to be a contact – my friends are my friends. So I don't get around into the various organisations.   (303)

The owner-controllers' strong sense of individualism shapes their attitudes towards the state and the role of trade unions. As with small employers, they do not regard the state as a 'neutral arbiter' between various groups in society, but, rather, as part of a 'collectivist' package which usually incorporates the interests of organised labour. This, they argue, accounts for the growth of state-funded social welfare which had undermined the will to work.

> The sad thing about our country is that a good many people have lost the will to work. I don't think you'll get people to do anything any good unless their backs are against the wall . . . People are too spoon-fed now. Life is too easy. If you don't work you get plenty of money – not plenty, but enough from the state and that's basically the downfall of this country . . . Everyone's lost their feeling of purpose – it's all too easy.   (308)

> Really, the amount of money paid out to people on social security should be dropped because it just isn't fair on the working man. Your employee is never going to really work hard for the same money that you can get for stopping at home – and that is certainly ruining the country.   (318)

In a nutshell, the will to work has been undermined by successive governments . . . other countries don't have such high social services generally. There are too many things that you don't have to pay for and everybody's become complacent. It's 'Oh well, the state will do this' and 'The state will do that'. But why should it? Take the dole queue . . . they're obviously not that bad off for a job. I think it's disgraceful, I don't see why all these things should be paid for. People should get off their backsides and do more work. But the way the system has gone, they don't have to – that's the tragedy.   (319)

Such views would seem to have their origin in the nineteenth-century doctrine of self-help. In particular, they are reminiscent of the verities expounded by Samuel Smiles:

Help from without is often enfeebling in its effects, but help from within invariably invigorates. Whatever is done for men or classes, to a certain extent takes away the stimulus and necessity of doing for themselves; and where men are subjected to over-guidance and over-government, the inevitable tendency is to render them comparatively helpless.[26]

The state, then, undermines work commitment and so indirectly challenges the efficiency of the market economy. But according to many owner-controllers it also has a more direct impact because it creates a large amount of unproductive work and, at the same time, subsidises inefficient businesses. In so doing, it interferes with the 'free' operation of the market system. The comments of two respondents were typical of many:

There are too many civil servants. There's not enough people earning money. This is the problem – it can't be anything else when you think of the number of people there are in government . . . I have got on my desk the census of production. They want to know every bit of material I've bought, every subcontractor I've had and how much I've paid them . . . It's all non-productive . . . it's not helping the gross national product . . . If there were more people actually laying bricks it would help the whole country. But no one wants to do it . . . there are far too many people organising what we ought to do instead of getting on and doing it.   (325)

I think that if a lot of businesses were left in private enterprise they would either go to the wall or look for alternatives. A private

business, be it large or small, does not have a bottomless pit. Take
British Leyland when it went to the government and said they were
going to wrap up unless they were provided with X million pounds.
If they'd been left alone they would have sold off bits of it which
by now could have been running as profitable independent
businesses.   (308)

If this is the 'problem', the 'solution' for many owner-controllers is to
administer the state as though it were a business; for them the familiar
rhetoric of 'balancing the books' had a particularly strong appeal.[27]

It's my naive opinion that running the country is very much like
running a small business, or any business. You can't spend what you
haven't got. Yet they seem to constantly do this in this country.
It's great having a socialist state if only you can afford it — but we
bloody well can't.   (309)

Government expenditure ought to be controlled. I've been involved
with a continuing analysis of what this company is doing, how it's
doing it and whether it's doing it efficiently. I don't believe that the
government do enough of this. They should do some time-and-
motion studies to see whether there's a better way to deal with work
than by just increasing staff all the time.   (302)

The trade unions were also seen as a restraint upon business
efficiency because they explicitly prevent workers from being more
productive; if left to their own devices union members would, according
to our respondents, be prepared to work harder to advance their own
self-interests.

There is a place for unions — I don't think they ought to be
abolished. What I'm saying is that they should keep a sense of
proportion. They shouldn't regard profits as a dirty word . . . There's
a lot of 'Them' and 'Us' and it's unfortunate . . . In a capitalist
country, workers should expect employers to make a profit, be
happy about it and work for it. I'm not talking about my own
employees, because they work very well and I've got no complaints.
But generally, people in this country don't work anywhere near hard
enough . . . and a lot of it is the fault of the unions.   (304)

I rely on my men to apply themselves. There's a lot of responsibility

thrown on their shoulders and they respond.. . . I rely on their
integrity . . . Trade unions don't get too involved in my business. In
general, it will be nice when the unions eventually come into the
twentieth century . . . They're so far apart from their members'
attitudes . . . It's the few that control the many; they are not a
democracy . . . The leaders have to face up to the realities of life . . .
No-one can ever convince me that they're good for their members
when other countries, which don't have a high trade union membership, are much better off financially.   (320)

Clearly, then, owner-controllers adhere to an ideology which
emphasises the desirability of individualism, free competition and the
market. As a result, they are offended by the development of the
'collectivism' which trade unions and the state are seen to represent.
However, they are also hostile towards another aspect of the corporatist
economy; the growing domination of large-scale businesses. For them,
an ideal economy would be self-regulating and characterised by 'free'
and 'fair' competition between medium- and small-size companies. Their
opposition to big business often stems from the view that efficiency
declines with organisational growth. As two respondents commented:

I think the problem is that the bigger a firm gets the more inefficient
it becomes both on the management side and for the working chap.
There's an awful lot of waste with the bigger firms . . . whereas with
a small business you are always on your toes – you have to be
because you haven't very much to fall back on. The bigger you get,
the bigger are your assets and perhaps you're not so pushed or
worried.   (307)

Certain businesses become so big they are difficult to manage by
any one person. As soon as there is more than one person trying to
manage it, it becomes a problem. Certain big companies are just too
big; they're unwieldy and uneconomical. Nobody knows what's
going on and this sets off other fringe problems . . . The reasons why
a lot of these companies get bigger and bigger is to minimise the
market risks; to monopolise it so they can get a higher price for the
product and make more money.   (319)

The commitment to free competition, however, is more an outcome
of their material circumstances than simple ideological preference.[28]
Whereas the self-employed and the small employers are able to 'opt out'

of the market by servicing regular customers, owner-controllers are confronted with severe competition, often from larger companies which trade 'down-market' during periods of economic recession. In this sense they are caught uncomfortably in the middle – in competition with each other and subject to 'undercutting' by both smaller and larger businesses. For these reasons, and despite their rhetorical commitment to market competition, many of them would seem to have views similar to those noted by Wright Mills:

> When small businessmen are asked whether they think free competition is, by and large, a good thing, they answer, with authority and vehemence, 'Yes, of course – what do you mean?' If they are then asked, 'Here in this, your town?' still they say, 'Yes', but they hesitate a little. Finally: 'How about here in this town in furniture?' – or groceries, whatever the man's line is. Their answers are of two sorts: 'Yes, if it's fair competition', which turns out to mean: 'If it doesn't make me compete'.[29]

In view of our evidence it is to some extent justifiable to regard owner-controllers as the 'survivors' of a bygone era; that of competitive capitalism. Released from direct involvement in manual labour, their sole function is to manage their businesses in a profitable way. To do this it is necessary to develop rational, cost-effective forms of administration and employee control. This they do, largely by themselves, and hence their strong commitment to individualism and self-reliance. But if business growth continues, there comes a stage when the scale of an enterprise no longer enables the owner-controllers singularly and solely to perform these functions. Management then becomes a collective activity and it is to this that we now direct our attention.

Notes

1. The literature on entrepreneurship and entrepreneurial ideologies is extensive. General-based historical discussions are available in R. Bendix, *Work and Authority in Industry*, New York, 1956; D. C. McClelland, *The Achieving Society*, New York, 1961; M. W. Flinn, *Origins of the Industrial Revolution*, London, 1966; H. Perkin, *The Origins of Modern English Society, 1780–1880*, London, 1969.
2. C. W. Mills, *White Collar*, London, 1951, pp. 35–6;
3. Ibid., p. 34.
4. The importance of *labour* as a means of business growth reflects the low capital-intensiveness of the building industry.
5. Our respondents had, for example, ONC and HNC qualifications in building

and civil engineering and some had passed the Institute of Building examinations. Subsequent occupational experience included employment as contracts managers, surveyors and structural engineers.

6. The acquisition of qualifications and experience outside the family firm is a means by which nepotism can be disguised. See Chapter 7 for a further discussion of this practice.

7. For evidence of 'employee-inheritance' of businesses amongst French bakers see D. Bertaux and I. Bertaux-Wiame, 'Artisanal Bakery in France: How it Lives and Why it Survives' in F. Bechhofer and B. Elliott (eds.), *The Petite Bourgeoisie*, London, 1981.

8. Of course, the self-employed and small employers can also undercut owner-controllers by trading at a lower price *in cash*, thus avoiding taxes and other overheads.

9. Evidence from the recession in the building industry during the 1970s provides some support for this claim. The total number of private contractors in 1978 with 0–7 employees was 96 per cent of the 1973 figure; for those with 115–599 employees the equivalent figure was 86 per cent. The number of contractors with between 25 and 59 employees (the nearest equivalent to our category of owner-controllers who had an average of 38 employees) was, however, only 83 per cent of the 1973 total. See Department of the Environment, *Private Contractors' Construction Census 1978*, Table 1.

10. Owner-controllers often diversify into building-related activities although this is not always the case. The particular capabilities and aptitudes of children are frequently an important influence on the direction of diversification.

11. A. Fox, *Beyond Contract*, London, 1974a.

12. Ibid., p. 19.

13. Ibid.

14. The classic location of low-discretion work is the vehicle assembly line. The experiments of Volvo represent one recent attempt to redesign such work but there have been many other less-known schemes. See, for example, V. H. Vroom and E. L. Deci (eds.), *Management and Motivation*, Harmondsworth, 1970; A. Fox, *Man Mismanagement*, London, 1974b; D. A. Buchanan, *The Development of Job Design Theories and Techniques*, Farnborough, 1979.

15. Fox, *Beyond Contract*, p. 30.

16. Ibid., pp. 74–5.

17. R. Blauner, *Alienation and Freedom*, Chicago, 1964 cited in A. Fox, *Beyond Contract*, p. 23.

18. For a discussion of 'central' and 'peripheral' employees see A. Friedman, *Industry and Labour*, London, 1977.

19. Many have previously been self-employed but with age have reverted to working for others albeit with a considerable degree of autonomy.

20. Friedman, *Industry and Labour*, p. 110.

21. Labour-power is an indeterminate commodity, infinite in its potential but limited in its realisation. The concept, introduced by Marx, is discussed in H. Braverman, *Labor and Monopoly Capital*, New York, 1974, Chapter 1 and T. Nichols (ed.), *Capital and Labour*, Glasgow, 1980.

22. Braverman, *Labor and Monopoly Capital*, pp. 60–1. A useful historical survey of subcontracting arrangements in British industry is provided in S. Pollard, *The Genesis of Modern Management*, Harmondsworth, 1968.

23. Direct Labour Collective, *Building with Direct Labour*, London, 1978, p. 40.

24. In this, owner-controllers resembled the small shopkeepers studied by Bechhofer and his associates. It should be noted, however, that their sample concentrated upon, in our terms, the self-employed and small employers. The

discrepancy is possibly explained by the greater reliance of shopkeepers upon property. See Chapters 1 and 4 for further discussion.

25. This contrasts with the conventional middle class life styles portrayed in the literature. See, for example, M. Stacey, *Tradition and Change: a Study of Banbury*, Oxford, 1960: C. Bell, *Middle Class Families*, London, 1968; J. Raynor, *The Middle Class*, London, 1969; J. M. and R. E. Pahl, *Managers and their Wives*, Harmondsworth, 1972.

26. S. Smiles, *Self-help*, London, 1908 cited in P. D. Anthony, *The Ideology of Work*, London, 1977, p. 78.

27. The monetarist policies pursued by the Conservative government elected in 1979 laid particular emphasis upon the desirability of spending only what could be 'afforded'.

28. Their support for competition, then, is *economically* grounded rather than a 'free-floating' preference.

29. Mills, *White Collar*, p. 36.

7 OWNER-DIRECTORS AND FAMILY-OWNED FIRMS

In this chapter we discuss those enterprises in which the owners delegate areas of decision making to managers and supervisors. Thus, although ownership is largely retained by owner-directors and their families, control is — to some extent — subdivided and allocated to others. By definition, these enterprises have developed organisational structures within which certain managerial tasks are delegated since the scale of activities precludes the possibility of owner-directors *personally* undertaking all managerial functions. Consequently, there is an increasing dependence upon bureaucratic and impersonally-defined rules and regulations although, on their own, these are insufficient as a basis for organisational integration. Thus, within these larger family-owned firms, paternalism often provides a further normative support within which bureaucratic rules operate. However, this is often a source of considerable tension since managerial authority based on technical competence may conflict with employers' strategies of paternalism. One of the major problems facing the owner-directors of expanding enterprises, then, is the tension between traditional legitimacy, upon which many control procedures have been established, and the increasing need to introduce more rational-calculative forms of control.[1] As Newby has argued:

> The tendencies towards increasing rationalisation under capitalism . . . threaten the efficacy of paternalism . . . The universalistic characteristics of capitalist development . . . rendered traditional forms of authority inappropriate and lead to a search for new methods of social integration and rationality. What the growth in size achieved was to render less effective and less possible the management of the contradictions inherent in traditional authority . . . Effective paternalism is therefore related to size, for above a certain size, personal, traditional modes of control break down . . . bureaucratic control becomes unavoidable.[2]

Paternalism, then, is most pronounced within smaller enterprises but is generally inappropriate in large organisations.[3] On the basis of our evidence, it is most likely to be found within owner-director enterprises rather than in any of the other categories. There are various reasons for this. On the one hand, owner-director enterprises are too large to enable employer control to be exercised through the *fraternalist* strategy, while on the other, they are small enough for control to be exercised through personal relationships rather than according to bureaucratic rules and procedures. Further, if size is one factor, the nature of local labour markets is another. Thus, owner-directors may use paternalism as a means of retaining workers whose skills are in short supply.[4] This, then, polarises the labour force between 'central' craft employees and 'peripheral' semi-skilled and unskilled workers who are more exposed to the vagaries of the market.[5] For the latter, it is unnecessary for owner-directors to develop paternalist strategies since it is sufficient to pay the market rate. Paternalism, then, can be a function of both size – which renders *fraternalist* and bureaucratic strategies of control inappropriate – and of labour market conditions.

It is now necessary to illustrate these points by reference to our data. We studied twelve enterprises, ranging in annual turnover from one to twenty million pounds; the average was six million. In the smallest company there were 30 regular employees while in the largest there were 1200; the average was 300. This variation can be partly explained by the level of trading and the extent to which subcontractors were used. On average, 20 per cent of all employees were white-collar staff and the remainder were manual operatives. Of the twelve enterprises, four were controlled by five 'founder-owners' and the remaining eight by ten active proprietors, all of whom were 'family-inheritors'.[6] In addition, ten senior managers were interviewed in order to acquire information about the delegation of proprietorial control.[7]

Our data confirm that owner-directors often cultivate a strategy of paternalism which is then increasingly challenged by the bureaucratisation of procedures associated with business growth. The importance of paternalism as a means of recruiting and retaining labour in the face of market competition was stressed by several owner-directors:

> We have a lower labour turnover than most national contractors who are a little bit soulless. We can listen to their family problems . . . talk to them, know their problems. I mean this morning I walked into one of our carpenters who's been on the firm for some time . . . We had a chat and as far as I'm concerned, he's part of the team . . . we're all in the same thing together . . . It's sometimes difficult for a firm like ours to attract people to stay . . . Money, of course, is one thing but a lot of people like working for a firm like ours because

we are a family-type firm and we talk to one another. They can walk into my office any time . . . At the present time a national contractor is recruiting labour — they want to finish a contract on time and so there are big bonuses involved . . . That attracts them away from firms like us because we can't compete with that kind of money . . . We've also lost a few recently who've gone self-employed . . . but they're back now with us. They want the stability that a firm like ours can offer . . . You see, we'll be here long after this contract's finished. So by talking to the chaps, knowing them and their family problems we can do things, We treat the staff, at all levels, as best we can.   (413E)[8]

I've never longed for an enormous firm. I just wanted to increase steadily so that it would still be a family business — I think that's the best way of saying it . . . I reckon we are a pretty good old family team where we try and keep everybody happy. We're knit together and are a terribly friendly crowd . . . If a chap wants a car desperately then we loan them money and deduct it weekly. We try and help them out. It's just knowing people, because in a lot of bigger firms the chap in charge would pass somebody in the street and not know whether he was working for him or not. A lot depends on how you look after them . . . There's an awful lot in treating people properly. You can get a lot more work out of them if you know how to handle them.   (401A)

Similarly, two senior managers argued:

I've always thought — and I know the owner does too — that if you can engender a sort of team spirit you get much better effort out of everybody. We've always prided ourselves in that we've been a very friendly company . . . We've tried to produce a team spirit — even the site staff, they're very much part of us all. I know them personally. When we have a 'do' in the office they're all invited in . . . The owner has engendered a family spirit amongst the whole firm. It's very apparent because my chaps working on various sites think it's particularly nice when the owner goes round and has a chat with them because he is *the* owner. You couldn't get that feeling in a firm where there isn't a particular owner . . . His father, too, is still highly respected and often appears on site and it's always very much appreciated . . . People may be away for months sick but we'll keep on paying them — the one month's sick pay is never adhered to. This sort of thing, it's because it's a family firm.   (409D)

> This is a family business ... The directors are all family members
> and they care about their staff – they participate ... You can't get
> too far removed from the workforce in building because of the very
> nature of the work ... And here the best elements of the family
> firm come out in the atmosphere that's created ... The owner knows
> more of the outside operatives than even I do!   (405A)

Paternalism, then, is an important employer strategy for the
purposes of obtaining the ongoing commitment of employees and, as
such, it enables medium-sized family-owned firms to compete effectively with larger national companies for skilled labour. Whereas the
latter can often offer higher wages they are less able to develop the
paternalistic strategies characteristic of owner-directors. But with
business expansion, there is an increasing dependence upon formalised
control procedures; although paternalism may remain a mechanism of
social integration, there is a growing need for more impersonal
supervisory systems. These systems vary according to a number of
factors including the extent to which owners are prepared to delegate.[9]
They are often reluctant to do this, as is illustrated in the following
comments of a son who had recently taken over his father's business:

> I can remember when I first started, everything had to be checked
> by my father – really everything. Every order had to be checked by
> *him* before it left his desk. This was the sort of thing that worried
> me more than anything in the early years. Everything seemed to
> revolve around him making decisions about everything. I think that
> was one reason why, when the Building Advisory Service looked at
> the company, some of these things were delegated ... They advised
> us to recruit one or two managers from outside.   (402A)

Despite these criticisms of his father, this owner-director was subject to
the same accusation by the company secretary:

> The son is nervous ... because he's seen so many businesses collapse
> through not having the proper effective control from the top. He
> feels he ought to have his finger in all these things ... The weakness
> is the obvious one, there's too many reporting to one chap. Perhaps
> one might think he should have the confidence in the people here
> that could relieve him of some of his responsibility ... He's been

reminded of this fact several times – this isn't the way to operate a
successful business, although I suppose it is successful but it's
contrary to all of the textbooks.   (404A)

A similar point was emphasised by a senior manager in another
company:

> When two people effectively own 90 per cent of the shares every-
> body understands that, throughout the group. Every directorship is
> a personal appointment of theirs . . . The ultimate power is with the
> owners . . . I'm the only person who . . . can occasionally face up to
> the owners and say that I've made a decision whereas with the other
> directors there'd be all-hell to pay. Perhaps, because I'm an accoun-
> tant I have a certain independence. I can go and get a job anywhere
> . . . But these are the difficulties in family companies, the chief
> shareholder rules and you've just got to live with it. Even if we went
> partly public it would still be the same, the family would still retain
> control.   (425L)

Many of the owner-directors' fears about delegation seem to be
related to four major factors. First, they are in control of *family*
companies; they, often with other family members, own the substantial
majority of the shares. Although the ownership and control of enterprises can be separated – with the latter delegated to senior managers –
control is a resource which *potentially* can be used by managers against
the owners. Secondly, the market within which they trade is
characterised by considerable uncertainty such that 'formal' managerial
structures are inappropriate; during periods of economic recession they
can constitute expensive 'overheads'. Thirdly, there is an ideological
resistance to delegation because owner-directors feel that many
managerial tasks are unproductive. Finally, the rather 'haphazard'
process through which many of these companies have expanded, and
the owner-directors' lack of formal managerial training, encourages the
emergence of ill-defined, 'un-bureaucratic' management systems.[10] It is,
therefore, difficult to identify a predominant *type* of management
structure. Certainly, there was little evidence of those 'mechanistic'
forms sometimes described in management theory; on the contrary,
there was a tendency for 'organic' structures to predominate.
According to Burns and Stalker, 'mechanistic' management structures
entail detailed job descriptions, clearly specified rules and procedures
and the co-ordination of work tasks through a hierarchical system of

decision making.[11] They are most effective where the work process can be readily subdivided into repetitive, routine tasks and the market situation is characterised by a relatively high degree of stability. 'Organic' structures on the other hand, lack this precise specification of work tasks; procedures are broadly delineated and there is 'the adjustment and continual re-definition of individual tasks through interaction with others'.[12] Management is less hierarchically arranged and subordinates are vested with a considerable degree of autonomy and responsibility in the performance of their tasks. There also tends to be:

> a lateral rather than a vertical direction of communication through the organisation, communication between people of different rank, also, resembling consultation rather than command; a content of communication which consists of information and advice rather than instructions and decisions.[13]

The 'organic' form, then, tends to be more appropriate where flexibility and adaptability are required, fluctuating market conditions prevail and specialist products are made in 'short runs'. It is, then, particularly suitable for firms in building.[14] Indeed, in a detailed case study Foster found that despite attempts to establish a 'mechanistic' management structure, the nature of the work process led to the adoption of the 'organic' form which 'relentlessly evolved in response to circumstances'.[15]

In our study it was clear that organic structures enabled senior managers to enjoy semi-autonomy *without*, at the same time, challenging the owners' prerogatives. Although such structures appear to be more flexible and democratic than mechanistic forms, they actually serve to reinforce the owner-directors' control.[16] Sometimes this strategy is reflected in the creation of holding companies under which various subsidiary and associated enterprises are established.[17] Ownership of the holding company is typically confined to owner-directors and their families, while some share participation may be extended to non-family directors within the subsidiaries. The directors of these subsidiaries are often given day-to-day control over their enterprises but this is normally within parameters stipulated by the owner-directors.

The absence of formally-defined decision making processes was often referred to by the senior managers we interviewed. The following comments were typical:

> It is possible to plan and we have got to plan but it's not down on

paper anywhere. It's just telepathy between the owner and the two
senior directors – that's how the plan's developed . . . It's a very
nebulous situation because the owner, being the chairman and
managing director of the group, makes the final decisions. Usually
they evolve by conversation but if there is any uncertainty or doubt
or we don't see eye-to-eye then eventually he has got to make his
own mind up as to what he must do about it . . . We're in and out of
each other's offices all day, every day just generally chatting about
whatever is happening. It just comes out day-to-day, so I don't know
how I would define it really because it's such a casual arrangement
. . . I, also, as an individual, rely on people just working together and
if they don't fit in and so on, that's it – they go or I go – or
something happens. But I don't like it all written down because that
itself is capable of more abuse.   (422K)

We keep it all at a very informal level here . . . Anybody that wants
can come in here and sit down and discuss something with me. It
takes up an enormous amount of my time but we've always thought
it was the best way of doing it . . . When you get into very large
companies you get definite departments but a lot of us here are sort
of interchangeable . . . the staff do all sorts of different things and
they stay here a long time, I'm glad to say . . . You'll find that they're
all happy to be here. We do try to give them their heads a lot too, we
give as much responsibility as we possibly can. That makes them all
work better. We have a very open system of communication, the
whole staff is on a very friendly basis and it pays dividends . . . The
management structure is very ill-defined . . . particularly the
relationship between the associated companies and ourselves. You
can never find anybody to define that, it just sort of happened and
it seems to work.   (409D)

As we have already suggested, such informal practices are less 'open'
than they would at first appear. Without clearly-specified rules there are
greater possibilities for owners to exercise discretion and to implement
arbitrary decisions. Hence, the crucial influence of the owners'
personalities in determining the use to which *their* capital assets are
put.[18] This point was well understood by two senior managers:

There are some situations where, in a family company, the family
will have too much control over the company and the executives
aren't given freedom of movement. I was quite pleasantly surprised

by how much freedom I was given . . . and that identified very much with the son – as a younger man's approach. The older man in a family business doesn't give so much freedom and will tend to reduce your involvement . . . It's very much dependent upon the personality of the guy who owns the company.   (410D)

In a private company you must have control at the centre because, after all, the owner and his family have invested and they, quite rightly, don't want to see all their investment dissipated . . . The family of investors are obviously looking to keep their money intact. They're looking more directly at the people underneath them to see whether they're doing their job but intermixed with this is *personal* preference for people which you can't avoid . . . The personality of the people sitting at the head of the company is all-important . . . unless your views are somewhat akin I don't think you can live in a private company . . . If there's a clash of personalities then sooner or later something's going to go and there's only one thing *can* go. The investor's not going to go so the director's got to. Whereas in a public company, depending on size, the difference is that responsibilities are more clearly laid down and you have the ultimate discipline of the shareholders to back you . . . personalities play a part but they're not quite as important.   (411L)

Organic structures not only enable the owners to retain overall control, they also allow the financial performance of senior managers to be quickly assessed. The creation of subsidiaries as part-and-parcel of evolving organic structures is particularly conducive to this end.[19] As an owner-director told us:

Since the fifties we've become more specialised . . . and have set up different associate companies . . . (Once) you get these various companies it's much easier to set up separate cost-centres so you can measure the results of them . . . Originally, the joinery was part of the main company and figures didn't appear separately but if you form a separate company and put someone in charge you can really see what's happened at the end of the year . . . Each year we draw up a budget for all the companies and then during the course of the year you can measure what's going on.   (402A)

These comments were reaffirmed by his company secretary:

The subsidiaries encourage people to set their own results and to record their own achievements and then be rewarded accordingly. That is the main function . . . Should a surplus be made it goes into the general reserve – the profit-and-loss appropriation account. It's not left to the individual director to decide how he should spend his money, whether it's in work in progress or otherwise. Because we feel this is a principle which must only be done in consultation with the owner, because he can see the whole picture.   (404A)

Three senior managers of another company made similar observations:

We have a decentralised company situation . . . but once you start handing out control of cash collection and payment to the subsidiaries you really have got to watch things on a daily basis. The daily cash reporting comes back to us . . . It's a question of daily monitoring the balances at every location . . . (So) the company is centralised in it's controls, it has to be in construction. Our assets, if you like, are just people and our potential for profit is very small. But our potential for loss if people make mistakes is enormous. (425L)

This being a family business, if things aren't going too well we hear that if it wasn't for other parts of the business we would be in trouble and they hear likewise. But we never really know how that other part of the business is actually doing, which is bad . . . I think that the main board likes to keep a competitive side to the business and it wouldn't be too healthy for us to know everything that was going on in each other's subsidiary – especially when one business is held up against the others at appropriate times.   (424L)

The owner sits on the board of virtually all the subsidiary companies . . . He's entitled to interfere as a director *and* as an investor. But he has to be careful that he doesn't interfere too much. This is, obviously, sometimes very difficult . . . This is one of the problems where the investor is also concerned as a member of the board of directors. There is a conflict . . . The owner will often say, 'Look, I'm sitting here as an investor and telling you that this is good or this is not good'. At that point he is completely defined as an investor. But at another point, he'll talk as a director. And, of course, the managing director of the subsidiary then thinks, 'Well, *I'm* the managing director . . . I'm going to tell him what I'm doing about *this* business'. But he has to be careful what he says about 'my' business because it isn't his business and that's the problem. That's the real rub of the whole thing. Because, let's face it, somebody who's come up through the ranks and becomes a director, his livelihood, his remuneration, his benefits and his future are all locked up with the company. For the person who hasn't got finance to put into it, what he's going to get out of it is in the company. But he's not an investor. He is investing his time and energy for a remuneration but he's in a difficult position if he tends to think it's *his* company. You see, he's not laying £100,000 on the table and saying, 'That's my company'.   (411L)

In the last instance, then, it is *ownership* which primarily determines the extent to which control is delegated to those senior managers who are 'responsible' for subsidiary companies. Nevertheless, a degree of trust between owner-directors and their managerial staff is assumed since there is little potential for interpersonal rivalry. Either senior managers *accept* the owners' prerogatives or they must leave; hence, the commonly- observed 'happy atmosphere' of family firms is partly a function of this selective process.[20] Owner-directors deliberately recruit managers with 'personalities' compatible with their own. As one senior manager stated:

If your immediate superior happens to be the major shareholder and you can't get on, you might as well leave because as a team, you'll never hit it off.   (411L)

Accordingly, managerial appointments are not solely determined according to meritocratic or technical criteria. There is, in fact, a tendency for managers employed in these companies to lack higher educational qualifications.[21] This, in turn, is linked to the continuing dependence in construction upon a craft-based technological system.[22] All the senior managers we interviewed had completed apprenticeships and been employed as manual craftsmen before embarking upon managerial careers. The following career paths were typical:

I started life as a carpenter. I was indentured with a local company ... Within a couple of years I'd been to technical school and I'd established that I wanted to do something better than being a carpenter ... I wanted to be a builder's manager so I was busily swatting, doing national and higher national certificates and such like . . . Then I was offered a trainee surveyor's job . . . So, if you like, I was blooded from the trade background into this company . . . Now, I'm responsible for the marketing we do within the entire group.   (410D)

I've been with the company since I left school. My father was a small builder so, I suppose, from the time I could walk, building was in the blood . . . I went through technical school education and then came into this company in general office work. Then I did the estimating side of things, plans and specifications . . . Then, general surveying . . . and on to contracts managing . . . Finally, in charge of the planning department where I've been for fourteen years. (412D)

The advantages of this system were frequently argued by owner-directors and senior managers alike. In an industry where the work process is subject to considerable uncertainties, it is imperative that managers have personally experienced the practical difficulties which confront operatives. This is crucial for supervising workers and for assessing their efficiency,[23] as several of the respondents pointed out:

A manager has got to have a thorough knowledge of the business. That's absolutely essential. That's the greatest criterion, they must have a full understanding of the business . . . People who have not come through apprenticeship training have got more ambition and believe they can get to the top faster. But they lack the understanding of the business to enable them to get that far. They've got more drive — they want to be managers more than the guy who's come through the business . . . but I get better results from someone who's come through because they can motivate everybody right the way through . . . And when you're sitting at a meeting you've got to understand what is being said at the meeting. If you don't, things just don't happen . . . Managers without practical knowledge are unable to motivate . . . They're led by the people who they are supposed to be leading, rather than vice versa.   (424L)

You couldn't manage unless you've got an adequate building and construction background . . . You couldn't appoint someone with a technical qualification but no experience. You could do the reverse. You could give the job to a practical man who could develop the theory, if you like. But you couldn't really do it the other way round because there's no other way than seeing it happen over a period of years and practically building it up in your mind. You've got to have a practical knowledge, definitely.   (412D)

If somebody has been through the trade they know what they are talking about. They don't know much in theory but they know the practical side and I think that is more important. If you join a company, say from university, you know all the theory but it doesn't work when you get on to the site. So I prefer to see managerial staff come up from the other side. That's what we've always done.   (419I)

There are, however, limits to the career mobility which managers in owner-director firms are likely to enjoy; on the whole, positions which entail *overall control* are restricted to family members. In many of the companies that we studied, sons rather than senior managers were being trained to take control at a specified future date. This was often the basis for considerable tension among managers since it seriously blocked their own career opportunities:[24]

I think the career prospects in our structure are extremely limited. We tend to take on ready-made people for fixed positions and all the positions in the structure are filled. Therefore, there's no organic growth . . . It's very limited. We don't really have any development of staff at managerial level . . . and there is always the feeling that the structure of the company limits one's progress . . . Although the owner is not only responsible for everything that happens . . . there is the feeling that one isn't totally the master of one's own situation. In that way, I find it limited.   (422K)

My ambition in life was to have my own company. But there comes a point in your life where you have to decide whether it's going to be your own company or whether you are going to be an employee . . . I decided that I had an opportunity within a family company to be the boss and that's what I aimed for. And I got to be the boss but it hasn't taken very long to find out that it's not the same – nowhere near the same as being the boss of your own company . . . You have to answer for everything . . . One has to make essential decisions, yet you have to answer for almost every decision you make. And this can be very overbearing.   (424L)

> One experiences minor frustrations in having to seek advice on every minor issue because when the firm is family-owned, obviously, the governor is close to the people in the organisation and he's always there . . . I'm looking for something more. I'm 31 years of age and I haven't reached my optimum level. I want something more. I'm less sure of where I'm going to get it at the moment because I've gone to the top fairly quickly — or at least, to the level where I am now . . . Maybe admission to the main board is the next step but I'm not too sure of my chances.   (403A)

The nepotism that characterises the transfer of family-ownership and control between generations is often concealed by owner-directors insisting that their sons obtain experience in other companies before taking over control. After working for other firms they normally assume lower-grade supervisory positions within the family business and subsequently pursue a reasonably predictable career, gradually acquiring control from their fathers. One owner-director outlined this process as follows:

> If you bring very young sons into a business you've got to ensure that they go and work for other people to start with — that's vitally important. And they must be bright and really have the ability and having proved they have ability at a low level in your existing company, then give them a tiny business to run. Having worked for somebody else, if they've made a success, then give them a slightly bigger one. But to give somebody a very big business straight away can be disastrous.   (421L)

Two 'family-inheritors' reaffirmed this view in recollecting their own careers:

> I left technical college and worked for a building company on the south coast, to gain experience. I really feel this period should have lasted longer . . . because it's always best to get experience in another company before starting up or taking over the family business. But the death of my father and another director meant I had to come back and take over as contracts manager after only a year.   (416F)

> When I first left school I wanted to take employment with another building company. I thought it was interesting and useful to do . . .I did intend, in the end, of course, to come into this business but I

wanted to get some outside experience first.   (406B)

Even within craft-based technological systems of the sort which
predominate within the building industry, work experience becomes
insufficient as owner-directors expand their companies. Business growth
necessitates a greater emphasis upon technical rationality and this, in
turn, can be the basis for considerable tension within management
structures. The influence of technical experts such as accountants and
marketing specialists, for example, increases as the more practical
experience of owner-directors becomes less appropriate. As a result,
owner-directors are more dependent upon hired experts and this has
repercussions for the exercise of their own personal control. One senior
manager recognised this as a problem common to many family-owned
firms:

> The owner has come up the hard way and he has no professional
> qualifications. He's got to the point now where he can't handle it
> and his policy is to employ professional people in all departments to
> run it for him . . . Hence we have a chartered accountant looking
> after plans, an architect as well to design things and myself. I have
> professional qualifications for building . . . The tendency is for more
> professionally-trained people rather than coming up through the
> ranks. That's probably the general situation in the industry. Owners
> don't know the new management techniques, particularly if they've
> come up from the working-class and been perhaps a bricklayer or a
> craftsman.   (418H)

In a sense, organic management structures are functional because, on the
one hand, 'expert' managers are able to preserve a degree of personal
autonomy while on the other, owners are able to retain overall control.
This helps to accommodate tensions between 'experience' and
'expertise'. But, as with owner-controllers, some managerial problems
can, alternatively, be overcome by subcontracting labour and specialist
services. Most estimates indicate that at least one-third of all construction work is subcontracted, but that this figure 'is higher in new
building, particularly on large and complex projects'.[25] As a recent
investigation into the building industry suggests:

> Discontinuity of production means that even the largest firms
> cannot guarantee work to a wide range of specialist activities.
> Subcontracting of specialist work is a way of overcoming the

problem at a minimum cost to the contractor. It also ensures that such specialists will be actively employed for longer periods of time than would otherwise be the case.

Moreover, for even the largest firms, work levels vary enormously. If subcontracting did not exist, it would be exceedingly difficult for contractors to adjust to such variations. It takes time to build up a workforce, and to acquire plant and materials. This can be avoided through subcontracting the work, which considerably increases the flexibility and ability of contractors to adapt to changing workloads. As a result, the costs and delays involved do not fall on one contractor alone.[26]

Subcontracting *between enterprises*, therefore, affords a degree of flexibility which is particularly useful for owner-director firms.[27] During periods of market depression, small subcontractors may be 'squeezed' and if they go bankrupt their larger trading partners can easily take their trade elsewhere. Owner-director enterprises, then, can resolve certain managerial problems and cope with market uncertainties by subcontracting to 'weaker' and smaller firms. In this way, the larger firms overcome problems of managerial control by, in a sense, avoiding them; subcontracting represents an alternative to the development of managerial and supervisory structures.

If subcontracting offers very direct advantages to specific enterprises, the cost within the industry as a whole, tends to be borne by labour. Unskilled and semi-skilled workers employed by small specialist subcontractors are doubly disadvantaged because they are both marginal to their own and their employer's employer; that is, to the main contractor. Friedman has put the point as follows:

> The flexibility which large firms acquire from their co-operative relations (with smaller subcontractors) means hardship and insecurity for workers in smaller supplier and distributing firms . . . The unskilled and semi-skilled manual workers working for these firms are therefore peripheral workers on two counts. They are peripheral to these firms as are semi-skilled and unskilled workers in larger firms, but they are also employed in what might be considered peripheral firms.[28]

Such 'hardship and insecurity' manifests itself within the building industry in a number of ways. A recent investigation attributes poor work and safety conditions to the fact that 'site control . . . by both management and trade unions is considerably weakened by the existence of transient subcontractors, who come and go at various stages of the project'.[29] On most large construction sites the existence of several labour-only and specialist service subcontractors makes the effective imposition of safety controls difficult. A recent Health and Safety Executive Report, analysing one hundred deaths in the industry, concluded that over two-thirds were attributable to inadequate management; that labourers were most at risk and that small contractors and subcontractors offered particularly poor safety training facilities.[30] In the long term, the health of building workers suffers and the subcontracting system which 'thrives upon the use of a young adult workforce prepared to work long hours in poor conditions' eventually produces 'unemployable' workers who, long before retirement, have poor health and job prospects.[31] Their plight is made worse by the fact that many of them have received little or no formal training — a further reflection on the generally poor employment conditions in the industry.[32]

Owner-directors, then, who rely heavily upon subcontracting both in the provision of labour and specialist services, contribute to the creation of a dual labour market and a system of 'dependent' relationships between enterprises.[33] The economic viability of a large number of small firms, and their employees, is contingent upon the requirements of larger enterprises, many of which occupy a 'dominant' position within local trading markets. Owner-directors legitimate this system by reference to three major factors. First, they argue that it is a consequence of market fluctuations over which they have no control; because of these they feel unable to bear the costs of employing a large, permanent labour force. Secondly, they claim that many specialist tradesmen are difficult to supervise and that it is more cost-effective to pay for their services through the market rather than within the employment relationship. Finally, it is argued that subcontracting encourages the formation and growth of small businesses. This, in turn, reinforces an ideology of 'business opportunity' which conceals many of the exploitative aspects of the relationship that exists between small and large firms. As an owner-director told us:

> People that set up on their own tend to be enterprising although not often very qualified. They've had some experience in the building industry, possibly as a subcontractor, and it appeals to them to start on their own . . . There's so many small businesses around and many of their friends are used as small specialist subcontractors or small businesses.   (418H)

The advantages of the subcontracting system for owner-directors were typically described in the following terms:

> The major problem in the industry is the continual up-and-down . . . Everything goes crazy, then all of a sudden, bang, it all drops off and you're left holding the baby . . . Of course, this affects the labour. Everybody likes to have a reasonably steady job but when the trade goes down the business goes down and the labour is obviously disposed of. Ninety per cent of them might go and work in a factory and won't come back into the trade . . . With direct labour you've often got to be behind them all the time, otherwise they waste your time. Then you've got all the problems with the unions – what you can do and what you can't; whether you can sack them and whether you can't. The output is nowhere near what you'd get from somebody who's got incentive. If you have a subcontractor he's doing a job for X amount of money and, therefore, he wants to get the job done as quickly as possible. So he works hard. It's in your interest to get the job done as quickly as possible, and you know what you've got to pay for it. So, all you've got to do is to control it and the ideal controlling staff are on the job. They have got the problems because they're employing all the men . . . Now, we tie every subcontractor to a contract with specific dates . . . We hold a retention on all the payments and then if they're behind we threaten them with bringing in other people and they lose their retention.   (419I)

> The type of thing we are looking for is minimum direct involvement ourselves. If I can give you a mix of a job, let's say, a nominated content of two-thirds to one-third builder's work, that, to us would be very attractive because although we've got to *manage* we don't have to *do* it. Managing is one thing and doing is totally different. Obviously, if you reduce the amount you do, you reduce the amount of risk but you use your own expertise in management.   (410D)

Owner-directors, then, abdicate many managerial responsibilities through the market without risking the control and ownership of their capital assets. Despite this, they are more exposed to market forces than the self-employed and small employers who can more readily develop a satisfactory level of trade with a number of regular private customers. The size and complexity of owner-director companies demands that they develop efficient marketing methods in order to obtain contracts through the contract-and-tender system. However, some enterprises are able to reduce these risks because they occupy positions of market dominance within specific geographical areas.[34] In this way, they are able to determine the nature of the market in terms of prices and wage payment systems. An alternative method of reducing market risk is to acquire smaller established businesses in different geographical localities. Thus, it is possible to 'buy' local contacts, acquire 'goodwill' and obtain an established labour force. As two owner-directors stated:

> It's important to buy yourself into companies rather than set yourself up. We tried very hard, funnily enough, to do this a little while ago. We were interested in getting a small works section on the south coast. I was looking around for another company to buy so that we had a readymade set-up. You know, the bus was moving, as it were. But to start cold is difficult.   (408D)

> The purchase of a building company already in existence in Sussex gives us scope for covering the county to the coast . . . We took them over lock, stock and barrel . . . It's difficult to get sufficient skilled men within the industry on a directly-employed basis . . . We obviously have got to have a nucleus of regular staff and to try and enlarge it is very difficult . . . Taking over another company is one way, of course, of increasing our turnover and getting more labour. (414E)

Some companies spread their risks by creating subsidiaries as part-and-parcel of a process of product diversification. Their core activities focus around general building but they expand into plant-and-tool hire, 'do-it-yourself', vehicle leasing and property speculation. Although the general direction of investment varies, one factor is always emphasised: the use of labour. Thus, owner-directors tended to give priority to ventures which involved minimum labour requirements in their search for market security.[35]

> There's such a demand for transport in this area – we need it ourselves – that we are thinking of setting up a separate company for vehicle leasing . . . We have space on the premises . . . We may also start manufacturing staircases and windows – that sort of thing. Again, this is because we're unable to buy them economically in this area so we decided to make our own . . . Our policy is to diversify into anything allied to building . . . The problem,

inevitably, is getting the right labour to run it – to staff the thing satisfactorily. We just can't find people of experience and competence. Hence, with the joinery . . . we are going to spend a lot of money on expensive automatic machinery . . . so that an imbecile can work them.   (418H)

Our insurance company started because in the old days you had to get a fire insurance for a mortgage and the usual thing was for the builder to be the agent for the insurance company. This is how the owner started . . . in a very small way with just an agent and it grew into a separate company . . . Obviously, the firm has vehicles and it has to carry large public liability insurance. So it's very profitable and very efficient administratively for us to have our own insurance broker . . . We've also formed a technical design company . . . which, in this case, is a way of employing or harnessing the talents of the owner's son . . . Finally, we recently purchased a wholly-owned subsidiary building company . . . A company must grow and spread in order just to survive . . . Nevertheless, our main future is always going to be the building industry . . . You can grow too quickly without enough skilled staff . . . We've got to make sure that the company doesn't outgrow our ability to manage. Lots of companies have gone into liquidation simply and solely because they've developed into a form which they couldn't maintain and manage . . . We make sure we don't outgrow our ability to run whatever company or work we are trying to do. That's definitely a limiting factor to the growth of any company.   (413E)

One of the major limitations to business growth is owner-directors' perceptions of their own personal competence.[36] Amongst the firms we studied, there was a tendency for expansion to occur only in those directions where they felt able to retain overall personal control. As one of them admitted:

The major obstacle to expansion is the competence of myself. My ability to control the whole business. We have tried to expand in an area which I knew nothing about. The business went wrong and it failed. That's one example of why I think that my competence will restrict the expansion of this business.   (415L)

Even the use of highly-qualified managerial staff is seen to be fraught with difficulties because they usually demand work autonomy and, therefore, need to be carefully recruited if owner-directors' objectives are to be achieved.[37] As a senior manager claimed:

> The key to diversification is the selection of the personnel in whom you are going to place the responsibilities ... If, as we've done, you diversify and allow autonomy you then have to be extremely careful how you select the person to whom you give responsibility. If you are not careful you can give autonomy to a person you have wrongly selected, then you could end up by, amongst other things, losing a lot of money and ruining that particular venture.   (411L)

In general, most of the companies in our study were committed to trading consolidation rather than business expansion if only because of inflation and uncertain market conditions:

> We aim for steady growth linked to inflation, obviously otherwise we'll stand still. We'll also diversify into other fields allied to the building industry ... but in general, we'll just keep going as we can.   (418H)

> The only forward plan we have is not to expand at all because we don't want to be in the power game of great expansion. The building industry is a monumentally risky business to be in for a start. It can go extremely well or extreme badly ... I want to enjoy the *status quo* really.   (408D)

> We've had steady controlled growth ... a steady growth in assets, a steady growth in profit, a steady growth in dividend. It's been a controlled, steady expansion and not a runaway one ... We've got to keep pace with inflation in real terms.   (420J)

Sometimes these strategies are accompanied by the deliberate cultivation of local 'social' contacts by owner-directors, senior managers and their families.[38] This was explicitly stated by one owner-director and two of his senior managers:

> I would have thought that there are a lot of advantages in being involved with the community. With the building business, if you are known locally and involved with people they will say 'Well, we know this firm, we'll go to them'. I always thought that builders should take part in the community because of this.   (402A)

All the people in the management team here are encouraged to join local associations and the expenses are paid by the company. Two or three of us are members of the BIM and there are various people that belong to the Masons and Rotary. The owner is now a JP and a member of various golf clubs in the vicinity. This is encouraged because by rubbing shoulders with senior managers of either companies in these associations, this can do nothing but good. (404A)

There are occasions where we have to represent the company at a social function and do entertaining as a couple from time to time. Perhaps when there's a particular client that wants looking after. Also, I've become quite good personal friends with several architects and, of course, we meet each other's wives and share the odd drink and meal together. It's all very pleasant and helps the company. (403A)

It is within this context that the role of owner-directors' wives can be understood. They tend to be involved in a wide range of clubs, associations and community activities which, in effect, serve to enhance the reputation of their husbands' enterprises. Although such involvement does not directly produce trade, it gives prominence to the local image of owner-director companies.[39] These points were appreciated by two of the wives we interviewed:

I think the wife should be involved in her husband's work . . . She should be adaptable . . . She should be able to go out to dinner and mix with her superiors on their level . . . you feel you want to for your husband, regardless of what you really feel yourself . . . It may sound hypocritical and two-faced but if it means the company does well and your husband gets on then you shoud be able to adapt. (414EW)

I believe socially the wife should fulfil a function with her husband's company – although not with the actual work, of course. I've been with my husband on opening ceremonies and this sort of thing . . . Yes, socially I'm in favour of involvement – in fact, we entertain quite a lot.   (423KW)

However, some of our respondents felt that increasing competition had tended to render this approach redundant. Although community involvement was often seen to be good for company image it was no longer regarded as necessary:

> Apart from the odd game of cricket my whole time is devoted to the business . . . If you are efficient in the office and your prices are right, you'll get as much work as you want. You don't have to go and see Joe Bloggs at the golf club. No – I don't believe in that at all.   (419I)

> There's a reluctance to accept that the world is changing – you can't swim against the tide . . . The relationship with another businessman where, you know, I went to school with him, we've mucked about together over the years, and he's always going to give us his business – that doesn't happen any more . . . These contacts only give you the *opportunity* to do the business . . . You see, there are very few people that phone up and say 'I want you to build me a house or a factory' and not ask about how much it's going to cost. (425L)

> We do a certain amount of entertaining. We see new clients in restaurants but we don't believe that the best business comes from that. It's your ability to perform as a company and your reputation which counts.   (421L)

Owner-directors, then, develop different orientations to the market as well as distinct strategies of managerial control. On the basis of these two factors – as they emerged in our interviews – it is possible to construct a simple typology of owner-directors. This may be presented diagrammatically as follows.

Table 7.1: A Typology of Owner-directors

		Development of control system	
		+	–
Market orientation	+	Managerial (1)	Entrepreneurial (2)
	–	Paternal (3)	Family custodial (4)

(1) Managerial

Of the 15 owner-directors we studied, four fall into this category. Managerial owner-directors tend to have inherited enterprises from their fathers. By definition, they are highly geared to market opportunities and in response to them, complex organisational structures emerge. These tend to be 'organic' in form and there are tensions surrounding the delegation of owner control. On the one hand, there are formal rules and procedures while on the other, owner-directors retain the right to make arbitrary decisions and, in the opinion of their managers, are often too involved in day-to-day practices. These owner-directors give total priority to profit maximisation and take considerable pride in their ownership of efficient organisations. There is no pretence of paternalism; instead, importance is attached to being seen as a 'good employer' who pays a 'fair wage' in return for a 'fair day's work'. They do not regard themselves as having paternal responsibilities for their staff outside work. *At* work, employees are viewed as members of a 'team' within which there is no place for conflict; they therefore see themselves as better placed than trade unions to deal with any problems. Managerial owner-directors are aware that they have acquired their business through inheritance but they do not legitimate their position in these terms. On the contrary, the development of successful companies, they claim, is sufficient demonstration of their personal achievement and competence. In other words, they argue, even without birthright they would still have *achieved* their present position. The managerial approach was reflected in the comments of one owner-director:

> You've got to train yourself to be a manager. I don't think there's any good in entrepreneurial skills unless you can perform as a manager in developing those skills. It's no good me saying it's a brilliant idea to get involved in a new aspect of business which we know nothing about because that would be an entrepreneurial idea but a major disaster. The world is full of companies run by entrepreneurs who will go bust because they can't carry their entrepreneurial ideas through into profit.   (421L)

These owner-directors often recognise the need for government intervention for the purpose of establishing market stability. Further, they stress the desirability of co-operation between companies to facilitate collective representation. Thus, there is only limited commitment to the virtues of the 'free' market since it can create difficulties for corporate planning. Several owner-directors in our study felt that successful capitalism had to be 'managed' and 'planned' in an orderly manner:[40]

It's quite absurd that the industry hasn't got a more united stronger voice to deal with the government . . . One of the big snags about the industry is that small firms, medium-sized firms, larger firms – they're all too fragmented. We don't work together enough . . . to provide a unified voice to work with the government . . . Of course, one accepts the fact that in our system you need plenty of government administrators to keep people employed. So it's fair enough that a government, inevitably, has got to have so many millions of pounds and must run these things . . . The civil service and their offsprings are, I think, ninety-nine per cent honest and better than most . . . I've found them easy going, actually . . . The civil service is just part of the inevitable machinery of government . . . When you actually get to see someone – the tax people, rating and valuation, local authorities – nine times out of ten, they're helpful.   (407C)

We're dependent upon what is a highly volatile market . . . If we could have a relatively static market, one could plan much more easily. From a political point of view we are not in a strong industry. There's no political muscle in the way in which the farmers have political muscle. We are, therefore, more easily used as a political football.   (421L)

(2) Entrepreneurial

Four of the owner-directors could be categorised as entrepreneurial. Although they are highly market-oriented, their businesses tend to have underdeveloped control systems. They are likely to be founder-owners who have rapidly expanded to a high level of trading and who often subcontract to avoid the problems associated with development of complex management structures. They do not, then, regard themselves a as managers; as entrepreneurs they are inclined to abdicate responsibility for the welfare of their workers since they define the employment relationship strictly in terms of the wage nexus. They are likely to offer few formal fringe benefits and all their decisions are legitimated by reference to the market.[41] Workers are seen to be responsible, in the last instance, for their own wellbeing; if they are dissatisfied, they can seek employment elsewhere or take the necessary risks and start their own businesses.[42]

Generally, they subscribe to anti-bureaucratic beliefs and are strongly committed to the virtues of the market economy. They are opposed to government intervention in the economy since the market guarantees business efficiency and encourages the 'survival of the fittest'. Entrepreneurial owner-directors are dedicated to work and rarely participate in community activities. Some of these points were reflected in the comments of the following respondents:

> It's not profitable to have your own direct labour because you've got to motivate them. Subcontractors get a price for a job, you let them do it and pay the price . . . They're more go-getting and at their age they're prepared to work harder. They're bringing up families and all the rest of it. That's generally the pattern that I see . . . Even apprentices don't stay loyal to the company where they qualified. They leave to seek their own fortune . . . There's one-and-a-half million out of work. They are the unemployable − they don't intend to work . . . I can guarantee that what the Job Centre send me for interview is not worth employing . . . They're troublemakers . . . They only come because they've been unemployed for so many weeks they've got to take a job just to satisfy the labour exchange . . . I think the government ought to make it easier for small businesses to survive. The amount of paperwork and returns which we have to deal with is getting depressing . . . They should forget all the forms, take them away from us and let us get on with it . . . All this employment protection and the jungle of paperwork and problems we have − the government should just leave us alone.
> (418H)

> With the health and safety legislation they are asking for an impossibility. With the employment protection . . . there's a lot of people wasting their time needlessly. And it's costing the government and the employers a lot of money in situations which would never have arisen had the Act not been enforced. When it comes to planning permission and building regulations, there's far too much bureaucracy. Things could be dealt with in a much quicker manner . . . Private monopolies are no better nor worse than government monopolies. All of them tend to be rather inefficient. If the competition is not there and you know you can't go elsewhere . . . they're going to be able to say exactly how you can go about doing business with them. They ask you for your money first . . . Some industries should be de-nationalised and broken down into smaller units. Then, you might get a little bit more competition and efficiency.　　　(406B)

Government interference with any industry is totally wrong. We were concerned over the last couple of years whether we were going to be nationalised . . . because I don't think the government can run the business as efficiently as people who know the business and know what they are doing . . . Unions have got far too much control . . . they've got overinvolved with running the country and that's not what they're to do. They should stick to negotiating fair wages and conditions for the worker. We should leave it all to the market. (419I)

In private business your own money is on the table largely. If it folds you've lost your job . . . Ever since the war people have said that it's difficult to start your own business but people have started. People who come out of school with nothing have now got big businesses. I'm sure for a man of enterprise and intelligence, opportunities will always be there – until we get a communist state! An essential freedom is the freedom to come and go as you please. I'm glad to see we've got back the freedom to be able to move capital about, in and out of the country . . . There's been a tendency to rely far too much upon central state planning.   (417G)

(3) Paternal

Five of the owner-directors may be regarded as paternal. All of them had inherited long-established businesses.[43] The history of their companies could be traced over several decades during which time their expansion had been either slow or non-existent. Their orientation to the market was low. Despite this, they have developed control systems within which paternalism was used as the predominant strategy. Despite the existence of formal rules there is, among paternal owner-directors in general, a heavy reliance upon the social obligations of the employment relationship which extends beyond the cash nexus. In return for employee loyalty, they are concerned for their general welfare. Consequently, these owner-directors regard their businesses as more than solely profit-making economic enterprises. Instead they are seen to have important *social* obligations to employees, customers and the wider society. As a result, many feel it is their duty to be involved in voluntary, community-based associations. State functions are seen to have grown by 'default' because of the failure of employers to satisfactorily fulfil their wider responsibilities. Many of the state's activities are either 'unnecessary' or are a potential 'threat' to individual liberty which could be reduced, they argue, if employers developed a more 'caring' approach. These points were emphasised by a number of our respondents:

> This is a very liberal and generous firm. We treat the staff at all levels as best we can. To stay competitive in our business we treat the staff as best we can . . . We're fortunate that we have a large number of men who were brought up in the old school . . . Their attitude is that they'll give eight hours' work for eight hours' pay, whereas the younger men are not interested . . . Recently, one of our managers – a very pleasant chap and a very good worker – wanted to buy a new car and was a bit short of cash so we lent him the money at very favourable rates . . . We'll do that for a good worker . . . We're currently looking at the idea of joining all the senior managers into BUPA, again, as a perk . . . We've got a good bunch of people working here. They like to work for us because of this homely attitude. They're not under constant pressure, I mean we demand efficiency but we don't ask them to sweat blood . . . Our men are in demand – our tradesmen in particular . . . they're snapped up . . . We believe in training . . . The founder-owner was very keen on putting back into the industry something in way of helping the young and it's a policy we still follow very carefully, even now. We have an above-average number of apprentices . . . People at our firm have to be trained and taught that they don't have to strike to get a rise . . . They will get a rise for good work. When our profit figures for the current financial year are produced, our first thoughts, as administrators, will concern how we are going to share that in salary reviews, bonuses, fringe benefits and perks . . . We have an annual dinner and dance for our staff including the related companies within the little empire . . . and we do have a few social functions which are mainly aimed to link the staff together more than anything else, to be quite honest. (414E)

> As a business in the town we do have a role to fill. We certainly do our best in terms of supporting local charities, for instance, and supporting the local chamber of commerce, and doing our bit generally towards the local scene. I think it's true to say that a business like this sees this as a responsibility more so than a branch of a big public company. People prefer this sort of set-up than working for a big public company. I sit, deliberately, right in the middle of this office block on the ground floor. The door is always

open and I know everybody in this business and they just pop in and out . . . I think they would say this is the reason why they like to work for this sort of outfit.   (408D)

There are, of course, things one tries to support locally . . . You just do what seems right to support the local issues as they crop up. But apart from that one first needs to be recognised as providing an honourable service, a good quality result and something that is value for money . . . My father and grandfather were mayors . . . I've been involved in the local trade association . . . particularly in the field of training . . . This, I think, is putting something back into what one's drawing out of the capital of the industry.   (420J)

(4) Family Custodial

Only one respondent in our study could be regarded as a family custodial owner-director. Such enterprises tend to have been in existence for several generations but will have experienced little growth over recent times. Through either choice or competence, these owner-directors control companies which have a low market orientation and poorly-developed organisational structures. They represent examples of companies where ownership is passed to heirs who are not committed to business growth. In such firms, there is a tendency for paternalism to prevail and for traditional and well-established practices to persist regardless of their operating efficiency. Further, they tend to delegate many of their control functions to well-trusted, long-serving managers in order that their own business involvement can be limited. Consequently, they often cultivate life styles based upon community organisations, local politics and various cultural activities. In this way, inherited family assets are used to enable owner-directors to develop 'gentlemanly' life styles; they are often the patrons of local cultural and artistic interests. The implications for their enterprises of these preferences are significant; unless a more committed, business-oriented heir or manager takes over, the company either declines or is bought by another firm. Although there was only one such enterprise in our own study, it did possess many of these features as the following comments of its owner-director suggest:

I've no intention to expand the business . . . It's bloody hard work keeping still, let alone expanding . . . The returns from business are pretty low and sometimes it hardly seems worthwhile keeping it going . . . It's a dodgy business but, to some extent, we're protected by our land bank which we've been gradually building on for over thirty years . . . We once used management consultants but all they did was come in and tell us about our own problems which we knew already! . . . I probably know about eighty per cent of my workmen by name but this side of the business is dying out – people just don't want to get themselves involved in that manner. We don't run a social club or anything like that – the personal factor is more important . . . I work between nine and five and don't really want to have too much to do with the business after that . . . For a company of this size you have to work in it to ensure things run properly although I'm considering bringing in a good manager to run things . . . These days the opportunities for small businesses are limited . . . Big Business has got too big but nothing can really be done about it – after all, I suppose the goal of industry is to expand . . . I'm fairly active locally in the golf club and the speakers' club and I also like to spend quite a bit of time in the community. (416B)

These, then, are the four types of owner-director that may be identified. Although the categories are rather crude they illustrate how an interplay of 'market orientation' and 'control strategy' is conducive to different managerial styles. Despite these differences there is, however, an inherent tension within *all* owner-director enterprises brought about by the need to retain *personal* ownership and yet develop *social* forms of control. These become more acute as their businesses expand, such that ownership, as well as control, becomes a social function because there is a growing need for capital which owner-directors are increasingly unable to meet. Thus, the logic of capital accumulation demands that owner-directors socialise partially, if not always wholly, the ownership function by going public. Such a process was under way in one of the largest companies that we studied:

One of the reasons for going public is so that the company can become more broad-based. That's very important indeed in our business because finance plays a number one role and it's a large financing operation. If you are a family company you're very limited in terms of finance. There's the bank and so on, but people are reluctant to lend you too much money because the security isn't quite as strong as it is with a public company. Once you're a public company there are many avenues of finance and, from the lender's point of view, far greater securities.   (423H)

This discussion completes the presentation of our empirical data. We hope to have demonstrated that our four types of business owner – the self-employed, small employers, owner-controllers and owner-directors – are characterised by distinct market and employment relationships. Indeed, the manner in which they cope with these largely determines the survival of their enterprises and their membership of the entrepreneurial middle class. It is, then, now appropriate to summarise briefly our evidence and broaden our discussion to consider, once again, the reproduction of the entrepreneurial middle class in modern society. This is the task of our concluding chapter.

Notes

1. The terms are, of course, derived from Weber's classic discussion of charismatic, traditional and legal domination. See H. H. Gerth and C. W. Mills (eds.), *From Max Weber*, London, 1961. For an empirical case study drawing upon Weber's theoretical framework see A. W. Gouldner, *Patterns of Industrial Bureaucracy*, New York, 1954.

2. H. Newby, 'Paternalism and Capitalism' in R. Scase (ed.), *Industrial Society: Class, Cleavage and Control*, London, 1977, p. 72.

3. As Newby points out there are exceptions to the rule. See ibid. and for case studies, T. Lane and K. Roberts, *Strike at Pilkington's*, London, 1971; R. Martin and R. H. Fryer, *Redundancy and Paternalist Capitalism*, London, 1973.

4. This use of the paternalist strategy is quite different from that observed amongst East Anglian farmers who are able to draw upon relatively abundant supplies of labour. See H. Newby, C. Bell, D. Rose and P. Saunders, *Property, Paternalism and Power*, London, 1978.

5. See A. Friedman, *Industry and Labour*, London, 1977.

6. The number of proprietors exceeds the number of enterprises because in three cases companies were jointly owned and controlled. In all twelve enterprises, ownership was extremely concentrated. Only in three companies did it extend beyond three individuals but in each of these cases family members owned over 60 per cent of the shares. In addition to the interviews referred to in the text, two owner-director wives were separately interviewed.

7. Most of the senior managers were non-shareholding directors responsible either for a particular function (e.g. marketing, finance, etc.) or a specific division or subsidiary (e.g. contracts, joinery, etc.).

8. In this chapter the twelve enterprises studied are identified by a letter placed after the number of the respondents.

9. The problems of delegation are discussed in the *Report of the Committee of Inquiry on Small Firms*, (The Bolton Report), Cmnd 4811, London, 1971, Chapter 10. See also, the discussion of the 'power culture' common amongst small firms in C. Handy, *Understanding Organisations* (2nd edn), Harmondsworth, 1981, pp. 178–9.

10. See *Report of the Committee of Inquiry on Small Firms*, (The Bolton Report), Chapters 2, 10; Handy, *Understanding Organisations*, pp. 178–9, 185–8.

11. T. Burns and G. M. Stalker, *The Management of Innovation*, London, 1961.

12. Ibid., p. 121.

13. Ibid.

14. See, in particular, the discussion in Tavistock Institute of Human Relations, *Interdependence and Uncertainty: A Study of the Building Industry*, London, 1966.

15. C. Foster, *Building with Men*, London, 1969, p. 128.

16. See Handy, *Understanding Organisations*, Chapters 4 and 7.

17. Ibid., p. 179.

18. Some of these issues are discussed by reference to empirical material in M. Stanworth and J. Curran, *Management Motivation in the Smaller Business*, Epping, 1973.

19. There are, of course, other considerations which influence whether or not subsidiary companies are established; in particular, the tax situation of individual enterprises is of some importance. See R. Scase and R. Goffee, *The Real World of the Small Business Owner*, London, 1980.

20. For a detailed analysis of employee selection practices in small firms see J. Curran and J. Stanworth, 'Self-selection and the Small Firm Worker – a Critique and an Alternative View', *Sociology*, vol. 13, 1979a.

21. See *Report of the Committee of Inquiry on Small Firms*, (The Bolton Report), Chapter 2 and M. Stanworth and J. Curran 'Growth and the Small Firm – An Alternative View', *Journal of Management Studies*, vol. 13, 1976.

22. See Chapter 3.

23. This reflects once again the general inability to extend *real* control over the work process in building.

24. For an extensive discussion of these issues see J. Boswell, *The Rise and Decline of Small Firms*, London, 1973.

25. National Economic Development Office, *How Flexible is Construction?*, London, 1978, p. 20.

26. Direct Labour Collective, *Building with Direct Labour*, London, 1978, p. 47.

27. See Friedman, *Industry and Labour*.

28. Ibid., pp. 114–15.

29. Direct Labour Collective, *Building with Direct Labour*, p. 47.

30. Ibid., p. 42.

31. Ibid., p. 43.

32. For evidence see E. H. Phelps Brown, *Report of the Committee of Inquiry into Certain Matters Concerning Labour in Building and Civil Engineering*, Department of Employment and Productivity, Cmnd 3714, London, 1968; National Economic Development Office, *How Flexible is Construction?*, Evidence from an interim report of a survey recently conducted by the Office of Population and Census Surveys for the Construction Industry Manpower Board apparently constitutes 'a devastating indictment of the working conditions and labour practices experienced by building workers'. See 'Lumping It', *New Society*, 13 March 1980, p. 553.

33. For a general discussion of dual labour markets see P. B. Doeringer and M. J. Piore, *Internal Labour Markets and Manpower Analysis*, Lexington, Mass., 1971. The model has recently been applied to the analysis of women by R. D. Barron and G. M. Norris, 'Sexual Divisions and the Dual Labour Market' in D. L. Barker and S. Allen (eds.), *Dependence and Exploitation in Work and Marriage*, London, 1976.

34. See Direct Labour Collective, *Building with Direct Labour*, p. 56.

35. Proprietors' attitudes to the employment of labour are reported in R. Clifton and C. Tatton-Brown, *Impact of Employment Legislation on Small Firms*,

Research Paper No. 6, Department of Employment, 1979.

36. See Stanworth and Curran, 'Growth and the Small Firm'; Handy, *Understanding Organisations*, pp. 178–9;

37. There is an extensive literature on the autonomy sought by those in managerial and professional occupations. Two well known empirical investigations are M. Dalton, *Men Who Manage*, New York, 1959; S. Cotgrove and S. Box, *Science, Industry and Society*, London, 1970.

38. For an illuminating discussion of the linkages between 'business' and 'social' life in one local community see M. Stacey, *Tradition and Change: a Study of Banbury*, Oxford, 1960.

39. For an analysis of the marital strategies pursued by business students in France and the associated gains in 'social', 'economic' and 'cultural' capital, see J. Marceau, 'Marriage, Role Division and Social Cohesion: the Case of Some French Upper-middle Class Families' in Barker and Allen (eds.), *Dependence and Exploitation in Work and Marriage.*

40. They subscribed, therefore, to the 'corporatist' ideal. For a general discussion see J. T. Winkler, 'Corporatism', *European Journal of Sociology*, vol. 17, 1976.

41. 'Informal' fringe benefits (e.g. shorter working hours when jobs are completed; personal use of building materials, etc.) granted at the discretion of owner-controllers are, however, more common.

42. It should be stressed that these attitudes are not confined to the building industry. For evidence of similar practices in another sector of the personal services see, G. Mars and P. Mitchell, *Room for Reform: a Case Study of Industrial Relations in the Hotel Industry* (Open University Industrial Relations Post-Experience Course, Unit 6), Milton Keynes, 1976.

43. These enterprises often had their own 'in-house' magazines and three had commissioned short histories tracing the formation and development of the family business.

8 CONCLUSIONS: ENTREPRENEURSHIP AND THE MIDDLE CLASS

The middle class has long been the subject of conceptual dispute, if only because it includes a diversity of occupational groups which display a range of attitudes, beliefs and life styles. Marxist definitions, which place particular emphasis upon the extent to which a class 'in itself' may, under certain circumstances, evolve into a class 'for itself', question whether the concept 'middle class' can even be used at all.[1] This is because Marxists are primarily concerned with the designation of classes as forces of struggle and, hence, of social change. Most sociologists, on the other hand, normally use the term to describe non-manual occupations.[2] Thus, in this study we hope to have located — on the basis of a materially-grounded theoretical framework — some of the key sources of diversity within the middle class.[3] Consequently, despite the existence of various forms of differentiation, it is possible to identify *two* major sources of cleavage.

First, it is helpful to distinguish between the use of *capital* and *labour* as resources for determining life chances.[4] This, in turn, enables the middle class to be separated into its *entrepreneurial* and *salaried* components. The former, at the most simple level, utilises *both* capital *and* labour for the purpose of economic gain. The latter, by contrast, are essentially wage labourers and although they possess marketable skills, they work within organisations owned by others, whether they be private, family-owned enterprises, state bureaucracies or multi-national corporations. Thus, the crucial difference between the *entrepreneurial* and the *salaried* middle class is that whereas the former are owners of capital and (except for the self-employed) *buyers* of labour, the latter are *sellers* of their labour power.[5] Upward mobility within the *entrepreneurial* middle class, then, is in terms of the degree to which proprietors extend their ownership over an increasing volume of capital assets and exercise control over larger amounts of labour. Entailed in this process of capital accumulation are a number of factors of which the *employment relationship* is one of the most crucial. For the *salaried* middle class, on the other hand, upward mobility is by way of increases in earnings and positional promotion within organisations. This is obtained through the acquisition of marketable skills and work experience.[6]

185

Secondly, it is possible to differentiate between the *established* and the *marginal* sectors of the middle class.[7] Some actors are more permanently *structured* within the middle class than others; a factor which is reflected in both intra- and inter-generational mobility patterns. As far as the entrepreneurial sector is concerned, *structuration* is largely determined by the amount of capital assets utilised. In our terms, *owner-directors* and *owner-controllers* are more firmly rooted within the middle class than either *small employers* or the *self-employed*. Although the latter positions provide avenues of mobility out of the working class, there are a number of factors that prevent further personal advancement through entrepreneurship. These tend to hinge around the employment relationship and, in particular, the extent to which proprietors can cease, themselves, to be direct producers and become solely 'capitalists' and supervisors of labour.[8] In other words, until their enterprises are firmly *structured* upon *capital* rather than *labour*, the position of proprietors within the middle class is tenuous. Thus, the *marginal* sector of the entrepreneurial middle class is characterised by relatively high rates of both inter- and intra-generational mobility.[9] Because there are few capital assets which can be inter-generationally transmitted, the life chances of the children of small employers and the self-employed are little better than those of property-less employees.[10] Among owner-directors and owner-controllers, on the other hand, the likelihood of children experiencing downward mobility is less because they typically inherit capital which can be used for the purposes of entrepreneurial, professional and other forms of self-advancement.[11] Thus, capital is the crucial resource of the *established* entrepreneurial middle class and it is hardly surprising that it should be the basis for attitudes and beliefs that differ significantly from those found within the salaried middle class.[12] It is in this sector, for example, that resistance to state legislation affecting property ownership and transmission – such as capital transfer, wealth and inheritance taxes – is most vehement.[13]

It is similarly possible to differentiate between the *established* and *marginal* components of the salaried middle class. The basis for this distinction, however, is not capital ownership but credentialism; that is, the possession of academic, professional and technical qualifications. Consequently, the *established* salaried middle class consists of administrators, managers, highly-qualified scientists and employee professionals, while the *marginal* includes various routine non-manual, lower-professional, supervisory and technical workers. It is this *marginal* sector that has expanded most rapidly during the post-war era,

providing avenues of upward mobility for working class children.[14] At
the same time, however, an alleged process of proletarianisation has led
to claims that the division between the *established* and *marginal* sectors
of the salaried middle class has widened.[15]

It can be argued that the position of the *established* entrepreneurial
middle class is more firmly structured than its salaried counterpart.
Although among the latter, inter-generational class, inheritance is high,
credentials cannot be transmitted within families as easily as capital.[16]
Whereas, on the whole, the state legally protects private property
ownership and, hence, the inter-generational transmission of capital,
there is no such provision for credentialism.[17] This is so, despite
'reformist' attempts to reduce the concentration of capital ownership
through tax legislation. Indeed, the sociological implications of legal
title to property have been seriously under-researched in view of their
far-reaching effects on the dynamics of class structure.[18] Sociologists
have correctly emphasised the importance of control relationships
within the productive process and their obvious similarities in family,
joint-stock and state-owned enterprises but in so doing, they have
neglected the social and economic consequences of legal ownership for
which this control is exercised.[19] These differences highlight the
distinctive structural premanence of the *established* entrepreneurial
middle class by comparison with its salaried counterpart. Owner-
directors and owner-controllers can, inthe last analysis, pass on their
capital assets to their children. Salaried managers, by contrast, may
similarly control productive resources but they cannot transmit these
to their heirs. This crucial difference in the relation to property
ownership is a major source of cleavage within the middle class; indeed,
it could be argued that it questions the extent to which proprietors
and salaried managers can be subsumed within the same class. However,
since both exercise control in the productive process and enjoy many
common privileges, each can be reasonably regarded as 'middle class'.[20]

We have, then, outlined two major dimensions of cleavage within the
middle class which produce on the one hand, the *entrepreneurial* and
the *salaried* and on the other, the *established* and the *marginal.* These
distinctions, it should be emphasised, are structured within the
productive process rather than upon patterns of consumption and may
be illustrated, albeit in a crude manner, as shown in Table 8.1.[21]

Obviously, these are not 'watertight' compartments;[22] there are
many positions that are in the interstice between the entrepreneurial
and salaried sectors. Many 'classical' occupations of the *established*
middle class, for example, those of the 'independent' professions

Table 8.1: Typology of the Middle Class

	Entrepreneurial	Salaried
Established	Active proprietors of productive assets, for example: (A) Owner-directors (B) Owner-controllers	Managers, professionals and highly-qualified technical employees
Marginal	Active proprietors of petty productive assets, for example: (A) Small employers (B) Self-employed	Lower-grade managerial, professional, technical and routine non-manual employees

(solicitors, accountants, private doctors, etc.), may be regarded as of this sort.[23] Similarly, within the *marginal* sector, 'freelancers' – for example, many journalists, writers, photographers, sales consultants and franchise holders – occupy a comparable intermediate location.[24] Nevertheless, in a general sense, the typology does enable us to identify cleavages within the middle class – related as these are to positions within the occupational structure – that account for the diversity of 'middle class' life styles, attitudes and beliefs.

In our own analysis the focus has been upon the entrepreneurial middle class and, specifically, the processes whereby it is reproduced. This, in turn, has led to an examination of those sectors of the economy where there are ongoing possibilities for small-scale capital accumulation by which wage-labourers may be upwardly-mobile through proprietorship. Four different categories of business ownership have been identified which enable the investigation of paths of entrepreneurial mobility and the identification of major divisions within the accumulation process. Thus, proprietorship offers opportunities for upward mobility for those who are unable to obtain entry into various salaried middle class occupations. This is not a novel assertion; several writers have emphasised the importance of self-employment and small-scale proprietorship as avenues of self-advancement for deprived and disadvantaged groups.[25] As such, proprietorship has been seen to appeal to various 'subordinate' or 'marginal' groups because it offers an alternative to the experience of deprivation in the labour market. However, these 'escape' routes are more available in some sectors of the economy than others; where production is labour-intensive as, for example, in the building industry, conditions are particularly favourable for self-employment and small business formation. Similarly, the growth of personal services, subcontracting and the increasingly important 'black economy', continue to provide contexts within which small-scale business enterprises are likely to emerge. In view of this, current Marxist analyses, entwined as they are in debates about *stages, forms* and *modes* of production, are largely unhelpful in describing these *ongoing* empirical processes. Of course, it must be accepted that modern societies are increasingly characterised by the domination of large-scale corporations that determine the parameters within which small-scale capital accumulation occurs. Nevertheless, the social and economic processes conducive to the formation of small businesses and, hence, to the reproduction of proprietorship need to be further explored. As we have shown, the persistence of labour-intensive production continues to provide opportunities for small business formation. Further, managerial attempts to extend *real* control over the work process can provoke *individual* rather than *collective* resistance. In response to attempts to curtail their autonomy, employees can 'opt out' of the capitalist work process and become self-employed proprietors.

Proprietorship, however, does not constitute an 'open' avenue for upward mobility; there are divisions that constitute substantial barriers to the movement from one form of proprietorship to another. Thus, as we have attempted to demonstrate in this book, there are a number of *social* as well as *financial* and *market* factors which limit sustained capital accumulation.[26] Within the labour-intensive sectors of the economy where most small business are formed, these factors surround the employment relationship. Problems inherent in the management and supervision of employees severely limit the upward mobility of proprietors through small-scale capital accumulation. The self-employed, for example, trade with their labour and, as former employees, frequently lack the skills necessary for the purposes of supervision. Similarly, small employers and, to some extent, owner-controllers encounter problems in the employment of staff which limit their potential for, and predisposition to, business growth. Unable to extract sufficient economic surplus from their employees' labour, they fail to acquire further capital assets and, therefore, to be upwardly-mobile within the entrepreneurial middle class.

These problems can be attributed to three major factors. First, there is the proprietors' own occupational experience; many lack the 'technical' skills of management which their *salaried* equivalents have acquired. Only those previously employed as managers have the necessary expertise to cope with the large-scale employment of labour. Secondly, one of the more important motives for proprietorship is a desire to escape the constraints of employment. Thus, for the self-employed, work autonomy is a major goal; to employ labour not only creates problems of supervision but infringes upon this autonomy. Similarly, small employers are, in a sense, *self-employed with employees* since they have often hired labour only because of obligations to customers. Essentially, they value productive work and can often only cope with the employment relationship by *acting* as fellow employees and cultivating a strategy of fraternalism. Thirdly, the employment relationship can be an obstacle to business growth because it is shrouded in *distrust*. There is a widespread view, shared by many proprietors, that the employment of labour *inevitably* creates managerial difficulties and consequently, they are often reluctant to expand their enterprises.[27] Thus, increased production and additional profits may only be pursued if they do not require the recruitment of extra staff. It is for these reasons that subcontracting is so attractive to many proprietors; in addition to 'offloading' a number of administrative overheads and financial costs, it enables them to abdicate partially, if not wholly, many facets of the employer role.[28] Clearly, then, the employment relationship is a major determinant of cleavage within the entrepreneurial middle class. Our own typology of proprietors is based upon their work role as this, in turn, is related to distinct employment relationships. In this sense, the four types provide the basis for a sociological understanding of small business growth and, therefore, of the entrepreneurial middle class.

We have, then, outlined the processes which explain the reproduction of the entrepreneurial middle class, described its various subcategories and shown how it offers a channel for individual mobility. It is now necessary to summarise the major functions that the entrepreneurial middle class fulfils within the modern economy before, finally, suggesting directions for future research. First, and most importantly, the entrepreneurial middle class legitimates private property ownership. As a class it consists of proprietors who own varying amounts of property and capital assets; thus, any upward mobility through entrepreneurship entails the *further* acquisition of assets through the accumulation process. However, as we have argued, the commitment to private property ownership is not uniform among *all* proprietors. The self-employed and small employers own few assets and their overall dependence upon labour power can often generate ambivalent and even oppositional attitudes towards private property ownership. Among owner-controllers and owner-directors, by contrast, there are no such uncertainties; their commitment to the 'natural right' of property inheritance and the inter-generational transmission of resources is unswerving. The entrepreneurial middle class, then, legitimates personal ownership if only because without it, proprietorship would cease to exist; there would be no privately-owned resources available for the purposes of production and capital accumulation.

Secondly, the entrepreneurial middle class upholds the capitalist economy because proprietors use their assets for the purposes of producing commodities which are sold in the *market*. This material circumstance is reflected at an ideological level in their commitment to 'risk', 'chance', the virtues of 'free competition' and their opposition to the growth of the state, trade unions and business monopolies which are seen to challenge their conditions of existence. However, despite this ideological commitment, proprietors often cultivate strategies designed to subvert the market even though they are dependent upon it for their survival.

Thirdly, small-scale proprietorship sustains capitalist society by providing a potential channel of upward mobility for deprived groups within the occupational structure. Although resentment is often expressed in a collective manner, it can also be articulated through various individual strategies. Thus, resentment generated by factors associated with the logic of capital accumulation can lead to individual responses that reinforce the reproduction of this same dynamic. Although subjectively the self-employed and small employers may express 'antagonistic' and even 'oppositional' sentiments, *objectively* they are attached to the logic of capital accumulation through their commitment to the petty production of goods and services for the market. Proprietorship, then, offers an avenue of mobility for those excluded from entry into the *salaried* middle class. If, through lack of credentials or explicit discrimination, some groups are less able to compete equally with others for occupational preferment, the market provides an apparently 'open' alternative. It offers the promise that personal success will be primarily related to the producer's capacity to provide goods and services for an impersonal and anonymous market. For these reasons, members of minority groups who experience discrimination in the labour market often seek economic gain through proprietorship.

Finally, the entrepreneurial middle class functions to legitimate capitalism by providing a material basis for certain 'system-maintaining' values. Despite sources of differentiation, proprietors tend to emphasise the desirability of the market, personal ownership and profit as the major means whereby resources can be rationally allocated in society.[29] This is reflected on the political plane by the existence of 'rightist' parties which, in turn, shape the parameters of political debate and, thus, core elements of the political culture.[30] Accordingly, forms of collectivism which represent the interests of subordinate groups are often regarded as threats to the 'natural rights' of man.[31]

In view of these points, there would seem to be a number of areas which are appropriate for further research. There is, for instance, a need to explore more fully the reasons why individuals choose to embark upon entrepreneurial careers. What are the specific facets of *employee* resentment and the *particular* attractions of work autonomy that lead to proprietorship?[32] As yet these issues remain largely unexplored, as do the family relationships within which such decisions are typically made. It would be useful, therefore, to investigate more fully the nature of conjugal relationships, the role of savings within the 'immediate' and 'extended' family and the importance of women within small-scale capital accumulation.[33] The formation and growth of *women*-owned enterprises is an almost totally neglected area of research and yet a number of issues might fruitfully be studied.[34] To what extent, for example, are women confronted with greater difficulties in obtaining credit from financial institutions? Further, what problems do they face as employers because of their socially-defined subordinate position in society? In short, what would be the findings of a comparative analysis of business*men* and business*women*?[35]

Further research should also explore differing ideological perspectives within the entrepreneurial middle class as these are linked to various stages in the accumulation process. We have shown how the self-employed and small employers, dependent as they are upon labour rather than capital assets, are more likely to express 'radical' and 'oppositional' attitudes. Our typology of proprietors provides a potential framework within which contradictions and diversities of this sort can be explored. Further, in order to provide results of a more general relevance, it would be desirable to undertake comparative studies of the entrepreneurial middle class. It would, for example, be useful to compare the formation and growth of small businesses between different sectors of the *same* economy as well as to conduct *cross-national* studies.[36] The latter could highlight the extent to which the reproduction of the entrepreneurial middle class is affected by variations in the development of the capitalist mode of production, the role of the state and the emergence of corporatism.[37] The differences between countries in the material conditions under which proprietorship persists and small-scale capital accumulation occurs must be explored if our *general* understanding of the entrepreneurial middle class within present-day capitalist society is to be enhanced.

This leads to our final two points. If fruitful research is to be undertaken, it will be necessary to develop relatively refined theoretical concepts and methodological categories. Hopefully, our own typology could serve as the basis for more detailed analyses, although it needs to be extended and tested within the more capital-intensive sectors of the economy.[38] Further, it must be recognised that a too rigid distinction between *actor* and *position*, as reflected in much research into social mobility, may have some validity in the study of careers within large-scale bureaucratic organisations but is of less value in the study of entrepreneurial careers.[39] As we found in our own research, it is difficult to distinguish between *actor* and *position* if only because proprietorship is 'carved' out of a process of capital accumulation. An *actor* acquires capital which, in turn, determines *position* within the entrepreneurial middle class; they are, in other words, virtually indistinguishable. Although, therefore, it is possible to differentiate conceptually the *category* of self-employed from the *actors* within it, to overstate the distinction is to detract from an understanding of the processes whereby the *actors* themselves contribute to the reproduction of the *positions* which they occupy.

There are, then, methodological problems in the study of the entrepreneurial middle class. Clearly-defined categories useful for the purposes of measuring upward and downward mobility within the accumulation process are largely absent. Of course, there are a number of conventional measures — such as number of employees, value of capital assets utilised and level of annual turnover — but these do little to enhance the *sociological* understanding of proprietorship.[40] The use of such measures is analogous to attempting to understand salary and wage earners solely by reference to their levels of income. What is needed, therefore, is the formulation of a methodology derived from the study of the entrepreneurial middle class and designed for its further research. In this context qualitative methods of the sort that we have used may be more appropriate than solely quantitative measures, if only because they encourage a contextual approach within which the social as well as economic dimensions of proprietorship and small-scale capital accumulation can be understood.[41] Comparative anlaysis, on the basis of qualitative research could, then, make a useful contribution to existing knowledge of the dynamics which determine the reproduction of the entrepreneurial middle class.

Notes

1. See Chapter 1.
2. This once included routine white-collar work; see, for example, F. Parkin, *Class, Inequality and Political Order*, London, 1971. More recently this category has been excluded but the term retained to refer to a mixture of managerial, professional and technical employees in public and private enterprises. See K. Roberts, F. G. Cook, S. C. Clark and E. Semeonoff, *The Fragmentary Class Structure*, London, 1977; J. Westergaard and H. Resler, *Class in a Capitalist Society*, Harmondsworth, 1976.
3. It should be stressed that our analysis is based upon position in the productive process rather than patterns of consumption or life styles.
4. We use this term to refer to an individual's ability to acquire valued economic and social resources.
5. The *amounts* of capital owned by the self-employed and small employers may only be small, but this does not entirely detract from its significance as a determinant of economic position and social behaviour. To equate petty owners of capital with categories of wage or salary earners is, in our view, unacceptable.
6. For a discussion of (1) the bureaucratic work orientation see J. H. Goldthorpe, D. Lockwood, F. Bechhofer and J. Platt, *The Affluent Worker: Industrial Attitudes and Behaviour*, Cambridge, 1968; (2) the concept of career see H. Wilensky, 'Orderly Careers and Social Participation', *American Sociological Review*, vol. 26, 1961. Two British empirical investigations indicate the central importance of the bureaucratic career for salaried employees. See C. Sofer, *Men in Mid-Career*, Cambridge, 1970; J. M. and R. E. Pahl, *Managers and their Wives*, Harmondsworth, 1972. However, economic recession has recently reduced possibilities for upward mobility through the 'conventional' channels and led to a reassessment of the career concept. See, for example, J. Hearn, 'Towards a Concept of Non-career', *Sociological Review*, vol. 25, 1977.
7. This distinction is derived from that drawn recently by Goldthorpe on the basis of the Oxford social mobility study findings. See J. H. Goldthorpe, 'Comment', *British Journal of Sociology*, vol. 29, 1978b.
8. According to Marx it is only after this transition that the small employer becomes a 'pure' capitalist:

> Capitalist production only then really begins . . . when each individual capital employs simultaneously a comparatively large number of labourers; when consequently the labour process is carried on on an extensive scale and yields, relatively, large quantities of products. A greater number of labourers working together at the same time, in one place (or, if you will, in the same field of labour), in order to produce the same sort of commodity under the mastership of one capitalist, constitutes, both historically and logically, the starting-point of capitalist production . . . the amount of surplus value (thus) produced might suffice to liberate the employer himself from manual labour, to convert him from a small master into a capitalist, and thus formally to establish capitalist production.

K. Marx, *Capital* (vol. 1), London, 1954, pp. 305, 312.
9. See Goldthorpe, 'Comment', p. 437; J. H. Goldthorpe, *Social Mobility and Class Structure in Modern Britain*, Oxford, 1980, Chapters 2, 5 and 9.
10. Ibid.
11. 'Large proprietors and independent professionals . . . will often be in a position to pass on businesses or practices to their sons; and furthermore they . . . are likely to be able to aid their sons' occupational chances substantially by the use of their relatively large incomes and accumulations of wealth – for example,

by buying them a privileged education, extensive training, or indeed a business or practice of their own.' Goldthorpe, *Social Mobility and Class Structure*, p. 100.

12. For a discussion of differing business ideologies amongst directors and senior managers see T. Nichols, *Ownership, Control and Ideology*, London, 1969.

13. A defence of hereditary wealth and critique of state measures which interfere with this transmission can be found in R. Scruton, *The Meaning of Conservatism*, Harmondsworth, 1980.

14. For statistical evidence see, for example, D. V. Glass (ed.), *Social Mobility in Britain*, London, 1954; A. H. Halsey, A. Heath and J. M. Ridge, *Origins and Destinations*, Oxford, 1980; Goldthorpe, *Social Mobility and Class Structure*.

15. See D. Lockwood, *The Blackcoated Worker*, London, 1958; Westergaard and Resler, *Class in a Capitalist Society*; H. Braverman, *Labor and Monopoly Capital*, New York, 1974; Roberts *et al.*, *The Fragmentary Class Structure*.

16. This is not to deny, of course, that the inter-generational transmission of credentials – and other 'cultural resources' – is not well established. See Halsey *et al.*, *Origins and Destinations.*

17. As Parkin points out:

The continuous raising of academic hurdles and certification barriers as a means of controlling entry to the professions carries with it a strong element of risk that large numbers of children from professional families witl not make the grade. The reliance upon written examinations does, as earlier argued, work in favour of those expensively schooled or otherwise socially advantaged, thereby reducing the hazards of competition quite considerably. Nevertheless, that troublesome factor known as intelligence can never quite be ruled out of the reckoning, especially that unknown quantum of it contributed by the throw of the genetic dice. Dense children of the professional middle class, despite heavy investments of cultural capital, will continue to stumble on the intellectual assault course set up largely for their *parents*' own protection.

F. Parkin, *Marxism and Class Theory*, London, 1979, p. 61. If the transmission of credentials can be problematic this is less likely to be so in the case of capital. As Goldthorpe suggests:

the surest advantages and the most decisive barriers in regard to inter-generational class mobility (considered independently of supply and demand factors) are those represented by economic resources and requirements. This is so, firstly, because economic resources can be more reliably transmitted inter-generationally than can cultural or social resources; and secondly, because, unlike the latter, they predominantly take the form of 'exclusive' rather than inclusive goods – that is, ones which if possessed by one party cannot be possessed by another.

Goldthorpe, *Social Mobility and Class Structure*, p. 100.

18. A similar point is made by Westergaard and Resler, *Class in a Capitalist Society*. See also R. E. Pahl and J. T. Winkler, 'The Economic Elite' in P. Stanworth and A. Giddens (eds.), *Elites and Power in British Society*, Cambridge, 1974.

19. This is evident in discussions of 'authority relationships' as well as in comparative analyses which stress the common features of capitalist and state socialist societies. See, for example, R. Dahrendorf, *Class and Class Conflict in Industrial Society*, London, 1959; R. Crompton and J. Gubbay, *Economy and Class Structure*, London, 1977.

20. It could be said, therefore, that they both fulfil the functions of capital. See G. Carchedi, 'On the Economic Identification of the New Middle Class',

Economy and Society, vol. 4, 1975; Crompton and Gubbay, *Economy and Class Structure.*

21. Our typology deliberately excludes, therefore, *rentiers* 'passively' living off revenue.

22. Given the 'closure' of careers within the salaried middle class as a result of economic recession it could be argued that there will be greater intra-generational mobility between the entrepreneurial and salaried sectors. Handy, for example, envisages 'spliced careers' made up of a 'mix of employment and self-employment'. C. Handy, *Understanding Organisations* (2nd edn), Harmondsworth, 1981, p. 401. In this context, recent 'management buy-ups' of companies that would otherwise be liquidated are of particular interest.

23. For these occupations, credentials are obviously important in the sense that it is impossible to work without them. Nevertheless, independent professionals operate in the market where they utilise both their expertise and private capital for the purposes of economic gain.

24. Although apparently 'independent' many freelance workers are little more than subcontractors working for one or two major customers; in a similar manner to the salaried middle class their security and prospects are dependent upon organisations in which they have no ownership stake.

25. For a review of this literature see M. Stanworth and J. Curran, *Management Motivation in the Smaller Business*, Epping, 1973; J. Boissevain, 'Small Entrepreneurs in Changing Europe: Towards a Research Agenda', unpublished paper presented at the European Centre for work and Society, Utrecht, 1980. A recent empirical investigation is reported in H. Aldrich, 'Asian Shopkeepers as a Middleman Minority' in A. Evans and D. Eversley (eds.), *The Inner City: Employment and Industry*, London, 1980.

26. These social factors have an independent causal effect, which is rarely recognised in the literature, on small business formation and growth.

27. In this way media presentation of industrial relations, for example, determines rather than reflects social attitudes and behaviour. For detailed empirical analysis see Glasgow University Media Group, *Bad News*, London, 1977.

28. The autonomy thus granted to subcontractors may, in the long run, allow them to use their expertise and become fully independent. This reinforces the small firm 'dynamic' which we have referred to in earlier chapters.

29. The self-employed in particular, can be 'agnostic' on some of these issues. See Chapter 4.

30. A comparative discussion of the relationship between the entrepreneurial middle class and political parties can be found in S. M. Lipset, *Political Man*, London, 1960. See also F. Bechhofer and B. Elliott, 'The Voice of Small Business and the Politics of Survival', *Sociological Review*, vol. 26, 1978.

31. Such views do not, however, necessarily reflect unqualified support for the existing *status quo*; instead, they may be indicative of a *general* disillusionment with the established social order.

32. It may be possible, for example, to differentiate between new proprietors in terms of their adherence to 'conventional' or 'unconventional' norms and values and their market orientations. This distinction was suggested, during the course of a seminar discussion at the University of Aston, by Professor Colin Bell.

33. Detailed suggestions for further research on these topics are provided in Boissevain, 'Small Entrepreneurs in Changing Europe'.

34. The authors are currently undertaking a small-scale exploratory study of businesswomen with the aid of a grant from the Nuffield Foundation.

35. Reference to work in this area is available in Centre for Women Policy Studies, *Bibliography on Women Entrepreneurs*, Washington, DC, 1974.

36. See F. Bechhofer and B. Elliott (eds.), *The Petite Bourgeoisie*, London, 1981.

37. For an insightful analysis of these themes see, N. Mouzelis, 'Capitalism and the Development of the Greek State' in R. Scase (ed.), *The State in Western Europe*, London, 1980.

38. It must be accepted that financial factors – and, in particular, the availability of credit – are of more significance in capital-intensive sectors. Nevertheless, we would maintain that the dynamics surrounding the employment relationship are often a more important determinant of business formation and growth than credit availability. Evidence of managerial inadequacies within such firms is abundant. See, for example, J. Boswell, *The Rise and Decline of Small Firms*, London, 1973. The role of finance is examined in detail in *The Financing of Small Firms*, (The Wilson Report), Cmnd 7503, London, 1979.

39. For a general discussion of these issues see A. Stewart, K. Prandy and R. Blackburn, *Social Stratification and Occupations*, London, 1980.

40. The shortcomings of statistical definitions of the sort adopted in The Bolton Report are discussed in J. Curran and J. Stanworth, 'Self-selection and the Small Firm Worker – a Critique and an Alternative View', *Sociology*, vol. 13, 1979a.

41. For a discussion and application of this approach see N. Elias and J. L. Scotson, *The Established and the Outsiders*, London, 1965.

METHODOLOGICAL APPENDIX

Methods

As with all social research, the methods adopted in this enquiry were largely dictated by the nature of the research problem. We set out to study the *dynamics* of small-scale capital accumulation and the *social processes* which account for the reproduction of the entrepreneurial middle class. In addition, it was our intention to define more precisely the *nature* and *interrelationships* of the constituent groupings within this class. The complexity of these issues did not favour quantitative investigation; in our view a qualitative approach was more appropriate. This preference was based upon three considerations. First, the research was exploratory; given the dearth of available empirical evidence our aim was to *generate* hypotheses which could subsequently be quantitatively assessed. Secondly, the heterogeneity of the population under investigation would have made it both difficult and expensive to draw an adequate representative sample. Instead, a more practical aim was to document, according to a number of specified criteria, the range and variety of proprietorial positions within the entrepreneurial middle class. Thirdly, the emphasis upon the *dynamics* of accumulation — and the opportunities and constraints generated by the *social relationships* which surround it — encouraged us to adopt research methods which were sufficiently flexible to capture the nature of these processes.

Consequently, we undertook an intensive study of a limited number of proprietors using semi-structured interviews which were, to a considerable extent, shaped by the personal experiences of the respondents. Interviews of this sort are often said to be less reliable than those which are more formally structured and standardised. However, the 'gains' of *reliability* have to be set against the 'losses' in terms of *validity*. Highly structured interviews may simply enable the consistent (and, therefore, reliable) replication of 'meaningless' responses on a large scale. This risk is greater, we would argue, when the issues under investigation are relatively complex and the existing body of knowledge is limited. Of course, the determination of validity cannot be based solely upon 'technical' considerations which apply universally to all types of research. To a large extent, the success of a particular methodology must be assessed in relation to the empirical evidence and theoretical hypotheses which it is able to generate in specific research investigations. Our decision to lay greater emphasis upon the quality, rather than quantity, of the data collected must be judged accordingly.

A Study of Building Proprietors

The data in this study were taken from interviews with business owners and their wives in the building industry. The reasons for selecting this industry are discussed in Chapter 3 and 'basic' information on the respondents and their businesses is given in the various chapters. Here, further details are provided on the way in which the respondents were chosen, the interviews conducted and the material analysed; and the background of the respondents.

Our initial enquiries were limited, for reasons of cost, to Kent-based firms which seemed to fit into each of the four categories of business proprietor. Letters were sent to them explaining the objectives of the research and requesting interviews, which were subsequently arranged by telephone. As a result of these initial contacts, a number of proprietors were excluded because they were specialist labour-only subcontractors. But some proprietors recommended others who might fit our specifications and as a result the 'target' number of 100 respondents equally divided between the four categories was quickly achieved. Our fears that proprietors might be hostile to academic research proved groundless; the overall response rate was 83 per cent.

The interviews were conducted during the summer and autumn of 1979. Most were completed in the respondents' homes although some – particularly those with owner-directors and senior managers – took place at work. The interviews typically lasted between one and three hours. Separate questionnaires were designed for each of the four categories of business owner and all the interviews were tape recorded and later transcribed. In addition, we interviewed twelve wives; as earlier, these were also tape recorded and transcribed.

Every transcript was analysed by both authors and, with 25 male respondents in each category, it was possible to become very familiar with each account. As the selection of the respondents was neither random nor representative the data could not be used for statistical generalisations. Further, the semi-structured nature of the interviews limited the scope for quantitative analysis. But this was because our primary aim was to collect a detailed set of personal accounts which could be used to illustrate the central themes of our research. We feel that the verbatim extracts produced in Chapters 4 and 7 provide valuable insights into the nature of the social processes underlying the formation and growth of small-scale capital and the associated reproduction of the entrepreneurial middle class, probably more so than a sophisticated statistical analysis. We are fully aware, however, that the representativeness of our claims must await a more quantitatively-based research programme.

Despite our emphasis upon personal accounts rather than statistical aggregates, it is possible to present the tabulated information in Table A.1 on the respondents and their businesses.

In addition to the 90 proprietors included in Table A.1, ten senior managers, drawn from four owner-director enterprises, were interviewed. Their evidence provided useful insights into the way in which control was *collectively* exercised within *privately-owned* companies. Of the wives who were interviewed, five were married to self-employed proprietors; five to small employers and two to senior managers in owner-director enterprises. The limits of time and finance prevented further interviews and, given these constraints, we focused primarily upon the wives of the self-employed and small employers who generally made a *direct* contribution to the running of the businesses.

Wherever possible, extracts from the interviews have been reproduced verbatim without any form of editing. However, repetition or exceptionally poor grammar sometimes forced us to alter statements which might otherwise have appeared incomprehensible. In addition, some sections of the extracts have been excluded if they were considered irrelevant to the issue under discussion in the text. Where parts of a statement have been omitted in this manner, it is indicated by (. . .). *Any* form of editing interferes with the authenticity of first-hand accounts; nevertheless, every attempt has been made to retain the original sense and 'feeling' of respondents' statements. This is often difficult when interview evidence and theoretical discussion are inter-woven, but it should be remembered that even those studies which rely almost entirely upon the reproduction of first-hand evidence are highly selective in their procedures.

All statements have been attributed to particular respondents in a numerical fashion in order to preserve their anonymity. This procedure also makes it possible to identify the responses of those individuals who have been quoted more than once. In all, we have used 276 quotations from business proprietors and their wives and their distribution between the four categories is shown in Table A.2.

As every respondent has been cited at least once in the text the

Table A.1: Background Information on the Proprietors and their Businesses

Category of proprietor	Age of proprietor (years)		Age of business (years)		Annual turnover (£)		No. of employees	
	Average	Range	Average	Range	Average	Range	Average	Range
Self-employed (N = 25)	41	31–60	14	1–33	14,100	6,000–25,000	–	–
Small employer (N = 25)	49	35–65	24	4–150	71,700	10,000–250,000	6	1–35
Owner-controller (N = 25)	47	28–77	37	3–90	500,000	100,000–1 million	38	25–125
Owner-director (N = 15)	52	30–68	90	9–250	6 million	1 million–20 million	300	30–1200

Notes: 1. The relatively high average age of the businesses owned by the self-employed and small employers suggests that our sample may be weighted towards well-established enterprises. However, we were able to include in the categories, through personal recommendations, proprietors who had only recently set up businesses. Thus, amongst the self-employed, eight businesses were less than eight years old and among the small employers, seven were less than ten years old. Further, it should be noted that if one enterprise, which was 150 years old, is excluded from the small employer category, the average is reduced to eighteen years. 2. The lower limit of employees in the owner-controller category is explained by the fact that several enterprises made extensive use of subcontractors. Seventeen of the firms in this category did, however, employ at least 25 men on a regular basis.

Table A.2: The Number and Distribution of Quotations

Category of proprietor	No. of quotes
Self-employed	79
Small employers	78
Owner-controllers	58
Owner-directors (and senior managers)	61
Total	276

average number of quotes per person is approximately 2.5. In general, the quotations were deliberately drawn from a wide spread of the respondents; only three individuals have been cited more than five times as Table A.3.indicates.

Table A.3: The Distribution of Quotations

No. of respondents	No. of quotes
42	1
25	2
23	3
11	4
10	5
1	6
1	7
1	8
Total 114	

Note: The total of 114 includes 100 business proprietors and senior managers; 12 wives interviewed separately; and 2 wives present at the original interview with their husbands.

BIBLIOGRAPHY

Aldrich, H., 'Asian Shopkeepers as a Middleman Minority' in A. Evans and D. Eversley (eds.), *The Inner City: Employment and Industry*, London, 1980

Anthony, P. D., *The Ideology of Work*, London, 1977

Bannock, G. and Doran, A., *Small Firms in Cities* (Economics Advisory Group Ltd for Shell UK Ltd), 1978

Barron, R. D. and Norris, G. M., 'Sexual Divisions and the Dual Labour Market' in D. L. Barker and S. Allen (eds.), *Dependence and Exploitation in Work and Marriage*, London, 1976

Batstone, E., 'Deference and the Ethos of Small-town Capitalism' in M. Bulmer (ed.), *Working ClasssImages of Society*, London, 1975

Batstone, E., Boraston, I. and Frenkel, S., *Shop Stewards in Action*, Oxford 1977

Bechhofer, F. and Elliott, B., 'An Approach to a Study of Small Shopkeepers and the Class Structure', *European Journal of Sociology*, vol. 9, 1968

—— 'Persistance and Change: The Petite Bourgeoisie in Industrial Society', *European Journal of Sociology*, vol. 17, 1976

—— 'The Voice of Small Business and the Politics of Survival', *Sociological Review*, vol. 26, 1978

—— 'Petty Property: The Survival of a Moral Economy' in F. Bechhofer and B. Elliott (eds.), *The Petite Bourgeoisie*, London, 1981

—— (eds.), *The Petite Bourgeoisie*, London, 1981

Bechhofer, F., Elliott, B. and McCrone, D., 'Structure, Consciousness and Action', *British Journal of Sociology*, vol. 29, 1978

Bechhofer, F., Elliott, B., Rushforth, M. and Bland, R., 'The Petits Bourgeois in the Class Structure: The Case of the Small Shopkeepers' in F. Parkin (ed.), *The Social Analysis of Class Structure*, London, 1974a

—— 'Small Shopkeepers: Matters of Money and Meaning', *Sociological Review*, vol. 22, 1974b

Bell, C., *Middle Class Families*, London, 1968

Bell, D., *The Coming of Post-Industrial Society*, London, 1974

Bendix, R., *Work and Authority in Industry*, New York, 1956

Bertaux, D. and Bertaux-Wiame, I., 'Artisanal Bakery in France: How it

Lives and Why it Survives' in F. Bechhofer and B. Elliott (eds.), *The Petite Bourgeoisie*, London, 1981

Blackaby, F. (ed.), *De-Industrialisation*, London, 1979

Blackburn, R., 'Social Stratification', unpublished paper presented to BSA Conference, Lancaster, 1980

Bland, R., Elliott, B. and Bechhofer, F., 'Social Mobility in the Petite Bourgeoisie', *Acta Sociologica*, vol. 21, 1978

Blauner, R., *Alienation and Freedom*, Chicago, 1964

Boissevain, J., 'Small Entrepreneurs in Changing Europe: Towards a Research Agenda', unpublished paper presented at the European Centre for Work and Society, Utrecht, 1980

Boswell, J., *The Rise and Decline of Small Firms*, London, 1973

Braverman, H., *Labor and Monopoly Capital*, New York, 1974

Brighton Labour Process Group, 'The Capitalist Labour Process', *Capital and Class*, no. 1, 1977

Brown, R., 'Work' in P. Abrams (ed.), *Work, Urbanism and Inequality*, London, 1978

Brown, W., Ebsworth, R. and Terry, M., 'Factors Shaping Shop Steward Organisation in Britain', *British Journal of Industrial Relations*, vol. 16, 1978

Buchanan, D. A., *The Development of Job Design Theories and Techniques*, Farnborough, 1979

Birgess, R. A. *et al.* (eds.), *The Construction Industry Handbook*, Lancaster, 1973

Burns, T. and Stalker, G. M., *The Management of Innovation*, London, 1961

Buxton, N. and Mackay, D., *British Employment Statistics*, Oxford, 1977

Carchedi, G., 'On the Economic Identification of the New Middle Class', *Economy and Society*, vol. 4, 1975

Centre for Women Policy Studies, *Bibliography on Women Entrepreneurs*, Washington, DC, 1974

Chesterman, M., *Small Businesses*, London, 1977

Chinoy, E., *Automobile Workers and the American Dream*, New York, 1955

Clifton, R. and Tatton-Brown, C., *Impact of Employment Legislation on Small Firms*, Research Paper No. 6, Department of Employment, 1979

Cotgrove, S. and Box, S., *Science, Industry and Society*, London, 1970

Crompton, R., 'Trade Unionism and the Insurance Clerk', *Sociology*, vol. 13, 1979

Crompton, R. and Gubbay, J., *Economy and Class Structure*, London, 1977

Crossick, G., *The Lower Middle Class in Britain*, London, 1977

Crozier, M., *The Bureaucratic Phenomenon*, London, 1964

Curran, J. and Stanworth, J., 'Self-selection and the Small Firm Worker – A Critique and an Alternative View', *Sociology*, vol. 13, 1979a

—— 'Worker Involvement and Social Relations in the Small Firm', *Sociological Review*, vol. 27, 1979b

Dahrendorf, D., *Class and Class Conflict in Industrial Society*, London, 1959

Dalton, M., *Men Who Manage*, New York, 1959

Delphy, C. and Leonard, D., 'The Family as an Economic System', unpublished paper presented to Institutionalisation of Sex Differences Conference, University of Kent, April 1980

Department of Employment, *Yearbook, 1975*

Department of the Environment, *Private Contractors' Construction Census 1976*

—— *Private Contractors.' Construction Census 1978*

Dilnot, A. and Morris, C. N., 'What Do We Know About the Black Economy?', *Fiscal Studies*, vol. 2, 1981

Direct Labour Collective, *Building with Direct Labour*, London, 1978

Doeringer, P. B. and Piore, M. J., *Internal Labour Markets and Manpower Analysis*, Lexington, Mass., 1971

Eden, J. F., 'Mechanisation' in D. A. Turin (ed.), *Aspects of the Economics of Construction*, London, 1975

Elger, T., 'Valorisation and Deskilling', *Capital and Class*, no. 7, 1979

Elias, N. and Scotson, J. L., *The Established and the Outsiders*, London, 1965

Elliott, B. and McCrone, D., 'Landlords in Edinburgh: Some Preliminary Findings', *Sociological Review*, vol. 23, 1975

—— *Property and Power in a City*, London, 1980

The Financing of Small Firms, (The Wilson Report), Cmnd 6703, London, 1979

Flinn, M. W., *Origins of the Industrial Revolution*, London, 1966

Foster, C., *Building with Men*, London, 1969

Fox, A., *Beyond Contract*, London, 1974a

—— *Man Management*, London, 1974b

Francis, A., 'Families, Firms and Finance Capital', *Sociology*, vol. 14, 1980

Friedman, A., *Industry and Labour*, London, 1977

Galbraith, J. K., *The New Industrial State*, Harmondsworth, 1972
Gasson, R., 'Roles of Farm Women in England', unpublished paper, 1980
Gershuny, J., *After Industrial Society*, London, 1978
Gershuny, J. and Pahl, R. E., 'Work Outside Employment: Some Preliminary Speculations', *New Universaities Quarterly*, vol. 34, 1979/80
Gerth, H. H. and Mills, C. W. (eds.), *From Max Weber*, London, 1961
Giddens, A., *The Class Structure of the Advanced Societies*, London, 1973
Glasgow University Media Group, *Bad News*, London, 1977
Glass, D. V. (ed.), *Social Mobility in Britain*, London, 1954
Goldthorpe, J. H., 'The Current Inflation: Towards a Sociological Account' in F. Hirsch and J. H. Goldthorpe (eds.), *The Political Economy of Inflation*, London, 1978a
—— 'Comment', *British Journal of Sociology*, vol. 29, 1978b
—— *Social Mobility and Class Structure in Modern Britain*, Oxford, 1980
Goldthorpe, J. H., Lockwood, D., Bechhofer, F. and Platt, J., *The Affluent Worker: Industrial Attitudes and Behaviour*, Cambridge, 1968
—— *The Affluent Worker in the Class Structure*, Cambridge, 1969
Gouldner, A. W., *Patterns of Industrial Bureaucracy*, New York, 1954
Halsey, A. H., Heath, A. and Ridge, J. M., *Origins and Destinations*, Oxford, 1980
Handy, C., *Understanding Organisations* (2nd edn), Harmondsworth, 1981
Hannah, L., *The Rise of the Corporate Economy*, London, 1975
Hannah, L. and Kay, J., *Concentration in Modern Industry*, London, 1977
Health and Safety Executive: Construction: *Health and Safety 1976*, London, 1978
Hearn, J., 'Towards a Concept of Non-Career', *Sociological Review*, vol. 25, 1977
Heath, A., *Social Mobility*, Glasgow, 1981
Higgin, G. and Jessop, N., *Communications in the Building Industry*, London, 1965
Hillebrandt, P. M., *Small Firms in the Construction Industry*, Research Report No. 10 (commissioned by The Bolton Committee), London, 1971
—— *Economic Theory and the Construction Industry*, London, 1974

Hilton, W. S., *Industrial Relations in Construction*, London, 1968

Hyman, R., *Strikes*, London, 1972

Ingham, G. K., *Size of Industrial Organisation and Worker Behaviour*, Cambridge, 1970

Jackson, J. A. (ed.), *Professions and Professionalisation*, Cambridge, 1970

Jenkins, A., *On Site, 1921–71*, London, 1971

Jessop, R., 'The Transformation of the State in Post-War Britain' in R. Scase (ed.), *The State in Western Europe*, London, 1980

Johnson, T., 'The Professions in the Class Structure' in R. Scase (ed.), *Industrial Society: Class, Cleavage and Control*, London, 1977

King, R. and Nugent, N. (eds.), *Respectable Rebels*, London, 1979

Klein, J., *Samples from English Culture*, London, 1965

Kumar, K., *Prophecy and Progress*, Harmondsworth, 1978

Lane, T. and Roberts, K., *Strike at Pilkington's*, London, 1971

Lenin, V. I., *Collected Works* (vol. 22), London, 1949

—— *The Development of Capitalism in Russia*, Moscow, 1956

Lipset, S. M., *Political Man*, London, 1960

Lockwood, D., *The Blackcoated Worker*, London, 1958

Lockwood, D. and Goldthorpe, J. H., 'The Manual Worker: Affluence, Aspirations, Assimilation', BSA Conference Paper, 1962 cited in G. MacKenzie, 'The Affluent Worker' Study: An Evaluation and Critique', in F. Parkin (ed.), *The Social Analysis of Class Structure*, London, 1974

Macafee, K., 'A Glimpse of the Hidden Economy in the National Accounts', *Economic Trends*, March 1980

McClelland, D. C., *The Achieving Society*, New York, 1961

McHugh, J., 'The Self-employed and the Small Independent Entrepreneur' in R. King and N. Nugent (eds.), *Respectable Rebels*, London, 1979

Mackenzie, G., *The Aristocracy of Labour*, Cambridge, 1973

Marceau, J., 'Marriage, Role Division and Social Cohesion: The Case of Some French Upper-middle Class Families' in D. Barker and S. Allen (eds.), *Dependence and Exploitation in Work and Marriage*, London, 1976

Mars, G. and Mitchell, P., *Room for Reform: a Case Study of Industrial Relations in the Hotel Industry* (Open University Industrial Relations Post-Experience Course, Unit 6), Milton Keynes, 1976

Martin, J. and Norman, A. R. D., *The Computerized Society*, Englewood Cliffs, New Jersey, 1970

Martin, R. and Fryer, R. H., *Redundancy and Paternalist Capitalism*, London, 1973

Marx, K., *Capital* (vol. 1), London, 1954

Marx, K. and Engels, F., 'The Communist Manifesto' (1848) in K. Marx and F. Engels, *Selected Works*, London, 1968

Mayer, A. J., 'The Lower Middle Class as Historical Problem', *Journal of Modern History*, vol. 47, 1975

Mayer, K., 'Business Enterprise: The Traditional Symbol of Opportunity', *British Journal of Sociology*, vol. 4, 1953

Merrett Cyriax Associates, *Dynamics of Small Firms*, Research Report No. 12 (commissioned by The Bolton Committee), London, 1971

Miller, S. M., 'Notes on Neo-Capitalism', *Theory and Society*, vol. 2, 1975

Mills, C. W., *White Collar*, London, 1951

Mouzelis, N., 'Capitalism and the Development of the Greek State' in R. Scase (ed.), *The State in Western Europe*, London, 1980

National Economic Development Office, *How Flexible is Construction?*, London, 1978

Newby, H., 'Paternalism and Capitalism' in R. Scase (ed.), *Industrial Society: Class, Cleavage and Control*, London, 1977

—— *Green and Pleasant Land*, London, 1979

Newby, H., Bell, C., Rose, D. and Saunders, P., *Property, Paternalism and Power*, London, 1978

Nichols, T., *Ownership, Control and Ideology*, London, 1969

—— (ed.), *Capital and Labour*, Glasgow, 1980

Nichols, T. and Beynon, H., *Living with Capitalism*, London, 1977

Norris, G. M., 'Industrial Paternalist Capitalism and Local Labour Markets', *Sociology*, vol. 12, 1978

Nyman, S. and Silbertson, A., 'The Ownership and Control of Industry', *Oxford Economic Papers*, vol. 30, 1978

Pahl, J. M. and R. E., *Managers and Their Wives*, Harmondsworth, 1972

Pahl, R. E., 'Employment, Work and the Domestic Division of Labour', *International Journal of Urban and Regional Research*, vol. 4, 1980

Pahl, R. E. and Winkler, J. T., 'The Economic Elite' in P. Stanworth and A. Giddens (eds.), *Elites and Power in British Society*, Cambridge, 1974

Parkin, F., *Class, Inequality and Political Order*, London, 1971

—— 'Social Stratification' in T. Bottomore and R. Nisbet (eds.), *A History of Sociological Analysis*, London, 1978

—— *Marxism and Class Theory*, London, 1979

Perkin, H., *The Origins of Modern English Society, 1780–1880*, London, 1969

Phelps Brown, E. H., *Report of the Committee of Inquiry into Certain*

Matters concerning Labour in Building and Civil Engineering,
Department of Employment and Productivity, Cmnd 3714, London,
1968

Pollard, S., *The Genesis of Modern Management*, Harmondsworth, 1968

Poulantzas, N., *Classes in Contemporary Capitalism*, London, 1975

Raynor, J., *The Middle Class*, London, 1969

Reekman, B., 'Carpentry: The Craft and Trade' in A. Zimbalist (ed.),
Case Studies on the Labor Process, New York, 1979

Report of the Committee of Inquiry on Small Firms, (The Bolton
Report), Cmnd 4811, London, 1971

Report on the Census of Production, (Summary Tables) 1973

Report on the Census of Production, (Summary Tables) 1975

Roberts, K., Cook, F. G., Clark, S. C. and Semeonoff, E., *The
Fragmentary Class Structure*, London, 1977

Routh, G., *Occupation and Pay in Great Britain 1906–79* (2nd edn),
London, 1980

*Royal Commission on the Distribution of Income and Wealth, Report
No. 8*, Cmnd 7679, London, 1979

Runciman, W. G., *Relative Deprivation and Social Justice*, London,
1966

Salaman, G., *Work Organisations*, London, 1979

Scase, R., *Social Democracy in Capitalist Society*, London, 1977

Scase, R. and Goffee, R., *The Real World of the Small Business Owner*,
London, 1980

—— 'Traditional Petty Bourgeois Attitudes: The Case of the Self-
Employed Craftsmen', *Sociological Review*, vol. 29, 1981

Schumacher, E. F., *Small is Beautiful*, London, 1973

Scott, J., *Corporations, Classes and Capitalism*, London, 1979

Scruton, R., *The Meaning of Conservatism*, Harmondsworth, 1980

Smiles, S., *Self-help*, London, 1908

Sofer, C., *Men in Mid-Career*, Cambridge, 1970

Special Task Force to the Secretary of Health Education and Welfare,
Work in America, Cambridge, Mass., 1973

Stacey, M., *Tradition and Change: A Study of Banbury*, Oxford, 1960

Stanworth, M. and Curran, J., *Management Motivation in the Smaller
Business*, Epping, 1973

—— 'Growth and the Small Firm – An Alternative View', *Journal
of Management Studies*, vol. 13, 1976

Stewart, A., Prandy, K. and Blackburn, R., *Social Stratification and
Occupations*, London, 1980

Stinchcombe, A., 'Bureaucratic and Craft Administration of Production:

A Comparative Study', *Administrative Science Quarterly*, vol. 4, 1959

Stone, P. A., *Building Economy*, London, 1966

Stothard, P., 'Trapped – Why Our Small Businesses are Still Struggling', *Sunday Times*, 10 February 1980

Sugden, J. D., 'The Place of Construction in the Economy' in D. A. Turin (ed.), *Aspects of the Economics of Construction*, London, 1975

Sykes, A. J., 'Navvies: Their Work Attitudes', *Sociology*, vol. 3, 1969a
—— 'Navvies: Their Social Relations', *Sociology*, vol. 3, 1969b

Tamari, M., *A Postal Questionnaire Survey of Small Firms*, Research Report No. 16 (commissioned by The Bolton Committee), London, 1971

Tavistock Institute of Human Relations, *Interdependence and Uncertainty: A Study of the Building Industry*, London, 1966

Taylor, F. W., *Scientific Management*, New York, 1947

Tomlinson, J., 'Socialist Politics and the Small Business', *Politics and Power* (1), London, 1980

Utton, M. A., *Industrial Concentration*, Harmondsworth, 1970

Vroom, V. H. and Deci, E. L. (eds.), *Management and Motivation*, Harmondsworth, 1970

Walker, C. R. and Guest, R. H., *The Man on the Assembly Line*, New Haven, Conn., 1957

Walker, P. (ed.), *Between Labour and Capital*, Hassocks, 1979

Warr, P. and Wall, T., *Work and Wellbeing*, Harmondsworth, 1975

Weir, M. (ed.), *Job Satisfaction*, Glasgow, 1976

Westergaard, J., 'Class, Inequality and 'Corporatism' ' in A. Hunt (ed.), *Class and Class Structure*, London, 1977

Westergaard, J. and Resler, H., *Class in a Capitalist Society*, Harmondsworth, 1976

Wilensky, H., 'Orderly Careers and Social Participation', *American Sociological Review*, vol. 26, 1961

Williams, W. M., *The Country Craftsman*, London, 1958

Winkler, J. T., 'Corporatism', *European Journal of Sociology*, vol. 17, 1976

Woodward, J., *Industrial Organisation*, Oxford, 1965

Wright, E. O., *Class, Crisis and the State*, London, 1978

Zimbalist, A. (ed.), *Case Studies on the Labor Process*, New York, 1979

INDEX

autonomy 9, 12, 14, 24, 45–6, 47,
    60, 61, 62, 64, 65, 70–5 *passim*,
    80, 88, 91, 94, 95, 110, 111, 130,
    140, 158, 166, 171, 172, 189,
    190, 192

Bannock, G. 65
Bechhofer, F. 11, 12, 13, 70, 94,
    107
'black economy' 70, 95, 188
Blauner, R. 139
Boissevain, J. 13, 15
bonuses 138, 155, 179
Boswell, J. 38–9, 40
Braverman, H. 44
Brighton Labour Process Group 46
Builders, Institute of 129
building 27, Chs. 3, 4, 5, 6, 7
    passim, 188, 199–202; Advisory
    Service 135, 156
bureaucratisation 9, 32, 95, 153,
    154
Burns, T. 157

capital accumulation 21–6 *passim*,
    64, 74, 95, 99, 181, 185, 188,
    189, 192, 193, 198
Carchedi, G. 18, 19
Chinoy, E. 70, 71
collectivism 121, 192
competition 13, 64, 75–6, 78, 133,
    134, 149–50, 173, 177, 191
concentration 21, 32–40
corporatism 121, 192
Crafts Council 73
craftworkers 11, 38, 46, 60–2,
    64–6, Ch. 4 *passim*, 98, 99, 139,
    140, 162
credentialism 186–7, 191
credit 25, 63, 98, 133, 134, 192
Crossick, G. 22
Crozier, M. 60

Doran, A. 65

Elliott, B. 11
employers, small 23, 24–5, 66, Ch.
    5 *passim*, 129, 130, 132, 169,

    186, 189, 190, 191, 192, 200
Employment Protection Act 141
employment relationship 98, 107–
    18, 126, 136–41, Ch. 7 *passim*,
    185, 186, 189–90; *see also*
    fraternalism, labour, paternalism

family inheritors 130–1, 136, Ch. 7
    passim, 186–7, 190–1; *see also*
    labour
farmers 11, 107–8, 117, 176
Foster, C. 158
Fox, A. 45, 46, 138
fraternalism 108–18, 136–7, 140,
    154, 190
Friedman, A. 34, 45, 140, 167
fringe benefits 112–13, 176, 179

Goldthorpe, J. H. 71, 75
government, relations with 121–3,
    175–8

Hannah, L. 32
Higgin, G. 59
Hillebrandt, P. M. 54, 56
Hilton, W. S. 59

ideology 9–10, 12, 60, 65, 94,
    126–7, 149, 157, 168, 191, 192

Jessop, N. 59

Kay, J. 32
Kumar, K. 14

labour 11, 23, 24, 45–6, 57–63,
    66, 81, Chs. 5 and 6 *passim*,
    168–71, 185, 189–90, 191;
    division of 15, 45, 53, 110, 136;
    family 23, 24, 25, 82–8, 103–7;
    legislation 117–18, 122, 133,
    141, 177; peripheral 140–2, 154,
    167; recruitment 114–15; *see
    also* subcontracting
Lenin 21, 22
Lockwood, D. 71, 75

Mackenzie, G. 71

management 9–10, 18, 25, 26, 44, 45, Chs. 6 and 7 *passim*, 186, 187, 189, 190, 200
Martin, J. 14
Marx, Karl 15, 16, 21
Marxist analysis 9, 15–23, 185, 189
Mayer, A. J. 22, 23
Mayer, Kurt 77
mechanisation 61–2, 64
Miller, S. M. 21–2
Mills, C. Wright 74, 126–7, 150
mobility, social 22–3, 25, 64–5, 71, 185–91, 193
monopolies 13, 17, 20, 35, 64, 177, 191
multinationals 13, 35, 185

Newby, H. 9, 10, 11, 107, 108, 117, 153
Norman, A. R. D. 14

owner-controllers 10, 18, 23, 25, 41, 66, Ch. 6 *passim*, 186, 187, 189, 190; – directors 23, 26, 66, Ch. 7 *passim*, 186, 187, 190, 200; founder – 127–30, 136, 154, 176
ownership 10, 11, 23, 42–4, 55, 71, 132, Ch. 7 *passim*, 185–93; concentration of 32–40

Pahl, R. E. 14
Parkin, F. 20
paternalism 107–8, 117, 153–6, 175, 178–80
Poulantzas, N. 16–20 *passim*, 94, 121
pricing 64, 78–9, 102–3, 134
proletarianisation 9, 15, 24, 81, 187

qualifications 49, 162–6, 186

Reckmann, B. 98
Reports: Bolton 34, 39, 41–2, 49, 55, 56, 73, 76; Health and Safety Executive 168; Wilson 34, 35

Scott, J. 34
self-employed 16, 23–4, 42, 43, 47, 48, 63, 64, 66, Ch. 4 *passim*, 98, 99, 100, 113, 129, 130, 169, 186, 188–93 *passim*, 200
size of business 11, 13–14, 34–6, 53–5, 108, 131, 135, 149, 153, 154, 169, 181; *see also* concentration

social contacts 115–16, 172–4
social security 122–3, 133, 146–7
Stalker, G. M. 157
Stinchcombe, A. 60
Stone, P. A. 61–2
subcontracting 140–4, 154, 166–9, 176, 177, 188, 190
subsidiaries 160–2, 170, 171
supervision 25, 45–6, 74, 76, 100, 111, 114, 126, 138, 139, 140, 142, 143, 156, 189, 190; *see also* management
Sykes, A. J. 65

taxation 15, 186; legislation 186, 187
Taylor, F. W. 42, 44
technology 14, Ch. 2 *passim*, 61, 98
trade unions 46, 47, 92–4, 146, 148–9, 168, 169, 175, 178, 191

unemployment 14–15, 72, 95
United States 60, 70, 71, 77, 126, 127
Utton, M. A. 35

Westergaard, J. 19
wives 82–8, 103–6, 132, 173, 200
women 192; *see also* wives
Wright, E. O. 17, 18, 19, 60

For Product Safety Concerns and Information please contact our EU representative GPSR@taylorandfrancis.com Taylor & Francis Verlag GmbH, Kaufingerstraße 24, 80331 München, Germany

Printed and bound by CPI Group (UK) Ltd, Croydon, CR0 4YY

01/05/2025

01858342-0003